S0-BTZ-338

30-DAY MONEY MAKEOVER

The No B.S. Guide to Putting More Money in
Your Pocket NOW.

Steven P. Sitkowski

Copyright © 2012 Steven P. Sitkowski
All rights reserved.

ISBN: 1-4392-2823-X
ISBN-13: 9781439228234

Visit www.booksurge.com to order additional copies.

Dedication

This book, like many of my endeavors, is dedicated to the memory of my mother, Jacky Sitkowski. My dad described her as the most honorable person he had ever known. No truer words were ever spoken. I am fortunate to be her son.

Acknowledgements

This book is the result of the years I have spent in the financial planning arena and the lessons learned from the school of hard knocks. But more than anything, this book is an extension of who I am, and therefore, anyone who has touched my life, has had a hand in crafting this text. I have lived a life blessed with many powerful influences and role models. Frankly, they are too many to mention, but I would like to send a special thank you to a select few.

To my wife Heather, without whom, this book would have never been written. The concepts and strategies contained herein are mine, but the words are hers. She is talented beyond description.

To my children for whom I strive to be a better example and role model each day. May the lessons I've learned the hard way be shared so that you can avoid the land mines upon which I have stepped.

To my dad who is my biggest fan, and I his.

To my sisters who continue to love me in spite of the fact that I wasn't always the easiest big brother with which to share a household.

To Charles J. Givens, my mentor and dearly departed friend.

To Larry Pino, the smartest man I have ever met. Thank you for giving me the chance to take center stage.

To Bob Proctor for teaching me about the Law of Attraction. It was my privilege to work with a living legend.

To George Mendez who taught me that not all brothers share the same parents.

To Dr. Robert Schuller who gave birth to my possibility thinking philosophy.

Table of Contents

Preface

I was doing some last-minute holiday shopping when I witnessed something that truly inspired me to take my strategies and ideas on managing finances and finally commit them to paper.

While waiting in a checkout line at my local Wal-Mart, I overheard the couple in front of me discussing whether they had sufficient funds to pay for the contents of their shopping cart.

They quickly took inventory of their cart, made some calculations, and ultimately concluded that the shampoo purchase needed to be deferred for another day. My heart broke as I watched the man discreetly remove the bottle of T-Gel from the other shopping items to set it aside for restocking.

In the wealthiest country in the world, hard-working people should NOT find it necessary to agonize over a seven dollar bottle of shampoo. As I gazed at the throngs of shoppers that day, I surmised that many of the shoppers were experiencing similar financial dilemmas to the one that occurred with the couple in line in front of me.

I had to ask myself, "Why?"

Why do so many people struggle to pay for life's basic necessities?

The answer was insultingly obvious.

People are taught how to make a living—but they are never really taught how to *live*.

There are a lot of books on the market these days that profess to teach the secrets of building fortunes, written by people who claim to have discovered the equivalent of the "Financial Holy Grail."

This is not one of those books.

If you are looking for a get-rich-quick program, guess what— I do not have one. If I did, I would be more than happy to share it with you.

Instead, this book is meant to teach anyone how to eliminate unnecessary financial stress and to provide lessons on how to create a solid, secure path to becoming wealthy and staying wealthy.

Being broke is painful.

And trust me, I have been there before.

Even though I have enjoyed great personal success during the second half of my adult life, the first half was a financial nightmare. I still wake up from old dreams about running out of money.

America is like Disneyland to someone with a fat wallet. But the fact of the matter is—life in the U.S. is downright depressing for someone short on cash.

When you are poor, you see other people living in homes you feel you could never afford, going to places you feel that you will never visit, and wearing clothes that you imagine will never grace your closet.

Sadly, many come to accept that mediocrity is just their lot in life.

But… what if you knew what the wealthy already know?

Then you could put yourself in a position to replicate their results.

All of a sudden, those *out of reach* things will not be out of *your* reach anymore.

It is possible.

It is even probable. But you have to start at the beginning. You have to be willing to learn new lessons and to change your old, ineffective ways. You must be willing to work, but it will take time, commitment, and perseverance for you to reach your goals and attain all that you want to attain.

Use this book as your guide. You will soon develop effective life skills and will soon gain the knowledge you need to accomplish your goals.

Introduction

Navigating the financial landscape in America can be intimidating and confusing. The average person is usually totally consumed with trying to make enough of a decent wage just to get by. As a result, many people feel that they are left with little time to develop a game plan that will ensure a better way of life and security at retirement age.

Even when finding free time is not the challenge, certainly the training and expertise required to make sound decisions may be lacking. With the plethora of financial products and services available to today's consumer, *where does one start?*

In the end, too many people simply throw their hands in the air and adopt a "whatever happens, happens" philosophy. They think, "Perhaps if I just keep my nose to the grindstone, it will all turn out OK."

No. Things will probably not turn out OK…if you adopt that kind of cavalier attitude.

In truth, ignorance is NOT bliss, and what you do not know *can* and *will* hurt you.

It is time to take control. TOTAL CONTROL over your life's direction. This book will be your guide map.

The purpose of this book is to help you build your personal financial blueprint by using its *30 Days'* worth of lessons. As soon as your plan is in place, it will serve you for the rest of your life. I want your finances running on autopilot so that you can move confidently and effortlessly into the future, knowing that the foundation for prosperity has been solidly built.

Once you understand the basics, you will probably be surprised at how financially capable you become. *You* will be the one to make your life a financial success!

The challenge for many people is that there are way too many mixed messages being sent out from advisors, agents, salesmen, advertisers, and so forth. It is hard to know which messages hold anything of value.

The harsh truth is that many of these agents are hoping to use *you* to make *their* financial dreams come true—not the other way around.

Instead, if you follow the simple steps contained in this book, I promise you will:

Save money on all insurance policies

Learn to cut your personal tax rates

Develop a systematic approach to saving and investing

Consider options for increasing personal income

Become a smarter consumer

Eliminate debt

Fund your retirement plans

Build an estate plan for future generations

Feel a sense of complete control and empowerment

And the best part is that you do not need any special talents, education, or expertise to follow these techniques and strategies.

They are spelled out in a very straightforward way so that anyone can implement them in just a few minutes each day. The goal is not to dazzle you with financial magic, but rather to provide you with **real solutions** that can work for anyone at any time.

Every strategy you will learn has passed the test of time and has made financial successes out of hundreds of thousands of people, many of whom started out just like you. Now, before you begin building your better tomorrow, I have a few words of caution that I cannot stress enough:

Do not try to move through this book too quickly.

You did not arrive in your present circumstances in one day, and it will take more than a day to restructure your finances. Thirty days is a mere blink of an eye in the grand scheme of things.

Introduction

One lesson per day is the formula for optimum results. It leaves time for consideration and execution. It is good to stop and think about why you are doing whatever it is that you are doing. When you leave yourself enough time to find those answers, it will inspire a sense of purpose.

This *30-Day* journey will inspire you as well.

Enjoy yourself!

Day 1

Creating Your Dreams List

Goals

Virtually every person who experiences any level of success is a goal-oriented individual.

As the saying goes, "If you do not know where you want to go, any path will lead you there."

Too many of us live like leaves that are carried around aimlessly by the wind.

Imagine a captain piloting a flight with no destination city—just cruising along without any sense of purpose or direction. Wandering aimlessly may not seem like such a horrible thing, but what happens if you run out of gas with no place to land?

For any of us, it is easy to get caught up in the daily mundane or fruitless tasks or distractions without pausing to ask whether any of our activities are leading us to brighter and richer tomorrows.

As children, we are natural goal setters, bright-eyed, curious, and ready for anything life has to offer. We naturally impose our goals on anyone around. A child is innately in touch with his or her desires.

WHAT HAPPENS TO US ON THE WAY TO ADULTHOOD?

How does *that* child, with the eternally optimistic, goal-oriented spirit, become a young adult who is unable to find any hope or is unable to cope with life's challenges?

Some cynics would say that *reality took hold*, and the child had to *grow up*.

I disagree with this reasoning. I submit that there is nothing sadder than watching the youthful luminescence of hope fade away. It does not represent *growth*. It is really an example of a magnificent bloom withering and *dying*.

I look into the eyes of some adults, and their essence is dominated by resignation, not resolve. They are going through the motions, but there is a total lack of inspiration or any feelings of power.

It is time to abandon the way of thinking that causes us to meander along listlessly without eagerness. Instead, we must choose to take total responsibility for everything that we experience and everything that we allow into our lives. By taking responsibility for ourselves, we regain passion, command, and a sense of ownership.

Begin this transformation by asking yourself an important question: "What would I do if I knew that I could not fail?"

The Science of Goal Setting

Goal setting is the process of realizing one's aspirations and subdividing the final objectives into a series of steps which, ultimately, produce the desired result.

In other words, we can turn any thousand-mile journey into a series of little steps that are easy to execute.

The trick to achievement or attainment is to take a future goal and determine what can be done TODAY that will move us closer toward that aspiration.

I have designed a system of steps which I apply to each one of my objectives.

Step 1: Establishing Your Personal Priorities

You need to determine what you want and what is most important to you.

This is a very personal assignment that will take considerable thought and comparative thinking.

No one else is capable of knowing what is right for you and for your life. **You cannot depend on others to make these determinations and decisions for you.** It is your responsibility because, as I have already mentioned, everything that you experience in life, and everything that enters or exits your life situation, is your responsibility and happens because of your decisions or your acceptance or rejection of another person's decisions.

To get started on this most important task, I suggest that you go to a quiet spot with a blank piece of paper and pencil (with an eraser). You may need the eraser because, at some point during this exercise, you may modify some of your choices. Of course, this task can be done on a computer as well; just make sure to save your completed list.

It is time to determine what is most important to you.

When you consider a choice, make sure to take the time to ask yourself *why* this item is important to you and *how* it became an important issue. You want to make sure that each item is something about which *you* truly care. You want to make sure that you are not making a choice based merely on the fact that someone close to you has already chosen it or because it is a choice that most other people seem to embrace as a priority.

As you construct your list, do not consider whether the things listed seem to be within your present ability for attainment. We will discuss that matter a bit later.

For now, use this as an exercise in self-discovery.

Next, you will see a sample of one person's wish list. This list was meant to be used as a sample, not as an example to be mimicked. Make sure to personalize your list.

No copying!

Sample Wish List
- New sports car
- Vacation cabin in the mountains
- Upgrade wardrobe
- College fund for Johnny and Lara
- Rolex watch
- Fishing boat
- Larger home

- Start a business
- Six months' living expenses in the bank
- Pay off credit cards
- Learn a second language
- Travel
- Early retirement

Create Your Wish List

As I suggested, choose a quiet spot where you will not be interrupted.

At the top of a pad of paper, write (or input into your computer) the following:

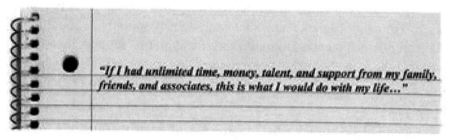

"If I had unlimited time, money, talent, and support from my family, friends, and associates, this is what I would do with my life..."

Then relax and let the ideas flow. Again, do not evaluate your potential for achieving each item at this time.

What you write should excite you, motivate you, inspire you, make you laugh, and, most of all, define your desires and dreams.

Write everything down that you could possibly wish for, no matter what it may cost in resources.

The ideas may come slowly at first, but the first step in turning dreams into reality is placing those dreams right out in front of you where you can see them and feel them! Have fun with this exercise!

(If you prefer, the next page has a blank form which you can copy and fill in.)

My Wish List

"If I had unlimited time, money, talent, and support from my family, friends, and associates, this is what I would do with my life..."

1. _____

2. _____

3. _____

4. _____

5. _____

6. _____

7. _____

8. _____

9. _____

10. _____

11. _____

12. _____

13. _____

14. _____

15. _____

As you review your list, you may find that there seems to be potential contradictions among the individual goals that you have listed.

Do not worry about this right now. This exercise is meant to be an open and unrestricted assignment.

As you continue to explore your personal values and priorities, you will begin to sort through your list and then give precedence to certain objectives.

Much like an eye exam where you are asked to look through a series of lenses and then choose the one that provides the best clarity, so, too, will life deliver a multitude of choices from which you will have to try to choose the best option. You will find yourself asking, "Is *this* option better…or is *that* option better?"

Sometimes, the answer will be difficult to determine because a conflict exists between choosing immediate or delayed gratification. Once you are able to define your priorities relative to all the available choices, the decision-making process becomes simplified.

In everything, remain mindful of your values and ultimate goals.

Step 2: Prioritizing Your Priorities

At this point, I want you to go through the wish list that you just committed to paper and begin putting your items in order with the most important listed as number one, the second priority as number two, and so on.

This task may be tough for some of you because it will require some real introspection.

Be honest with yourself as you prioritize your items. Do not base your priorities on another person's situation or desires.

Step 3: Be Specific

The next step in crystallizing your list is to take any items that are generalizations and make them more specific.

You should be able to visualize your objectives in minute detail. Visualization can work as a powerful motivator. On the other hand, it is difficult for the mind to imagine that which it cannot quantify.

For example, instead of writing, "I want to learn some foreign languages," you should write, "I want to learn to speak conversational Italian during the next eight months." As opposed to writing, "I want to change careers," you should write, "I want to become a real estate agent within the next three months."

The more specificity that you apply to your goals, the better the chances will be that you will be able to create a workable and efficient plan to achieve those goals.

Step 4: Price It Out

Your next step is to apply a *price tag* to each item in your list.

After reviewing each item and its cost, ask yourself whether the item truly seems worth that cost. Remember to consider any other options that you may have to forfeit (for now, at least) and what those forfeitures may cost you.

Consider my personal experience: as a kid growing up in Southern California, I used to salivate at the thought of owning a nice boat. As soon as I was financially able, I purchased a 42-foot sport fisher. It was magnificent. I invested around $200,000 into outfitting the boat to my specifications. As it turned out, I only used the boat ten times in three years. In my overzealous obsession with owning a boat, I had forgotten one very important fact: I get seasick!

During the short period that I owned my boat, I did have a handful of enjoyable and successful fishing excursions. However, I ended up selling the boat at a $100,000 loss.

If I had really given consideration to my purchase before spending all that cash, I could have avoided a very silly and expensive error in judgment.

On the other hand, I have never regretted the capital I have spent on any of my vacation homes.

My point is this: take sufficient time to evaluate your purchase before you reach for your wallet.

Once you are sure of what you want and what is best for you, it will be easier to build a plan that is capable of bringing you a greater feeling of fulfillment.

Additionally, realistic time parameters must be given to each goal. The guidelines in this book should allow you to create a plan that is both effective and achievable.

Staying the course will be the toughest part of the process. Let's face it—goal *setting* is the simplest part of the entire process.

Ultimately, however, you *will* come face-to-face with that four-letter action word → **W-O-R-K.**

Along the way, you may feel the urge to quit. We all feel that way from time to time.

Consider this: health clubs operate on a concept known as *breakage*. They are able sign up 400 members for a facility that accommodates 100 users because they know that 75% of the enrollees will not show up on a regular basis.

Most new members will visit once or twice but soon realize that the pursuit of a fitter body demands real effort and commitment. Most do not have the dedication to stick with a workout regimen.

I have long believed that the key characteristic of a winner is having the ability to do what needs to be done, even when the endeavor might not feel good or may not be convenient.

To make things a little easier, you should choose aspirations that inspire you so that your motivation carries you through the tougher parts of your journey.

My final thought on this subject is to re-emphasize the importance of aligning your goals and objectives with your values.

If you enjoy giving to others, your list should be dominated by things you would like to do for other people.

In my life, there have been few motivators greater than the feeling of fulfillment I've gotten from making a positive difference in another person's life. Figure out what motivates *you* the most, and keep that in mind as you review your own wish list.

Now it is your turn.

Open your notepad (or laptop), and open your mind.

In the following pages, you will learn the mechanics and skill sets required for turning your dreams into realities.

My Goals List
(Make as many copies as you need.)

Target Date

1. _____ _/ _/ ____

2. _____ _/ _/ ____

3. _____ _/ _/ ____

4. _____ _/ _/ ____

5. _____ _/ _/ ____

6. _____ _/ _/ ____

7. _____ _/ _/ ____

8. _____ _/ _/ ____

9. _____ _/ _/ ____

10. _____ _/ _/ ____

❖ ❖ ❖

Day 2

Taking Personal Inventory

Now that you have taken inventory of all of your *dreams and desires*, it is time to start the process of turning those ideas into realities.

We will start your financial makeover by examining what you already possess. To do this, we need to start collecting some important documents that you (hopefully) have somewhere in your home or in some easily accessible location.

I know this may be a tedious assignment for some of you, but trust me—it needs to be done before we move on to the next step in this process.

You may have to do some considerable searching and digging in order to find some of the needed records, but you cannot shortcut this assignment. Once you complete this step, you will never have to conduct another frantic or frustrating search ever again. One of the results of your *30-Day Money Makeover* will be that you will become a more organized person, and you will learn how to properly categorize and manage your financial records, forever and ever, amen.

The more painstaking this task is for you, the more it should be evident that you are in dire need of organization.

Here are the documents that you need to assemble:

Bank Instruments
- Checkbooks
- Savings accounts
- Money market accounts
- Certificates of deposit
- Retirement plan savings

Investment Accounts

- Brokerage statements
- Mutual funds
- Stock certificates
- Annuities
- Partnership interests

Retirement Plans

- IRAs
- 401(k)s
- 403(b)s
- 457s
- SEPs
- Keoghs
- Profit sharing
- Other

Insurance Products

- Life insurance policies
- Credit life
- Car insurance policies
- Homeowner's/renter's policies
- Disability coverage
- Health insurance
- Extended warranties
- Specialty policies

Loans

- Car notes
- Mortgage statements
- Personal loans
- Credit cards
- Lines of credit
- Student loans
- Department store financing

Tax Papers

- Last three years' personal tax returns
- Copy of W-2s

Estate Planning Documents/Personal Documents

- Wills
- Trusts
- Certificates (birth, marriage, divorce, death)

Once you have collected all the necessary documents, you should create an effective filing system. All items should be filed alphabetically in a secure location, such as a file cabinet or lockable container that is waterproof and fire retardant.

Then, whenever you need that marriage license or birth certificate, passport or closing statement, you will know exactly where it is, and you will be able to access it without any stress or any wasted time.

This assignment may really test your resolve. However, if you are not willing to retrieve the documents that we will need for review and modification, how can we begin to strategize?

Before you read any further, I want you to complete the "harvesting" process.

Only after you have found each and every vital document should you proceed to the next paragraph.

Now, go find those documents!

Record Keeping

In order to avoid any repeat of the fire drill that was (more than likely) necessary to retrieve the requested documents, I am going to suggest a simple method for storing these valuable pieces of information.

This system will save you time and aggravation.

Most families only need two places for maintaining records: a **safety deposit box** and a **waterproof/fire-retardant filing cabinet.**

In the safety deposit box, keep titles and deeds, collectibles, adoption papers, and video or photos of home contents and valuables (for insurance settlements).

Make sure that someone other than you is aware of the location of the safety deposit box and is given a key. I would recommend a trusted family member. It may be unadvisable to entrust a key to someone with whom you are romantically involved, as many intimate relationships dissolve and negative feelings develop which may generate acts of retaliation. However, in the case of a married couple, it is likely that joint accounts will exist, and, naturally, both account holders will expect access to all relevant account information.

Inside your at-home filing system, you should divide your record keeping into two basic categories: **immediate reference** and **long-term records.**

Obviously, the *immediate reference* files will contain items you use or refer to with greater frequency, such as recurring bills, installment notes, insurance premium notices, bank statements, current month's brokerage account statement, retirement plan statements, cancelled checks, recent receipts, and so forth.

The *long-term* section will contain recent years' tax returns, birth certificates, marriage certificates, divorce certificates, receipts for past home improvements or appliances, banking and billing statements from recent years, insurance policies, warranties, and so forth.

As a good guideline, you should keep most records for a period of anywhere from three to seven years. Some items should not be discarded, such as closing statements or certain receipts which help to establish your tax basis on a piece of property or a business.

On the following pages, you will find a detailed guide which will help assemble your comprehensive filing system.

You should keep the following items for three years:
- Household bills
- Credit card statements
- Proof of payment on minor purchases
- Year-end pay stub

(Option: At the end of each year, you can file all items collected throughout the past year in a separate fire-retardant and waterproof file cabinet or case, clearly marked with the respective year showing at the front of the container. Doing this will allow easier access to the current year's new collection of paperwork.)

You should keep the following items for seven years:
- Tax returns
- Receipts on deductible purchases
- Bank statements
- Canceled checks, if applicable

(Note: To keep from tossing out the *seven-year* items when you discard the *three-year* items, you should make sure to mark each item or file with the date upon which it can be discarded. This can be done by using bright, color-coded tabs or an indelible stamp to mark the file with the correct discard date.)

You should keep the following items until assets are sold or until an item becomes irrelevant:
- Insurance policies
- Legal settlements
- Home improvement receipts
- Estate planning documents
- Titles and deeds

On subsequent pages within this chapter, you will find a form entitled, "*My Financial Inventory.*"

If the format fits your situation, simply make a copy of the form and fill it in as you organize your files. If your situation calls for a customized form, use the provided form as a guideline to create your own financial inventory.

As you compile your documents and files, fill in each record's location information. Keep the form in a safe place where you will not forget it and where it will not be damaged or destroyed. The form acts as a master reference for everything you file away so that you are able to find items easily and return them to the proper place just as easily. Stop here and complete these tasks using the form found at the end of this chapter. Once you have everything filed and organized, read on.

❊ ❊ ❊

Back already?

OK then, take a deep breath.

The hardest part is done. You have successfully collected and filed all your documents!

I know getting organized does not put cash in your pockets immediately, but it will save time throughout your life.

And time is money.

I believe that any individual or family should handle finances the way a successful business handles its finances.

A well-organized business has an end-of-year goal in sight each year. There is usually a magic number, the company's *bottom line*, which it pursues in order to be profitable. If you run your finances like a successful business does, constantly evaluating your position in relationship to your objectives, then it will be easier, by far, for you to formulate the best plan to reach those goals.

Your seemingly unattainable dreams will begin to materialize.

The better you become at managing the *business* of your personal finances, the better you will become at achieving any goal.

My Financial Inventory

Bank Instruments	Location
____ Checkbook 1 ____ Checkbook 2 ____	
____ Savings accounts	
____ Money market accounts	
____ Certificates of deposit	
____ Retirement plan savings	
Investment Accounts	
____ Brokerage statements	
____ Mutual funds	
____ Stock certificates	
____ Annuities	
____ Partnership interests	
Retirement Plans	
____ IRAs	
____ 401(k)s	
____ 403(b)s	
____ 457s	
____ SEPs	
____ Keoghs	
____ Profit sharing	
Insurance Products	
____ Life insurance policies	
____ Credit life	
____ Car insurance policies	
____ Homeowner's/renter's policies	
____ Disability coverage	
____ Health insurance	
____ Extended warranties	
____ Specialty policies	

Loans	Location
___ Car notes	
___ Mortgage statements	
___ Personal loans	
___ Credit cards	
___ Lines of credit	
___ Student loans	
___ Department store financing	
Tax Papers	
___ Last three years' personal returns	
___ Tax returns/copy of W-2s	
Estate Planning Documents and Personal Identification Documents	
___ Wills	
___ Trusts	
___ Passports	
___ Birth certificates	
___ Marriage certificate	
___ Divorce papers	
___ Death certificates	
___ Adoption papers	
___ Titles	
___ Titles	
___ Deeds	
OTHER	

❖ ❖ ❖

Day 3

Finding Ground Zero

How are you doing so far? I know it may be hard to see how all these seemingly tedious exercises will help you reach your financial goals, but soon enough we will bring everything into greater focus, so hang in there!

Let's start Day 3 of your *30-Day Money Makeover*!

You have committed your dreams and goals to paper, and you have tackled (and finished) the chore of collecting every single financial document you will possibly need.

Now it is time to put your current status into perspective. To accomplish this, you will need to create a personal *financial statement* in order to compare your assets to your liabilities.

You do not need to be a mathematical genius to fill out a financial statement. Furthermore, with today's technology, completing a financial statement may be as simple as answering a few questions.

Your first task is to decide whether you want to invest in software, which will calculate most of the arithmetic for you, or whether you would prefer to stick with the pen and paper method.

If you decide to do this task without using any software, there are several places you can obtain a copy of a financial statement form. I have provided a sample financial statement at the end of this chapter. A hard copy of a financial statement can also be found at any bank or credit union. Additionally, for a couple of dollars, you can purchase financial statement forms at any office supply store.

However, if you would rather use a computer during this process, I would recommend purchasing a financial software program. This financial software is capable of doing much more than creating financial statements. It can help you set goals for yourself and keep track of your spending, too. In addition, the financial software will save you from the hassle of creating a financial statement from scratch whenever you have to update your information. With the software, you simply make any needed updates and save the new information.

Some programs, such as Microsoft Excel, provide a financial statement template which is easy to download (you need to be online). If you already own the Microsoft Office suite, then the financial template is provided free of charge. First, under **File** choose **New**. Then, under **New Workbook,** look for **Templates** and **Search online for**: . Then type *"financial statement"* in the search box. Microsoft will populate a list of possible documents for you to use. The first choice is usually the most appropriate. Click on the first available **personal financial statement** template, and a download preview should appear. Click **download** and save the file to your computer.

Also, there are several software packages available for about $30 which are simple to use. Here are a few for your consideration.

Microsoft Money

This might be the most popular money management software. It is very user-friendly and includes features that help you to manage your finances and budget, track your investments, bank online, and do some tax planning. The electronic checkbook feature allows bills to be paid online and keeps track of expenses so that financial statements can be created at the end of each month. This is a good way to keep track of your progress.

The software also includes other, more sophisticated features for those who wish to do more than just the basics.

Quicken

Quicken helps with banking, investing, taxes, financial planning, budgeting, and more. You can pay bills online, balance your checkbook, and reconcile your bank statement quickly and easily. The software makes it easy to see where your dollars are going and keep tabs on actual expenses compared to a set budget. Additionally, the tax data contained in Quicken can be transferred over to Turbo Tax for planning and calculation purposes.

Money Dance

This software is not as well-known as the Microsoft and Quicken products, but it is perfect for anyone who wants a basic program. It is not as complex as the other two platforms (which means that it cannot perform as many functions as the two previously mentioned programs). However, if simplicity is your primary preference, Money Dance may be the right choice. Money Dance can be used on Windows, Linux, or Mac operating systems.

Getting Started

The best way to start this task is to first think about how you spend money each month. What are your monthly expenses? If you use credit cards to pay for most bills, the job of assembling a list of monthly expenses may be much easier. You can use your end-of-month statement to begin your list. All you have to do is put each expense into a category (for example, auto, utility, grocery, insurance, and so forth).

Your checkbook register may be the next-best source for your list of monthly expenses.

In addition, do not forget to list recurring items that might be paid for in cash, such as road tolls, tips, cab rides, valet parking, or perhaps that daily gourmet coffee and sugary-sweet coffee cake. (You know who you are!)

To begin, itemize all your expenses.

For example:

1. Gas/Other Transportation Costs
2. Groceries
3. Rent/Mortgage
4. Electric/Gas
5. Cable/Internet
6. Car Payment
7. Water/Sewage
8. Daycare
9. Phone/Cell Phone
10. Entertainment
11. Miscellaneous

At a later point in this book, I will show you how to become a wise consumer so that you can make your dollars go further. For now, let's focus on your current expenditures.

This seemingly simple task may turn out to be more challenging than you expected.

When I had my financial planning practice in Newport Beach, California, I would sit down with clients each day to review personal incomes and budgets.

In almost every case, the client's income figures and proposed budget could not be reconciled.

For instance, a couple would report an after-tax income of $40,000 per year against a household budget of $25,000, and yet the couple somehow managed to save only $1,500 during the entire year and was unable to account for the "missing" income!

My clients' perception of their situations very often did not reflect reality. In my experience, most people cannot account for 20% of their outflow. That 20% can add up to be a huge amount of money each year!

Are you the kind of person who frequently wonders, "*Where did all my money go this month?*" If so, you are not alone.

It is time that we plug that money hole and begin to put all that lost money to good use! The only way to accomplish real progress is to first determine your *actual* spending (not the amount you *think* you are spending). And the only way to do this is to begin tracking each dollar you spend. For the next three months, you will account for each and every one of your expenditures.

You read that correctly. This process is tedious, but necessary. You need to be accountable for EVERY dollar you spend.

If you have to use a shoebox to keep your receipts, then do it. Just find something, anything that works for you. No excuses. If you live with other people who might inadvertently interfere with this process by throwing out your receipts or billing information, make sure to find a secure hiding place for all your records. It is your responsibility to keep a detailed record of your expenditures. I believe the easiest approach is to use checks and credit cards for nearly all of your purchases as they leave a paper trail that is simple to retrace.

The key to attaining an accurate figure will rely on your ability to track your cash purchases as well. Ask for a receipt for everything you buy. You can double check your math by taking your beginning checking account balance, adding deposits, then subtracting ATM withdrawals and all of your written and electronic checks, and then compare this number to your month-end balance to make certain that all expenses have been counted.

Compare the number you come up with to your cash receipts to see if everything balances. If it does, you have managed to keep an accurate tracking of your cash flow. If the figures cannot be reconciled, you will need to give a greater effort toward monitoring your cash expenditures. For example, you started the month with $100 cash in your purse or wallet. During the month you took out an additional $200 from the local ATM. At the end of the month, you still have $75. You should have cash receipts for $225 ($100+$200–$75). When the figures do not match, you have what I refer to as *leakage*. (Sounds messy, doesn't it?) It is this leakage which makes many household budgets unmanageable.

When hundreds of dollars per month fall through the cracks without any accountability, it makes it difficult to set a workable budget. The process of closely tracking your cash receipts must be repeated until your cash purchases can be reconciled at the end of the month. Only then will you have accurate numbers and an accurate assessment of your personal financial habits. Taking the time to create a current financial statement and an income and expense report should also prove to be an exercise in self-discovery. You may be amazed at what you find. I have had clients discover that almost $1,000 was being spent per month on food alone…for two people!

It soon became very clear they could afford to change some things and redistribute some of that money to their savings or investment accounts or even just for other things they'd wanted to buy, like computer software or housewares.

Once you have successfully completed today's exercises, the most difficult and painstaking parts of your *30-Day Money Makeover* will be COMPLETE.

Determining *ground zero* may take a significant amount of time, effort, perseverance, and above all…courage. After today, we will finally be ready to launch into strategies and techniques that will rapidly move you toward the financial security and lifestyle you desire.

Remember to go at your own pace with each chapter.

Get a good rest. Tomorrow will be an exciting day!

My Financial Statement

ASSETS	
Liquid Assets	**Value**
Cash	$
Checking Accounts	
Savings Account	
Money Market Accounts	
Savings Bonds	
Certificates of Deposit	
Mutual Funds Accounts	
Corporate Stocks	
Government Bonds	
Life Insurance Cash Value	
Prepaid Items	
Fixed Assets	
Personal Residence	
Vacation Home	
Investment Real Estate	
Total Personal Property (jewelry, etc.)	
Vehicles	
Employer Retirement Accounts	
Individual Retirement Accounts	
Value of Business	
Loan(s) Receivable	
Other Assets	
Total Assets	$

LIABILITIES	
Loans (Balance)	**Debt Amount**
Automobile	$
Recreation	
Furniture	
Credit Cards	
Mortgage (Balance)	
Home	
Vacation Home	
Investment Real Estate	
Other Liabilities	
Total Liabilities	**$**

My Net Worth

(Take your total assets and subtract your total liabilities to get your net worth.)

Total Assets $ (_____)
Total Liabilities $ (_____)
Current Net Worth $ (_____)

My Income and Expense Statement

Name:	
Date:	
Income	**Amount Allocated**
Wages or Salary (before withholding)	
Commission/Tips/Bonuses	
From Savings	
Interest and Dividends	
Bonuses	
Scholarship/Grants	
Government Grants	
Government Loan/Financial Aid	
Tax Refund	
Rental Income	
Loan From Parents/Relatives	
Other	
Total Income	
Expenses	
Fixed Expenses	
Federal Income Taxes	
City Income Taxes	
Medicare Taxes	

Day 3: Finding Ground Zero

FICA Taxes	
Personal Property Taxes	
State Income Taxes	
Savings and Investments	
Pension Contributions (ex: 401k)	
Individual Retirement Account	
Housing (rent/mortgage)	
Automobile Loan Payments	
Student Loan Payments	
Other Loan Payments	
Tuition	
Homeowner's Insurance	
Life Insurance Medical Insurance	
Automobile Insurance and Registration	
Installment Loan Payments	
Cable TV Bill	
Internet Bill	
Other	
Total Fixed Expenses	
Flexible Expenses	
Food (groceries)	
Eating Out/Snacks	
Utilities (gas, electricity, water, garbage)	
Telephone	
Gasoline	
Car Repairs/Maintenance	
Medical/Dental (not covered by insurance)	
Prescription Drugs and Medicines	
Child Care/Other Dependent Care	

Laundry	
Clothing and Accessories	
Spending Money	
Education/Books	
Professional Dues	
Household Furnishings/Repairs	
Magazines, Newspapers, etc.	
Television	
Personal Care	
Entertainment and Recreation	
Hobbies	
Gifts	
Contributions	
Vacations	
Credit Card Payment	
Savings and Investing	
Miscellaneous	
Other	
Total Flexible Expenses	
Total Expenses	
Discretionary Income	

Day 4

Taking Charge of Your Debts

There are few things in life more debilitating than mountains worth of debt.

Oftentimes, debts add up at such a fast pace that by the time people realize the mess they have created, they feel overwhelmed and completely helpless to do anything to fix the situation.

I know this feeling all too well.

Many years ago, when I was much less wise about personal finance, I managed to take on about $25,000 in installment obligations.

Back in those days, $25,000 represented a not-so-small fortune.

I remember lying in my bed, unable to get to sleep, feeling completely powerless about my terrible financial situation. I felt that the massive amount of loans that menacingly loomed above my head was going to come crashing down. Then I was reminded of an old allegory:

"How do you eat an elephant? One bite at a time!"

With that simple lesson in mind, I cleared my jumbled thoughts and began to consider how I could unburden myself from my mountain of debt. This *one bite at a time* method can be applied to any large problem. Think of each "bite" as a single step that will lead to a final solution.

Step 1: Make a List of Everything You Owe

This is an easy step for you because, as a participant in the **30-Day Money Makeover**, you have already completed this step. All the information can be gathered from your financial statement created on Day 3.

This time, however, we are going to go into more detail with regard to your liabilities. You will need an itemized list of the loan principle,

31

interest, terms, payments, and the number of payments you have left until the loan is satisfied. Do this for each of your liabilities.

Also make note of whether the loan is deductible for tax purposes.

Sample Loan List

Balance	Type	Interest	PMT	Terms in Months	Tax Deductible
$18,200	Car 1	8.5%	$365	37	No
$14,500	Car 2	3.2%	$260	31	No
$7,100	CC	16%	$100	300	No
$2,200	Store	9%	$324	7	No
$264,000	Mtg.	5.8%	$1752	287	Yes
$11,200	CC	14%	$220	300	No
$15,000	Dad	0%	0	Flexible	N/A

Use this sample list as a model in charting out your own debts.

Step 2: Prioritize Your Debt

Now that we have your total debt charted out, it is time to create a game plan.

Most advisors suggest paying down the loan with the highest interest rate first, but I would suggest that you consider the particular overall impact of each debt.

Look at the example above. Even though the store loan of $2,200 has a relatively lower interest rate of 9% compared to one of the credit cards which carries an interest rate of 16%, paying off the balance owed to the store will provide $324 in cash flow per month. That extra cash each month would help satisfy the next loan on your list.

Your goal is to carry debt on your mortgage and, possibly, a car loan. That is it.

Actually, the ultimate goal is to be COMPLETELY debt free.

You will no longer carry balances on high interest rate credit cards which waste your money through interest payments. Later in this book, we will explore additional options regarding methods for paying off mortgages and owning cars free and clear. True financial security comes only when you have achieved a debt-free way of life.

You cannot win the personal finance game if you are losing money to interest payments.

Let's look at our sample list of debts again.

The following payoff order represents my suggestion for how to best satisfy these debts.

$2,200 Store Loan

$7,100 Credit Card

$11,200 Credit Card

$18,200 Car Loan

$15,000 Loan from Dad

Can you see the pattern here? Aside from the loan from Dad, which can be paid at a flexible pace, the debts are being paid from the smallest debt to the largest debt. Each time a debt is eliminated from the list, extra money is made available that can be used for the purpose of repaying the next debt on the list.

Using this method, debt can be paid off quickly and easily.

You may have noticed that I left off two items from the previous list— the car loan of $14,500 and the mortgage of $264,000. First, notice the interest rate on the car. The rate is 3.2%. With such a relatively low rate, it usually makes sense to continue making the scheduled payments instead of paying off the loan. Your money can earn more than 3.2% in the financial marketplace. As for the mortgage, it is reasonable to expect that just about everyone will need to maintain the schedule of making monthly payments. Paying off the entire lump sum at one time usually falls outside of the financial capacities of most individuals. We will discuss property ownership and mortgages in more detail on Day

8. For now, take advantage of the fact that the mortgage payment is tax deductible.

Review the chart you created which lists all your debts. Using my example, determine the best sequence to use in paying off all of your debts.

Step 3: Consider Your Existing Resources

Sometimes we find that the answer to our problems has been staring us straight in the face for some time and that we have just overlooked it.

During Step 3 we will remove the blinders and critically evaluate any available resources.

I remember meeting with a client for the purpose of reviewing his financial statement. I immediately noticed that he had a considerable amount of credit card debt that carried an 18% interest rate, and yet he had enough money in his checking account (earning 0% interest) to pay off the entire credit card debt. I looked across my desk and asked him if he would be interested in an investment that paid 18% tax-free and with absolutely no risk. He replied, "Of course!" I pointed out that he was the one borrowing money at 18% and lending it out at 0% to the same bank. What a deal he had given his bank! Of course, before our meeting ended that day, he and I solved the inequitable business relationship he had going with his financial institution.

I understand that not everyone will have a simple cash flow solution sitting in his or her checking account. Most of the time, financial problem solving is not quite that easy.

Advertisers will tell you about the wisdom of taking a home equity line of credit to pay off those pesky credit cards in order to get out of debt as quickly as possible. This may or may not be a good strategy for you.

On paper, borrowing money with an interest rate of 7% that is secured by your home and using it to retire credit card debt with higher rates seems like a no-brainer. This strategy only works, however, when you have learned to exercise proper financial discipline.

On the other hand, if you use your home equity to pay off your credit cards and then at some future date, when you are feeling more relaxed about your financial condition, resume racking up new credit card debt— then you have a serious problem. Your financial ship is once again sinking, but this time, you do not have an emergency "money life-boat" to use as an escape. I have seen this happen to many, many people.

I would rather you consider some alternatives. They might seem a little more painful, but trust me—in the end, it will help you avoid major financial agony.

Question: What do you own that you would be willing to sell?

Can you get by with one less vehicle or drive a vehicle that is less expensive?

Is there a piece of jewelry you can live without? Do you really need that boat if you are having trouble making ends meet? Can you exist with one less television or without your golf clubs? Do you have any exercise equipment gathering dust around your house?

I told you this alternative might seem tougher. We allow ourselves to become attached to our possessions; therefore, we make it hard to let go of our collections. As I mentioned before, it is time to take the blinders off. Change your way of thinking. If you have not used an item in the last year, do you really think it is of great value to you? Go through your closet. If there is an item in your closet that you have not worn in a year, it could be sold if it is in good condition.

I know that almost everyone has heard of eBay. If you have never sold anything on eBay, it is time to learn how to use this giant cyber store. Whenever you want to sell something, eBay is an incredible technological tool. You may be amazed at what some of your "old junk" is worth! To get started, go to the Web site at www.ebay.com. To create a free eBay account, click on **My eBay** and then click on the **Register** button. The rest is self-explanatory.

Here is the real test. The money you make from selling something must be used to pay down your debt and not for anything else. It cannot be used to go out to eat, for new clothes, for your niece's birthday, for your coworker's going-away party, or for a round of golf. Remember your reason for making these sacrifices. Review your debt list. Try to imagine what it will feel like to be totally free of debt. That is your No. 1 goal.

If you cannot find anything around your house that you are willing to sell, and you are still short on cash, it is time to consider increasing your income through part-time work. Remember, it is a temporary situation, but it is necessary for your financial survival. If you do not have enough cash or assets to cover your debts, it is time to start increasing your income level. There is no point in being melodramatic or feeling negative. Find something that fits in with your schedule and other obligations, and have at it.

Step 4: Renegotiate Your Loans

You may be surprised to discover that your current lenders can be flexible on the pricing of their products.

Most consumers are totally unaware of this valuable little secret.

The business world refers to this practice as *price matching*. Price matching among lenders is no different than your local electronics store offering to match the lowest price available on a television. The key is to know what the competition is offering. There are a couple of Web sites that you need to explore. The first is www.cardweb.com. This site provides a list of the best rates on credit cards currently offered in the country. Use these rate listings as leverage with your current credit card lender. You can always take your money elsewhere if your lender is unwilling to negotiate.

The second Web site is www.bankrate.com. Bankrate.com is an excellent place to shop for mortgages and car loans.

Once you have discovered lower rates being offered by other institutions, call your lender and explain that you are prepared to keep your business with them, but only if they are willing to match the published rates advertised by the other lenders. You may be surprised by what happens. Most of the lenders will agree to your terms to keep from losing your business. If they do not agree to adjust your interest rates so that they are aligned with market competitors, you will have to act on your initial declaration. Move your loan to an opportunity that has better terms. Then, whenever you get that phone call from your now *previous* lender in which they ask for an explanation for your recent decision to move your money, you will have an informative little story to tell them. You gave them a chance to keep your business, and they refused to accept your offer. It is usually a very satisfying phone conversation—for you, that is.

Step 5: Prepay Principal

Did you know that most loans can be prepaid without penalty?

Each loan's terms vary, so you will need to read your loan terms carefully before you begin making extra payments, but if no penalties exist, prepaying principal can be a great way to eliminate your debt.

With each loan that is paid off, extra cash flow is freed that can be put to better use…like paying off another loan!

For instance, in our example where we paid off $2,200 that was owed on the store loan, an additional $324 per month was made available that could then be used to pay down the next priority—the credit card debt.

This pattern should continue until all debts are paid off. Once a debt is paid off, the extra cash flow created by that payoff should be applied to the next debt on your list. Your goal is to amortize your loans within the shortest possible time frame by using any and all extra cash for the purpose of paying down debt. Use this strategy until you are free and clear…of all financial anchors! Here is another trick to add to your bag of financial shortcuts. You can pay off any amortized loan in half the time by simply making the current month's regularly scheduled payment PLUS next month's principal-only payment.

This is a particularly good strategy you can use on mortgages in the first stages of the loan where the extra principal payment might only be a few extra dollars per month.

This strategy helps you build equity in your property at an accelerated rate. To obtain an amortization schedule (so that you get a clear financial picture of the principal and interest portion of each payment), simply contact your lender and request a schedule. Otherwise, you can go to www. bankrate.com, click the **Calculator** icon, and print one for yourself.

Sample Mortgage Amortization Schedule

Principal Payment No.	Payment	Principal	Interest	Balance	Month
60	$500	$20	$480	$49,000	1
61	$500	$20.30	$479.70	$48,979.70	2
62	$500	$20.70	$479.30	$48,959	3
63	$500	$21.20	$478.80	$48,937.80	4

When you write a check for payment number 60 in the amount of $500, write another check for $20.30 representing the principal-only portion of payment number 61. The next month, write a check for payment 61 for $500 and another check for $20.70 for the principal portion of payment number 62, and so forth. Get it? Each month, pay the principal for the following month.

This simple strategy can cut your mortgage term almost in half—without the cost of refinancing.

Step 6: Do Not Repeat the Sins of the Past

Borrowed funds can be used for one of two things: building wealth or building debt. A loan can be used for one of three purchase types: appreciating assets, depreciating assets, or consumables.

An *appreciating asset* could be something such as real estate or an interest in a business. It is something that is expected to grow in value with time.

A *depreciating asset* could be a car or new appliances. It is something that is expected to decrease in value with time.

A *consumable* would be a meal at a restaurant, those gourmet coffees, or a vacation. As soon as it has been enjoyed or consumed, its value ceases. You can no longer get any value out of it. Now, there may be some who argue the underlying (and ongoing) value gleaned from something like a vacation—in the form of pleasant memories, and so forth. In this context, however, we are speaking to the practical financial values of different asset types. With this in mind, here are some rules to live by:

Rule Number 1: NEVER FINANCE A CONSUMABLE

Period. End of story.

There are unwise people (and you know who you are) who go holiday shopping and pay for all their gift expenditures with credit cards and, therefore, continue to pay for these presents during the next several months (maybe years!). This type of behavior is financial suicide! They are pushing their money off a ledge to a gruesome end. Worse still, many of these same folks treat a night out on the town in the same fashion. They finance all their fun with revolving credit card debt. Long after the evening has been forgotten and (perhaps) the alcohol hangovers have departed, they are still paying for their night of so-called fun, and the nasty financial hangover remains—through interest rate costs!

Rule Number 2: FOR ITEMS THAT DEPRECIATE, PAY CASH

If you cannot afford to pay cash for a depreciating item, do not buy it! The only exception to this rule might concern transportation provisions. I realize that a car is a necessity in most living situations. However, do you really need a $30,000 car when your annual salary is $30,000? Explore some inexpensive alternatives before you finance an unreasonable sum of money relative to your level of income. Even though I feel like it should go without saying, I have to make sure that everyone knows not to finance furniture. It is hard for me to believe that anyone does this, but, apparently, plenty of people make this mistake. Make do with what you have until you can save enough money to pay in full at the time of purchase.

Rule Number 3: BEWARE OF FINANCING

There are situations in which financing an appreciating asset is acceptable, and many times, prudent, just as long as the cash flow or appreciation exceeds the interest rate on the debt.

Avoid borrowing money for ventures that offer high potential returns but carry high risk as well. To borrow against your home for the purpose of investing in a risky business opportunity is a financial recipe for disaster. During your *30-Day Money Makeover*, you will learn about smart ways to finance wise investments strategies.

Getting out of debt is simple. It may not be *easy* for some of you, but it is absolutely necessary in order to build a strong foundation for your personal finance empire. For some of you, it will consist of merely reallocating priorities and resources. For others, the road to freedom from debt may be a longer (and tougher) one, but it is a goal that is well worth any effort necessary.

You may be the sort who suffers from an inability to control yourself whenever you go into a store or pass by a car lot.

Here's a helpful tip: GET CONTROL OF YOURSELF!

It is just that simple. If you have bad spending habits, STOP spending now.

I have to assume that if you are reading this book, there is a good chance that you are, at the very least, a young *adult*. Regardless of your age, there is no better time than right this minute to begin taking responsibility for your own actions and, in doing so, gaining control over your life.

I have not overlooked the fact that some of you may have recently experienced a job loss or may have suffered an illness that has set you back to the point of hopelessness.

Do not despair.

Even in unusual circumstances, there are strategies that will get you back to the right path.

For those of you who are currently encumbered with a large amount of debt, it is time to call in reinforcements (emotional and otherwise), and it is probably wise to seek the advice of a credit counselor. Just be careful in your choice as there are a number of companies out there who claim that they will help you, but in the end they will only add to your debts as a future creditor. If your debts have grown to the point where you see no possible solution (even after reviewing this chapter in the book), I suggest you call the National Foundation for Credit Counseling at 800-388-2227, or visit them online at www.debtadvice.org.

They can refer you to a no-cost or low-cost consultant who can create a plan specifically for your individual situation.

In times of need, it is nice to have an expert in your corner. There are few things more satisfying than getting out of debt and back into good financial shape.

By following the steps and suggestions outlined in today's chapter, you will begin to see the sweet rays of financial solvency on the horizon.

My Debts Worksheet

(Make a copy of this form, and fill out the required information. Retain for easy reference.)

Loan Type	Balance	Type	Interest	Terms	Tax

❖ ❖ ❖

Day 5

Increase Your Net Take-Home Pay

Most Americans have gotten into the habit of overpaying the Internal Revenue Service each year by claiming an incorrect number of allowances on their employer's W-4. Then, when these "over-payers" receive an income tax refund, they act as if they have just won the lottery. These people unwittingly use the withholdings from their paycheck as a sort of forced savings account and consider their year-end tax return as "bonus money."

Bonus money?

Bogus money is more like it.

Where do you think that bonus money came from?

You earned it!

It represents cash out of your pocket from every paycheck that could have been used to pay your monthly bills or make timely investments!

Let me explain the pitfalls of overpaying the IRS.

Imagine that a bank opened up an office down the street from you and offered a money market fund that paid no interest, required ongoing contributions, and only permitted access to funds on an annual basis. Sound like a favorable offer?

I hope you answered this question with a disgusted sounding, "No way!"

Well then, if you would say no to *that* offer, why are you allowing a tax *refund* to occur each year? The resulting consequence is the same!

The refund that you receive is merely the return of your own money—your own hard-earned dollars that you were never obligated to pay the IRS in the first place. You received no benefit from this forfeiture.

You collected no interest. And while it was nice of you to extend Uncle Sam an interest-free loan, could you not have used that money to help pay your *own* debts? (Which, I am guessing, were not offered to you free of interest.)

It is time to turn the tables in your favor.

If you normally receive a tax refund every year, then pay close attention to this chapter.

Today's lesson will provide you with an easy way to free up extra cash flow each month so that you are better able to tackle those monthly bills. This strategy can be applied to your very next paycheck.

The Withholding Calculator

When you signed on with your current employer, you were asked to complete something called a W-4 form.

The "Employee Withholding Allowance Certificate" is used to determine the correct amount of federal income tax an employer needs to withhold from your pay. By law, a W-4 form must be completed for every employer with which you are employed. This form includes three types of information that employers use to calculate federal withholdings:

1. Whether to withhold at the single rate or at the lower married rate
2. The number of withholding allowances the employee can claim
3. Whether any additional amounts are to be withheld

Your goal is to ultimately claim as many allowances as possible in an effort to **BREAK EVEN** at year's end. Instead of receiving that $3,600 refund at the end of the year, you will get an extra $300 each month that can be used to pay down debt, or it could go toward investments.

A good guideline to follow is to always accelerate income and defer expenses whenever possible.

Day 5: Increase Your Net Take-Home Pay

You are probably thinking to yourself, "Sounds like a great idea, Steven. I know I have to fill out a W-4 form, but how will I know exactly what I should enter on the form? What if I make an error on my taxes?"

I understand your concern. Sometimes just looking at that tax form can cause a sensation of panic.

Relax. The IRS has made it easy for us to determine the maximum number of allowances that can be claimed. They are just going to make us do a *little* bit of work first.

To better understand today's lesson, make sure to have your most current pay stubs and last year's tax returns on hand. You should know exactly where these items are because you learned how to organize and file all your important documents on Day 3.

See, this book's lessons are paying off already!

Next, go to the IRS Web site at www.irs.gov/individuals. Find the search box (it is usually found in the upper-right-hand corner of the screen). In the search box, type the words *withholding calculator*. Click on the word **Search** next to the box and wait a few seconds for the computer to locate the results.

On your screen, you should see a list of relevant search results. Find the listing that reads **Withholding Calculator** (it should be the first listing), and then click on that listing. At the bottom of the page that appears, you should see the words **Continue to the Withholding Calculator**. Click on those words, and then follow the directions provided for you.

You will answer a series of questions that will determine your specific optimum withholding allowances. This will assist you in filling out your W-4 form correctly.

Do not forget to print out a copy of the online worksheet after you have completed filling it out so that you can take it to your payroll department as soon as possible. You want to start enjoying your tax-free "raise" as soon as possible!

A bit of advice: it is very important that you NEVER try to cheat the system such as attempting to claim more allowances than you are permitted by law. Eventually, the IRS *will* find the deception, and they will charge interest on the entire amount of money they determine you *should* have been paying all along. The interest compounds daily and begins on the day that the taxes were due and continues until the IRS receives its money. The interest rate is variable, based on the federal short-term rate plus 3%. It is recalculated every three months.

In addition to the interest charged on unpaid taxes, the IRS can impose a penalty under certain circumstances. There is a late payment charge of 0.5% of the tax owed for each month (or any part of it) that your tax goes unpaid after its due date. The penalty can increase up to 25% and can increase in 1% increments if you do not pay after you receive several IRS notices.

I am fully aware that most people are in the habit of receiving a nice, big, fat, "unexpected" refund check from Uncle Sam each year. That refund tradition might put a smile on your face and may help fund the purchase of a new piece of jewelry, a set of golf clubs, or a trip to the islands, but…you need to understand the imputed cost of this situation.

Check this out: the average annual tax refund equals about $2,500.

Most people do not even remember what they did with last year's check.

Let me show you the benefit of having access to the funds during each pay period instead of waiting until the conclusion of the tax period.

Let's assume that, in following the plan outlined in this chapter, you are able to increase the number of allowances you claim on your W-4. Let's further assume that this change increases your net take-home pay by $200 per month (the amount that most taxpayers are having unnecessarily withheld). Chances are that you will be gainfully employed for some 40 years during your career, so let's use that as our timeline for this example. We will now use a financial calculator to determine the value of $200 multiplied for 480 months (40 years) at 8% earnings. Hold on to your hat. The resultant number equals $702,856! Of the $702,856, there is $606,856 in pure earnings that most Americans forfeit simply by allowing too much money to be withheld from their paychecks.

By claiming your tax dollars now instead of later, and by employing them in a prudent investment plan, that money could propel you more than halfway to becoming a millionaire! I was startled when I made this revelation myself!

Now follow the steps in the "My W-4 Plan" to complete your daily lesson.

My W-4 Plan

1. Use the tax withholding calculator in this chapter to determine how many allowances you should claim.

2. Ask the human resources department to make the necessary adjustments on your W-4 form.

3. Commit to using the additional take-home pay that is created to retire debt or start an investment account.

Day 6

Become a Better Consumer

The easiest way to make your dollars go further is to spend less.

Let me repeat that.

The easiest way to make your dollars go further is to spend *less*.

Now, you understand what I am trying to say, don't you? We need to work on your *purchasing skills,* because the easiest way to spend *less* is to become a **smarter consumer**.

Being a smart consumer means getting what you want or need for the absolute lowest possible price. Some call this *stretching* your dollars. Doing this will require some forethought on your part.

I am going to dedicate Day 6 to teaching you to think *before* you spend.

To do this, I will give you a sequence of steps that will allow you to evaluate any buying decision and make the best purchase possible.

In addition, whenever your evaluation process leads you to a *buy* decision, I will show you additional ways to ensure that you never pay too much for any item.

First topic…

Salespeople!

Gotta love 'em. Or not. Lurking near any retail area, these individuals are caring, honest, and just want to be our friends…right?

Of course not! They only want one thing—to sell something, anything, to anyone at any time!

Remember: anyone selling you something is not your buddy, pal, or partner. Salespeople may look friendly, act friendly, sound friendly, and smile at you with adoring eyes, but do not fool yourself!

You will not *hurt their feelings* when you decline their offers (although you may wound their wallets). Too many consumers end up buying out of obligation or a sense of duty because they are duped into believing that a salesperson will suffer emotional damage if refused. This is nonsense. Salespeople play a game in which they have been well instructed. You should also know that the higher the stakes, the more skilled the salesperson is at closing the deal.

Does this mean that they are all bad people? Not necessarily. They are just doing a job. It can be a legitimate way to make a living. Some of the most highly skilled salespeople I have ever met market life insurance products. Top-producing agents easily make several hundred thousand dollars per year. They spend a good deal of their time and their personal income perfecting the art of selling, whereas your local convenience store clerk may need to invest little in his or her sales skills.

Do Your Homework

The first step to avoiding any con is to do your own research before you buy. To keep from being prematurely separated from your money, you should verify all product claims through an independent source not connected to the sale. You need to do your homework before you commit to anything, and with invaluable resources such as the World Wide Web and the Internet, conducting your own research is very easy.

Advertising

It is nearly impossible to avoid the constant barrage of advertisement that occurs each day. Everywhere we go, we are bombarded by marketing messages. It is the job of advertisers to create desire and perceived value where none existed before. Most people understand that advertisers try to control how we think. Marketers tell us what is chic, what is safe, what is valuable, how to become popular or "cool," and (my favorite) what we *deserve*. This is pandering at its best. Accomplished salespeople are masters at their craft. If you disagree, then do me a favor. Go look in your closet or your garage. If you have chosen a certain brand-name item, then you have been persuaded to purchase that brand over another through the power of branding and advertising.

Advertisers have convinced almost everyone that if they do not wear certain clothes, or do not shop at well-known stores, or do not choose to drive a certain vehicle, they are somehow lacking. If you really stop and think about this assumption, there is only one conclusion that you can reach: the whole idea is ridiculous! It is merely an illusion. But, because this illusion comes at you thousands of times a day from billboards, movies, magazines, flyers, television, and so forth, the illusion begins to seem like reality! Do not be fooled by sensational marketing. Do not allow advertisers to control your lifestyle.

I remember long ago leasing a Mercedes that came with an astronomical monthly payment. Again, this was a very long time ago, before I had learned any real financial lessons. At that time, I believed that if I drove a Mercedes, others would view me as a successful person. Clearly, the advertisers had done their job well. Now I understand that it is much better to drive an inexpensive car and have people *think* that you are poor (when you are actually wealthy) than it is to drive a luxury car to make people think you are wealthy (when, in reality, you are broke). Still, people choose the latter option all the time because their fear of being judged overwhelms their desire to become financially sensible and solvent. Crazy!

I learned later in life that many multimillionaires drive relatively modest vehicles. I find that those with a mind-set of wealth will not spend money just to impress others.

Quality/Price Ratio
Perceived value is a powerful weapon that advertisers use to tempt you. You have been taught that better quality items fetch higher prices. However, have you ever noticed that the price seems to increase at an accelerated rate as the quality increases?

For example, a flawless, one-carat diamond might retail for $50,000 while a diamond that looks just as good to the naked eye can be bought

51

for less than $10,000. Where did the extra $40,000 price tag come from?

It comes from the supposed resale value. In reality, the chances are not great that you will sell the stone yourself. And even if you decided to sell the stone, it is unlikely that you would receive anything close to the projected resale price.

You can purchase an excellently made new sedan for around $30,000, or you could pay $100,000 for a luxury or exotic vehicle with similar specs. What is the difference? Mostly show. In reality, both vehicles take you anywhere you want to go, which is the primary reason to own a car. I will admit that the luxury vehicle may have alluring details, but do those details mean that you should pay three times as much? Are you getting 300% more in satisfaction and benefits? Of course not! I know that there are going to be a bunch of you who will try to argue with me on this point. I am going to assume that you are still under the hypnotic trance created by the advertisers. Once you free yourself from their spell, you will be able to come to your senses and begin making sound purchasing decisions.

When spending your after-tax dollars, you need to become more concerned with value than ego. As a perfect example: someone I know once argued that it was absolutely necessary that she purchase a $50,000 luxury wagon based on the fact that she claimed she was thinking of her children's safety, and she needed seating for at least seven passengers. At the time, that year's wagon-type models which received the first- and second-place rankings, respectively, for the safest wagons on the market were non-luxury vehicles that were priced (new) at $20,000 less than her luxury wagon. The less expensive wagons also seated seven to eight passengers. Her ego cost her $20,000 just on that one purchase. Most likely, she made the decision based on the fact that her friends had purchased the luxury vehicle, so she convinced herself that she needed one too. Just think how far that extra $20,000 would have gone had she contributed it toward her children's college education!

Learn to Negotiate
Did you know that America is one of the few places in the world where people pay asking price for nearly everything? The markup on

most items sold in this country ranges anywhere from 20% (such as on a newly constructed home) to 300% (for a piece of fine jewelry).

Why not ask for a better price?

For most people the answer is simply that they do not know how to negotiate without feeling like they are offending the seller.

Here are a few tips to help you make the negotiating process a little easier on your psyche.

First, you need to realize that a seller would rather have an offer below asking price than no offer at all. I own a furniture store in Florida. The markup on our merchandise is 100%. A sofa that sells for $1,000 was bought from the manufacturer for $500. If a customer walked into my store and offered me $800 for that sofa, and we ultimately agreed on a price of $900, then that customer saved $100, and I still made a reasonable profit. Stated another way: the customer just earned $100 tax-free in five minutes! That is a pretty decent hourly wage.

Only the uninformed or the timid pay asking price. Here is a rule to live by: always make an offer. The worst that can happen is that you will be refused, and we are not talking about being turned down on a marriage proposal here, so…you'll live.

For this strategy to work, you need to make sure that you are talking to someone who has the authority to cut a deal. How do you establish a salesperson's clout?

Answer: you ask! Be straightforward. Ask, "Who in this store would be authorized to sell me your merchandise at a discount if I choose to buy something today?"

You may be told that the owner is the only one with that authority and that the owner is not in the store. To this response you say, "That's fine. I will leave you my name and number as I am interested in purchasing several of your pieces." Next thing you know, you will be speaking with the owner or with whichever employee has the ability to negotiate prices. The key is that you must have patience. Negotiations take time.

Guaranteed money from an interested buyer is worth more to an owner than an uncertain sale in the future. Almost everyone has a little flexibility in their prices for a serious purchaser. You will only find out if you ask! Unfortunately, asking for a better deal seems to be a big problem for most people. Here again, giving in to your ego will cost you money, maybe a lot of money. Consumers refrain from asking for a discount because they fear that they will look cheap or that their negotiating will offend someone.

Here is an approach that should help even the shyest (or most egotistic) shopper: simply compliment the merchant on the item of interest, and ask if a 20% discount would be possible if the purchase was made right away. If the proposal is rejected, give them a second opportunity by letting them know that you will need to shop around to determine if their price is the best one available. Chances are that the proprietor may relent in order to keep you from leaving the shop empty-handed.

Try it! You will be amazed at how many people will adjust prices in order to keep your business.

Purchase in Bulk

There are plenty of places that offer shopping in bulk now, and it is easy to save money when you shop this way. Costco, Price Club, and Sam's Club use this concept. Stockpiling might cost you more in the beginning, but the overall savings are worth the extra storage space you will use. However, do not overdo it. Why buy 20 boxes of oatmeal if you will never, ever eat 20 boxes of oatmeal? Too many people "overshop" at these bulk stores and end up wasting money anyway when their purchases go unused.

Buying out of Season

When is the best time to buy an umbrella? You buy it when the sun is shining, of course. The best time to buy ski equipment is at the beginning of summer. When should you buy Christmas lights and decorations? December 26!

This strategy may not be new to you, but most people do not take advantage of buying out-of-season items. Timing your purchases (instead of buying on impulse or buying items when their prices are at a premium) may save you up to 50% or more on just about anything. We will discuss this concept in more detail when we talk about car buying on Day 17.

Used or Damaged Goods

Did you know that you can save up to 90% off regular prices by purchasing items that are used or less than perfect? Some stores sell clothes that have been returned or that have slight imperfections for less than half of the original price. Furniture can be bought in nearly new condition for a total savings of 50%–75%.

The same goes for electronics, computers, CDs, and DVDs. All of these can be purchased for pennies on the dollar when you purchase them slightly used or "out of the box."

Again, forget your ego! Who cares if you buy used? Think of the money you might save and how you will be getting richer, faster than all those folks paying full retail. The only real concern you should have is to make sure that you are not buying junk (this is especially true with electronic items). You should make sure that the items work properly, and ask the seller about warranty eligibility.

Outlet Malls

Outlet malls are springing up all across America. High-end retailers are opening shops in these facilities to sell their excess merchandise in order to make room for incoming products. Brand names like Hugo Boss, Kenneth Cole, Nike, and Lennox are just a few examples of the kind of brand names you may find at the outlet malls.

Still, whenever you plan to purchase a brand-name item, make sure you do your homework before you shop—even before you shop at an outlet. Receiving $5 off of a $100 shirt is not a bargain. This is where the power of the Internet could save you a substantial amount of money on each purchase by allowing you to compare prices without much effort.

Let me give you another piece of advice. Just because you found a bargain does not mean that you should make the purchase. Even though you have just stumbled upon a stainless steel espresso machine for 50% off the retail price does not mean that you should buy it. Discount prices can help your budget, but they can also be hazardous to your financial health. Do not get in the habit of buying every bargain that you find. You will end up in debt all the same. (You will just end up in debt with slightly more stuff piled around your house.)

The Internet Is Your Friend

You will read this repeatedly in this book: use the endless resources found on the World Wide Web! Most retailers also have online stores.

There are incredible deals to be found online, and more and more retailers are paying for or discounting shipping costs which extends your purchasing power even further. Some items are available online only. You may be missing out on great deals if you never shop online. Additionally, you want to make use of resources such as the Federal Trade Commission's Bureau of Consumer Protection Web site. The site provides a wide array of consumer information such as product alerts and warnings, product safety tips, and a platform for consumers who need to file complaints about companies. The FTC's Web site can be found at www.ftc.gov/bcp/consumer.shtm.

Another consumer resource is *Consumer Reports* which provides consumer information on just about anything on the planet. This site can be an excellent source of information, but it is a subscription-based Web site. Its main page can be found at www.consumerreports.org.

Buyer Beware

There are many types of dishonest offers of which I want you to be aware. One in particular is the *deadline offer*—offers that claim that you must make a purchase **now,** or the offer *will be gone forever* (supposedly). Do not be pressured by that tactic. Nine times out of ten, the threat is bogus. Deadline offers are one of the oldest tricks in the (salesperson) handbook. Any offer put on the table today will, more than likely, be available tomorrow, regardless of what you are being told.

Final Thoughts

Remember our primary purpose: the motivation to become a better consumer should be tied directly to your principal desire for financial freedom. It takes discipline and forethought to achieve this goal. It means placing value above convenience, impulse, or ego. It means spending a little extra time shopping around and learning the art of negotiation...and, more importantly, RESTRAINT.

If you use the techniques provided in today's lesson, you should save several hundred dollars per month, depending on your current level of shopping. Those saved dollars can be used to pay off debt or to continue funding your investments. Compound this money over time, and you will achieve your financial goals at a much faster pace.

By implementing these lessons into your spending routine, you will soon find more cash each month to put to better use, which means you will be another day closer to creating a better life for yourself and your family.

My Savings Worksheet

List the items you plan to purchase in the near future. These are items that you now know could be purchased out of season, pre-owned or used, in bulk, through discount and online vendors, or by negotiating the price of any item. When you finally make the purchase, write down the retail price of the item, and then next to it, write down the price that you paid for it.

With your new smart consumer knowledge, you should see a significant difference between the two prices. If you cannot see a big difference, then read today's chapter again and work harder to apply its lessons to your next purchase.

Item	Retail Price	Purchase Price	Savings!

❖ ❖ ❖

Day 7

Saving Money on Car Insurance

Today will be devoted to the topic of auto insurance. Car insurance premiums can total thousands of dollars per year for owners with multiple vehicles, so it is important to find the lowest rate available, coupled with the proper policy coverage. For those who have to add teenage drivers into the equation, the value of today's lesson becomes even more significant.

First, this is a purchasing decision, so take advantage of the lessons you learned on Day 6.

Resist being swayed by flashy or humorous advertising. Just because the commercial says you can save a lot of money on your car insurance by switching (to you know who) does not mean that *you* will really save money.

In this chapter, you will find some easy-to-follow tips and strategies that can help you cut your car insurance premiums by 15%–30%. That savings could equal hundreds of dollars each year.

Know the Different Coverage Types

It is important that you know exactly what you are buying. You need to be able to identify which type of coverage is best for your situation.

Collision

Collision covers damage done to your car in the event of a collision or a vehicle rollover. Under this coverage, the insurance company pays the claim, minus your deductible.

Comprehensive

Comprehensive covers loss incurred by theft, fire, falling objects, or natural disasters. Whereas collision protects the value of your car in the event of an accident, comprehensive coverage will protect your car from just about any other type of vehicle damage.

Liability

This type of coverage serves to compensate others in the event that you are at fault in an accident. This coverage also provides protection in auto-related lawsuits. Liability is the most important part of your auto insurance policy and is required by law in virtually all states. Carry enough coverage to protect your net worth. If your net worth is $1,000,000, make sure you have a sufficient amount of liability protection. (Refer to your net worth statement from Day 2.)

Bodily Injury

If you are at fault in an accident and the accident causes injury to someone else, bodily injury coverage will pay for the injured person's medical expenses and lost wages. This type of coverage is also required by law in most states and comprises a critical part of your insurance package.

Property Damage

This coverage pays toward damage caused to another person's property including cars, homes, fences, and other items—anything that might become damaged in an auto accident. This is another form of liability coverage.

Medical Payments

Pretty self-explanatory—this coverage pays for medical bills and/or funeral expenses in the event that a covered driver or his or her passengers are injured or killed. The coverage pays regardless of who is at fault.

Personal Injury Protection (PIP)

This coverage is available in some states and helps to pay for medical costs, lost wages, or other accident-related expenses. It is very similar to medical payments coverage. This coverage is mandatory in some states.

Uninsured/Under-Insured Motorist

This coverage provides for medical expenses, lost wages, and general damage in the event that you are involved in an accident in which another driver is uninsured or under-insured. This coverage is mandatory in some states.

Rental Car Reimbursement Coverage

This is an optional coverage offered in some states. It will pay for the cost of a rental car in the event that your car is damaged or stolen.

Emergency Road Service

This coverage will pay for towing should your car become disabled. If you are already a member of a service like AAA or own a vehicle whose manufacture provides lifetime roadside assistance, this insurance option is unnecessary. You can save some money by dropping the coverage.

Tip 1: Comparison Shop Online

With today's technology, it is easy to shop insurance rates. There are several great Web sites that I suggest you visit in order to get some competitive quotes for your policies. Go to www.insure.com, www. esurance.com, www.comparisonmarket.com, www.progressive.com, and www.geico.com. These are just a few examples of Web sites that provide free quotes. If you have a good driving record, be sure and obtain a quote from www.allstate.com.

Just a few minutes' review of each Web site could mean a big cost difference in rates and result in a significant amount of savings year after year. I love strategies that you can implement one time that will save you money for a lifetime.

Tip 2: Raise Your Deductible

Unless you are getting into a car accident every three years, it is probably cost-effective for you to raise your deductible amount on the collision and comprehensive portions of your policy. For example: by raising your deductible from $250 to $500 (or possibly as high as

$1,000), you can save up to 40% on this portion of the premiums. By opting for a higher deductible, you assume more of the risk and lighten the load on the insurance company. A higher deductible lowers your monthly premiums, so this option pays off by increasing your monthly cash flow. You just need to make sure that you have the cash on hand to cover your deductible amount should an accident occur.

Tip 3: Drop Unnecessary Coverage

Take the time to learn how car insurance really works, what each coverage type protects, and how it is applied. You may find that you have elected some unnecessary coverage.

Collision and comprehensive will cover the value of your vehicle should you get into an accident or otherwise suffer a financial loss related to your auto. Here is a money-saving tip: if your car looks like it has already been in an accident, paying for collision and comprehensive may provide little value for you. In other words, if your car *is* a wreck, *collision and comprehensive* coverage will provide little compensation if you get into an accident. The insurance company will not buy you a brand-new car. Rather, they will only recompense you for the relatively small value of your current jalopy.

Once the value of your car dips below $3,000, it is time to consider dropping the collision and comprehensive coverage. Let's face it; when you get to this point, you really need to avoid wasting any money so that you can begin to *save* money to buy a newer car!

Tip 4: Avoid Coverage Add-Ons

If an insurance agent tries to tempt you with add-on coverage such as *towing*—beware! An add-on like this is just a high-profit item for the insurance companies. Stick with the coverages you need: *liability (bodily injury and property damage), collision and comprehensive*, and *uninsured motorist*. Watch out for so-called specialty products. Their sole purpose is to provide profit for the insurance company.

Tip 5: Choose a Car Carefully

The make and model and age of your car will, in large part, determine your insurance costs. Some cars are more susceptible to theft, and some have higher repair costs. In order to avoid getting trapped in a vehicle that is too expensive for your budget, you need to research *all* of its related costs before you buy your next vehicle. One of the most important cost factors is the insurance premiums.

A quick call to your insurance company will determine which cars are *premium friendly*, meaning your premium payments will be reasonable. Before you buy that luxury sports car or behemoth SUV, you need to find out what you will be paying in additional insurance costs *each year*. Also, Web sites such as www.edmunds.com can be an easy source for general information regarding insurance costs for every kind of vehicle.

Tip 6: Be a Safe Driver

Careless driving can cost you in a number of ways.

To keep your insurance costs to a minimum, maintain a clean driving record. Do your best to avoid moving violations and accidents. Learn how to become a defensive driver in order to anticipate bad situations around you. Go the speed limit. Stop completely at all stop signs. Do not assume that another driver will stop at a stop sign or stoplight. Make sure the intersection is clear before proceeding.

If you are juggling things like a cell phone, jumbo coffees, lunch, lipstick, or darling Fido in your lap, you will dramatically increase your chances of getting into an accident. Modern vehicles have become incredibly easy to operate, so much so that people mistakenly believe that driving needs little attention or effort. Do not allow yourself to become distracted while driving. More than any amount of money, your health and well-being is the most valuable asset you possess. Do not jeopardize any of these precious things by driving recklessly.

If your current driving record is marred, clean it up as soon as possible, and then keep it clean. You will establish yourself as a lower risk to the insurance company, which will result in lower premiums on your policy.

Tip 7: Maintain Good Credit

Maintaining a good credit score may save some serious dollars on your insurance costs. Insurance companies have found a correlation between a solid credit score and a good driving record. Paying your bills on time will lead to lower insurance costs, which, ironically, makes it easier to pay your bills on time.

Tip 8: Ask About Discounts

There are a multitude of reasons for which insurance companies will give discounts. Check for *multi-car, good student, good driver, senior citizen, long-term customer,* or *driving school completion* discounts.

No one is going to call *you* just to tell you that you now qualify for an insurance discount. You have to be the one to hunt down money-saving opportunities. Insurance agents get paid for selling insurance, not for saving you money.

Tip 9: Install Safety/Anti-Theft Devices

By installing an alarm and tracking device on your car, you can lower your risk profile to the insurance company.

The additional up-front expense that you will invest in installing this type of equipment may get paid back to you in a relatively short period due to the annual insurance savings you will enjoy. Plus, you will benefit from the immediate peace of mind provided by the extra security. Once you have installed an alarm and/or tracking device, make sure to tell your insurance company that you have added these mechanisms to the vehicle.

Tip 10: Keep Your Car(s) inside a Garage

Cars parked inside a garage are less likely to become targets for thieves, vandals, or other moving vehicles. Plus, you greatly reduce wear and tear by protecting your car from exposure to the elements. So, if you have a garage, make sure it is being used to house your valuable

Day 7: Saving Money on Car Insurance   autos. If your garage is currently serving as a self-storage unit, get rid of all the junk or storage items clogging up the space, or find a way to organize those items to create the parking space that you need.

Tip 11: Join Organizations and Auto Clubs

According to the AAA (American Automobile Association) Web site, this auto club provides emergency roadside services and maps as well as expert services in travel, financial services, car buying, and insurance. Besides freeing you from worries about flat tires, running out of gas, or engine failures, your AAA membership may also entitle you to a discount with your insurance company. Check out all the benefits of AAA on its Web site at www.aaa.com, or call 800-AAA-HELP (800-222-4357)

Auto insurance is an absolute need for any auto owner. In most states, it is illegal to drive without the proper insurance. Frankly, it is not smart to drive around without the proper coverage. One bad accident could clean you out financially. Use today's information to find the most cost-effective coverage available.

The extra money you will save each month makes it well worth the time and effort it will take to do some research. You can use the guideline on the following page to take notes as you make your phone calls.

My Auto Insurance Worksheet

Compare insurance rates to find the best offer.

Insurance Company	Monthly Rate	Types	Coverage	Misc. Notes

Day 8

Saving Thousands in Mortgage Interest

If you are like most people, the greatest expense you will ever incur will be the cost of buying your home and retiring your mortgage.

For the majority, it is financially unrealistic to pay cash for the entire cost of a home.

Therefore, almost every homebuyer needs to be astute about mortgages and all the legal obligations that a mortgage entails. Homebuyers also need to determine which type of mortgage is best for them.

There are many sound reasons for obtaining a mortgage. On Day 6 we learned ways to become better consumers. Well, a mortgage may represent the largest purchase of your entire life. Therefore, we want to use all the best research techniques and shopping strategies when the time comes to shop for a mortgage. In this purchasing situation, a smart consumer can save tens of thousands of dollars over the life of the home loan.

Again, the best plan to follow can be illustrated through a series of steps. Let's take a look at the proper approach to financing a home.

Step 1: Shop Around

Just as with any other major purchase, you must do detailed research and compare rates. This is one purchase in which your time and effort could pay off in a HUGE way.

Historically, most homebuyers use a mortgage broker whenever there is a need to purchase a mortgage. A broker acts as an intermediary between the borrower and the available lenders. They shop the market to find a loan that fits specific needs and means. For this service and the advice they offer, brokers are compensated through points, fees, or a percentage of the difference between the wholesale and the negotiated costs of the funds passed on to you, the borrower.

In the past, the borrowers looked for mortgages by talking with several different brokers or lending institutions and comparing loan offerings.

Today, technology has revolutionized just about every aspect of our lives, and shopping for a mortgage is no exception.

Online loan shopping is so simple; it only makes sense to begin the mortgage-shopping process at your computer instead of in a bank's branch office. Almost anyone with reasonable credit and a steady income can obtain a mortgage without paying any points and can enjoy a relatively low interest rate.

I suggest you check out some of the following Web sites to get the process started the right way: www.bankrate.com, www.eloan.com, www.ditech.com, www.quickenloans.com, and www.lendingtree.com.

Also, keep your eyes and ears open. There are new Web sites coming to the market all the time. You want to find the most competitive rates, so use your favorite search engine and start mortgage hunting.

Step 2: Compare Apples to Apples

Once you have at least five different offers on the table, it is time to compare each one in order to find the best loan package for your situation.

At first glance, you might find all the different terms and figures confusing. One offer might seem better at first. However, once you start *crunching the numbers*, you may find that the offer is not as good as you first thought. You need to be willing to take a little time to learn what the mortgage terms and figures mean.

You will find mortgage offers with *lower interest rates with higher points* and *higher interest rates with low or no points*. You will see *interest-only* loans and *adjustable-rate* loans. Are you familiar with all or any of these terms? Do you know how each one will affect your payments and total payoff amount?

Which one is right for you?

First, take a step back and look at *your* big picture.

- How long are you planning on staying in this house? This question is critical when determining whether it makes sense to pay points in order to obtain a lower interest rate.
  - If you plan to stay in your home *less than* seven years, it would not make good financial sense to pay the extra money on points, even if it provides you a loan with a lower rate of interest. (For those of you who are new to the mortgage market, a *point* equals 1% of the loan and is charged by some lenders as a service fee or to buy down a lower rate of interest. For example, a lender may quote a 6% rate of interest with *one point,* or 6.5% rate of interest with *no points.*)
  - If you plan to stay in the house for *more than* seven years, keep the long-term scenario in mind. Paying extra for points in return for a lower interest rate is probably the best choice for you.

When it comes to your mortgage, knowledge is financial power. Know *exactly* what each kind of loan will mean for your financial future. This awareness can save you tens of thousands of dollars.

Review the following mortgage components. You will need to understand each one in order to make the best mortgage choice.

A 15-Year Mortgage versus a 30-Year Mortgage

You may be under the impression that a 30-year loan is the standard that the average person chooses, so there must be no reason to consider anything else.

Wait a minute. You are reading this book so that you can do *better than* the *average* person, correct?

In order to do better than average, you have to be willing to learn more than the average person knows.

Let's compare the figures from a conventional 30-year mortgage and a 15-year mortgage.

30-Year Mortgage

If a buyer borrows $200,000 at 6% and pays the loan off over the full term of 30 years, the payments will total $431,000! In this loan scenario, you end up paying more in interest than principal during the life of the loan. It is like buying a house for yourself and one for the bank!

The monthly payment would equal $1,200, and the principal portion of your first payment would be less than $200. The entire remaining balance goes toward interest costs.

In fact, you will *not* make a payment where the principal portion exceeds the amount paid toward interest until payment number 222 out of 360 total payments.

For those who have not begun hyperventilating yet, please read that previous sentence again.

Can you believe it?

No wonder the mortgage business is such a lucrative enterprise!

Furthermore, in most cases, just about the time that the owner would start taking a bite out of the loan balance, it will probably be time to move. Most folks relocate every five to seven years. Then you start the process all over again with a brand-new 30-year mortgage. It can become a vicious cycle.

Allow me to give you an alternative to this scenario.

15-Year Mortgage

By electing to service the loan over a period of 15 years instead of 30 years, you could save an incredible amount of money.

The $1,200 monthly payment would increase to $1,687 per month, but the 15-year term saves more than $125,000 in total interest payments! The 15-year term also receives a more favorable interest rate, which saves even more money.

Your crossover point—the point where the amount paid toward principal equals the amount paid toward interest—would also move up from payment 222 (found in the 30-year mortgage example) to payment

42. (Obviously, with the 15-year loan the total number of monthly payments is reduced from 360 to 180.)

My point: if you can handle the increased payment imposed by the 15-year mortgage, it is to your extreme advantage to do so. It might crimp your financial style for the first couple of years, but you will adjust to the higher payment. If you cannot manage the small additional increase for each monthly payment, you need to make changes in your financial management as soon as possible. Each chapter in this book will teach you ways to either save money or make more money.

Adjustable-Rate Financing versus Fixed-Rate Financing

Let's take a look at both *adjustable-rate financing* and *fixed-rate financing* and compare the elements of each one.

An *adjustable-rate* loan will start with a *teaser rate*. A teaser rate is a very low interest rate offered at the beginning of the term of the loan. Adjustable-rate loans are tied to an index, like the prime rate, treasuries, or the LIBOR.

Most adjustable rates will allow you to lock in the interest rate for a specific period of time. The time frame normally ranges from one to five years. Thereafter the interest rate will float based upon the index to which it is tied.

The chances are strong that your adjustable rate on your mortgage will go up during the time that you own the property. The rate increase can raise the monthly payment significantly. The homeowner must be prepared for this increase—and be able to pay the higher monthly payment—or risk foreclosure on the property. This is the risk inherent in an adjustable-rate mortgage.

I do not want to advise you to avoid adjustable-rate loans altogether because, with the proper strategy, these loans can be used to your advantage. Whether you should choose a fixed-rate loan or an adjustable-rate loan depends upon the length of time that you plan to own the property and the prevailing interest rates.

If the plan is to own the property for *more than* five years, and you can obtain a fixed-rate loan with an interest rate of 8% or less, lock in your rate. If the interest rates are above 8%, take an adjustable-rate mortgage.

However, if the plan is to own a property for *less than* five years, it is statistically to your advantage to take the adjustable-rate loan. By the time the interest rates rise to the point where the rate is now disadvantageous (assuming rates move upward), your plan was to liquidate the property anyway, so this factor should not affect you. We will cover real estate investing in greater detail in a later chapter. In order to make a profit and stay out of trouble, you need to educate yourself and construct a reliable plan for each investment.

Interest-Only Loans

As the name implies, an interest-only loan is a hybrid that only requires that the borrower keep the interest current on a monthly basis, with no principal reduction built into the payment. These loans typically have a call feature and must be paid in full within five or seven years. At that point, the borrower would either need to sell, refinance, or pay off the balance with cash. Critical planning must be done in advance when obtaining this type of a mortgage. In the absence of appreciation, the owner does not have the benefit of any equity built during the holding period.

Balloon Payment Loans

A balloon payment loan calls for a lump-sum payment at some future date. In some cases, the balloon might represent 100% of the outstanding balance. In order for this type of loan to be appropriate for a borrower, the borrower must be a very savvy money manager with an iron-clad financial future. As you might imagine, I do not recommend these types of loans to many people.

Lender Fees

In addition to the interest and the *loan origination fees* (points) charged by your lender, there will be additional costs associated with obtaining financing for your property.

Some items are required by almost all lenders, such as *appraisal costs*, *title insurance*, and *recording fees*. Others items may simply translate into additional profits for the mortgage broker, like *document preparation fees* and *warehousing fees*.

It is always a good idea to obtain a written estimate—called a *good faith* estimate—detailing all of the costs associated with each lender's proposal before you commit to a particular loan.

Trust me—you do not want any last-minute surprises at the closing table.

Down Payment

How much of a down payment should be applied toward a home purchase?

I have heard various arguments as to what amount comprises the best proportion, but in my opinion, there really is no magic number that will apply to everyone or to every home-buying scenario. However, the down payment will affect how the loan is structured. Obviously, a larger down payment will create lower monthly payments, *and,* typically, it will lower the interest rate on the loan. Usually, the buyer will receive the lowest available interest rate if the down payment equals at least 20% of the purchase price or the appraised value of the property. This amount of down payment also avoids the necessity for Private Mortgage Insurance (PMI) which is a type of insurance some lenders require in order to offset some of the risk that is normally associated with property that has been highly leveraged. If the lender should foreclose on the property, sell it at auction, and take a loss, the insurance carrier would cover the loss with a payment to the lender.

With a 20% down payment, qualifying for a loan is relatively simple, provided you have a credit score of 680 or higher and a reasonable debt-to-equity ratio (ratio of all debt payments to income).

On the other hand, a smaller down payment translates into more cash in your pocket *now*, which could be used to invest in alternative ventures. If these investments could produce a higher rate of return than the interest charged by the mortgage company, you'd get to keep the overage. Please understand that this is a very aggressive posture that should only be considered by investors with a solid, long-term track record for making money in the marketplace.

We will discuss a variety of investment opportunities in later chapters.

Home Equity Lines of Credit

For most property owners, a home equity line of credit is an incredibly attractive method of securing funds. It provides immediate access to the equity in your home at relatively inexpensive rates, and the interest portion of the payment can be tax deductible.

Many borrowers use these funds to pay off high-interest credit card balances, car loans, and other personal obligations. This has become one of the most popular sources of debt consolidation in today's financial world.

However, like many other optional financing scenarios, there is reason to be very cautious when using this strategy.

It can be extremely hazardous to your personal security to replace unsecured debt with a loan that empowers a lender to take your home and sell it in order to satisfy the loan obligation (assuming you became incapable of making the payments).

I recommend staying far away from home equity lines of credit if you have any doubts about your financial discipline, or if you might be in any way unable to pay the loan in the case of emergency. If any doubt exists whatsoever, then do not proceed with attaining an equity line of credit on your home.

It is one matter to have a car repossessed or to default on a credit card account. Losing your home to foreclosure is a much more difficult experience from which to recover. Beyond the negative financial impact, the emotional scars and logistical nightmare that foreclosure can cause may take you many years to repair.

Final Thoughts

When it comes to selecting your mortgage, remember—take your time.

This may be the biggest financial decision you will ever make.

Shop around for the lowest possible interest rate coupled with the terms that best suit your specific plans for the property you are purchasing. Make sure that you receive written *good faith estimates* from each of the potential lenders. You do not want any nasty surprises after you have given a seller a non-refundable deposit.

By learning these mortgage strategies, you can save yourself more money in interest, over the term of the loan, than most American families save in a lifetime.

My Mortgage Worksheet

When the time comes to obtain a mortgage, follow these steps:

Step 1: Shop for the most attractive rates and terms at www.bankrate.com.

Step 2: Choose a 15-year mortgage versus a 30-year term if you are financially able to do so.

Step 3: If the plan is to live in the property for five years or more, choose a fixed-rate loan. If the plan is to live in the home for less than 5 years or if mortgage rates exceed 8%, choose an adjustable-rate loan.

Step 4: Remember: all lender fees are negotiable.

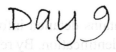
Day 9

Your Credit Profile

In the United States, we enjoy a free capital society.

Your personal level of enjoyment may depend upon your ability to borrow funds for personal use, real estate investments, or other business opportunities. The consumers who have better personal credit standings will find it easier to obtain money and will benefit from lower interest rates on borrowed funds.

You need to become diligent about maintaining your credit status in order to ensure that you achieve the highest level possible. To help you accomplish this, we will begin by exploring the various components that make up a credit score.

Credit Agencies

There are three primary credit agencies in the United States: Equifax, TransUnion, and Experian. These three organizations build a credit report card, so to speak, which is meant to reflect each consumer's creditworthiness.

It is interesting that these three entities probably have more data on your lifestyle and personal activities than perhaps any other organization, including the IRS. Yet, they are not part of a government agency, nor are they required to obtain your permission to track all of your financial transactions. The credit agency trinity members act like a self-appointed superpower that has the authority to affect almost every aspect of your financial life.

Whether you consider this situation fair or unfair is a discussion topic for another sort of book. For today's lesson in *this* book, I will explain the importance of learning how to deal effectively with the powers that be.

Your Credit Report

Your credit report contains detailed information about your financial history and personal identification. By reviewing your credit report, you have an opportunity to see yourself through the eyes of a potential lender.

The typical consumer credit report contains the following four types of information: public record, credit data, inquiries by others who have viewed your credit, and personal information.

Let's take a closer look at each of these information types.

Public Record Information

This information includes mortgages, liens, judgments, bankruptcy, and items such as overdue child support. Bankruptcy information can remain on your record for up to 10 years, tax liens for 15 years, and most other public information exists for approximately 7 years.

Credit Information

Credit information monitors specific account data such as the date an account was opened, credit limits, loan amounts, payments due, and payment record. This report also shows whether anyone besides you is responsible for a particular payment.

Active positive information may remain indefinitely while negative information can only remain on a report for a maximum period of seven years.

Requests to View Your Credit Report

On occasion, certain institutions will view your credit history. Whether you are being evaluated for a car loan or a mortgage, your credit report will be analyzed.

Your credit report will keep track of everyone who has viewed your credit history. This is a matter of federal law. According to the Fair Credit Reporting Act, credit grantors with permissible purpose may review your credit information without your prior consent. This activity may seem like an invasion of your privacy, but these are the rules. You should be aware of how the credit industry operates.

Personal Information

This information includes your name, current and previous addresses, telephone numbers, variations in your social security number, date of birth, and current and previous employers.

What it does not include is information regarding your race, religion, medical history, personal lifestyle, political affiliation, or criminal record. (Hey, at least *some* personal history and lifestyle issues are considered to be private information.)

You have the right to review your credit report at any time. If you are turned down for credit due to information contained in your report, a copy must be provided to you, free of charge. All you have to do is submit a request to the credit agency. Visit the credit agency Web sites at www.experian.com, or www.transunion.com, or www.equifax.com to submit a request online. You may also be entitled to a free copy of your report if you are unemployed, on welfare, or if you have reason to believe that your credit file contains inaccuracies due to fraud. At any time, each of the three primary credit agencies will allow you to access your credit report online for a nominal fee. You should check your credit report on an annual basis, at the very least. If you have not done so during the past 12 months, let's check it today. You can check your credit report annually, free of charge.

Federal law allows consumers to challenge inaccuracies and correct their credit files, also free of charge. Consumers also have the right to have a *statement of dispute* added to a credit history. A statement of dispute acts as a representation for the consumer's side of the story. It may help provide a potential creditor with information otherwise not contained in the report. Keep in mind that this statement will remain a part of your report for seven years.

Your FICO Score

One of the most widely accepted measures of your creditworthiness is your FICO score. This rating, developed by the Fair Isaac Corporation, is used by potential lenders to determine the likelihood that a borrower will repay a financial obligation.

A credit score attempts to translate a borrower's credit history into a single rating number. As you can imagine, this process can be challenging.

Your score is somewhat of a mystery because the credit reporting agencies are not required to disclose the formula that computes your score. Believe it or not, the Federal Trade Commission has deemed this approach to be acceptable.

Five Parts to FICO

While the formula varies for each credit report, the credit bureaus weigh the different types of information on your credit report with the following breakdown:

1. Your Payment History: 35%

Are you making your payments to creditors on time? If not, late payments or non-payment will hurt your credit score and will act as proof to lenders that you are not a reliable borrower.

2. The Total Amount That You Owe: 30%

How much debt have you accumulated? The amount that you owe can impact your credit score. The more debt you have, the less likely it will be that you will be able to take on any additional debt. Also taken into consideration is the amount you owe in proportion to the amount of credit you have available.

3. Length of Credit History: 15%

Have you had enough credit activity to provide substantial information regarding your spending habits? If you are a young person and have not built much of an independent financial record, your score may be low (or non-existent) due to lack of information. This situation can be frustrating to young adults who wonder how they will be allowed to develop a credit rating when they cannot seem to get anyone to extend them any credit...because they *lack* credit. Is there any way out of this vicious circle? Of course! Start with an easy-to-obtain credit card.

4. New Credit: 10%

Whenever you apply for a new credit line or open a new account, these actions affect your credit score. Depending on your financial history, new credit could affect your score in either a positive or detrimental way.

5. Other Factors: 10%

Other factors may affect your credit score.

Problems may arise when an individual has too many accounts open at one time. Lenders may view numerous open accounts as excessive portals through which you may get yourself into a financial bind.

Credit scores are determined by analyzing your credit history, taking into consideration various factors such as employment history, the length of time credit has been used, the amount of credit available compared to the amount of credit in use, payment record, and also more serious problems such as bankruptcies, charge-offs, and collections. Due to the fact that there are three credit agencies, you end up with three separate FICO scores. Some lenders will use one of the three while other lenders take an average of all three scores combined.

Improving Your Credit Score

Nothing improves your credit score like a sound understanding of the credit process and a good financial plan. If your credit score is suffering, do not wait for time to heal your wounds. That could take years. Let's take action now by examining your options.

There are companies out there who claim that they can restore your damaged credit immediately by getting any derogatory statements erased from your report. Be careful with these offers. I have spoken to many credit bureau representatives, and they have explained that many so-called *credit repair companies* are actually shams. Anything these organizations offer to do for a fee—like challenge a negative credit mark or present your side of the story—you can do on your own for free. With the knowledge you will obtain in this chapter, you will know what they know.

If you need to repair or improve your credit score, the following tips will get you headed in the right direction:

Tip 1.

Never attempt to hide from a creditor. If you cannot make a payment (or several payments) you will still do better by maintaining a consistent dialogue with your creditors. Some creditors may allow for some flexibility if you are willing to make an effort to contact them and explain any extenuating circumstances. They will not "let you off the hook" forever, but your communication efforts may prevent your accounts from being sent to collection agencies.

Tip 2.

Limit the number of inquiries to your credit report. Too many inquiries give the appearance that you may be trying to acquire too much credit.

Tip 3.

Reduce your loan balances. Reducing your loan balance improves your income-to-debt ratio. This act may have a significant and immediate positive impact on your credit score.

Tip 4.

Purchase a home. This may come as a surprise, but the purchase of a home is considered to be a good kind of debt with regard to your credit report. Lenders appreciate homeowners (as long as those homeowners are making mortgage payments on time, of course). On-time payments made on a mortgage will establish a good financial history.

Building a *Powerful* Credit Profile

1. *Pay your bills on time.* In order to pay your bills on time, all the time, you must learn how to budget and, perhaps, create special plans for unexpected lean times. Almost everyone experiences financial downturns at some point. Job loss, health issues, family emergencies, or family collapse—all of these issues can lead

to financial hardships. Do your best to establish some type of emergency plan so that, should an emergency occur, you will be able to survive without total financial devastation. It is a good idea to maintain three months' worth of living expenses in an interest bearing account for such events. With three months of covered time, you should be capable of developing and implementing a "plan B" in order to regain control of your situation without causing long-term credit problems during the interim.

2. *Avoid triggering an inquiry that will show up on your report.* As we have discussed previously, too many inquiries will cause concern for creditors.

3. *Take care not to have too many credit cards with high limits.* Lenders will assume that you may access these funds at any time and fold the potential debt into their calculations.

4. ***Never*** *co-sign a loan for* <u>*anyone*</u> *unless you are fully prepared to assume total responsibility for the repayment of the debt.* Anyone who needs another person to co-sign on a loan is not financially able to qualify for the financing on his or her own merit. Think about that before you co-sign. This is an issue that can cause serious strife among relatives. If you are asked to co-sign on a loan, you need to be sure that you have the ability (and willingness) to pay the debt on your own. If you have doubts about either issue, you need to refuse to co-sign. You do not want to chance the ruin of your own credit or destruction of personal relationships by entering into an inappropriate debt partnership.

5. *If you plan to get married, get a copy of your future spouse's credit report prior to the marriage.* I'm such a romantic! Right? I'm not recommending that you make this request during the actual marriage proposal...but, in all seriousness, you should discuss all financial topics in detail *before* you agree to marry your spouse-to-be. This book was not written with the intention of providing love-life advice. I will simply state that you should not dismiss your commitment to financial responsibility because of an emotional attachment. On the other hand, I am

not saying to exclude a partner based on a poor credit report; however, it is your right to know everything about the person to whom you will create a LEGAL (and financial) bond. In the event that your future spouse has a poor credit score and an unfortunate credit history, *your* future ability to borrow money may be compromised after the legal bond of marriage has been made. If you decide to proceed with the nuptials, you might want to consider any financing you will need for the near future and obtain that financing before the wedding occurs.

6. *Protect yourself from fraud.* Do whatever you can to avoid having your identity stolen. Do not allow your driver's license, social security card, receipts, or any account statements to be viewed by others, except when required by law.

7. *Review your credit report at least once a year.* Review every detail and check for anything that looks suspicious or anything that is inaccurate. Any errors should be brought to the attention of the credit bureaus, immediately. It is their job to represent you accurately, but it is your responsibility to make sure you are receiving the credit you are due (no pun intended). Additionally, if you are married, make sure that your spouse checks his or her credit report on a regular basis.

Credit Card Fraud

As of November 2012, the U.S. Federal Reserve reports that consumers owe more than $803.6 billion in credit card debt. With such a large balance and so many individuals holding credit cards, fraud is inevitable.

In the event that you become a victim of credit card fraud, it is likely that you will endure major inconveniences, including being forced to spend countless hours repairing harm that occurred due to no fault on your part.

There is no one definition of fraud, but some types of credit fraud include identity theft, identity assumption, and fraudulent spending.

Credit thieves can obtain your personal information by using your lost or stolen credit cards, stealing mail from your mailbox, looking over your shoulder while you are conducting a financial transaction, eaves-dropping on your phone conversations, sending unsolicited e-mail, tele-marketing, going through your personal records that have been thrown in the trash, or by hacking into an unprotected computer network.

The earlier you discover that a theft has occurred, the better the chances will be of fixing the situation. Some people remain unaware for years before they learn that they have been a victim of identity theft.

Here are some warning signs that may indicate that you have been a victim of credit card fraud:

1. *Your credit report contains information on accounts you never opened.* This is why it is extremely important that you check your credit report at least once a year.
2. *Unrecognized charges show up on your statement.* Check your credit card statements every month to make sure there are no er-roneous charges.
3. *Bills arrive from unfamiliar sources.* If you get a bill for an item you never purchased, chances are that you have been the victim of fraud. Give immediate attention to this problem! Procrastina-tion will definitely hurt you here.

In any of the above circumstances, notify the appropriate lender and the credit bureaus immediately. As part of your commitment to becom-ing organized, you should keep a master list of each of your creditor's names and contact information, as well as the relevant account numbers, so that you can address a problem as quickly as possible. Make sure this list is locked away with the rest of your private financial information. Your credit score is an invaluable tool that will decide your financial fate in almost every transaction.

And, even though this is not intended to be a book on personal re-lationships, perhaps, when it comes time to look for your one true love, instead of asking about that person's *sign*—maybe you should ask for his or her *score*. That latter kind of compatibility will prove to be much more important, trust me.

My Credit Worksheet

A. Getting Started—Your Current Credit Report

First, if it has been more than six months since you last pulled your credit report, go online to get a copy today. You can obtain one for free at: www.annualcreditreport.com/cra/index.jsp.

Once you have a recent copy of your credit report, continue filling out the following worksheet.

- My credit score is: _____
- Do you recognize, and can you account for, all the activity recorded on your report? _____
    - *If you find any erroneous item(s), call the appropriate lender immediately and contact the credit agency(s).*
    - If you do not find any errors or suspicious items, continue to the next section.

B. Improving Your Credit Score

You can:

1. *Dispute any discrepancies.* If you find a mistake, report it to your credit agency immediately.
2. *Tell your side of the story.* If there were extenuating circumstances regarding a negative mark that has affected your credit, it may help to contact the credit bureaus to present your side of the story. Make sure to include all relevant and important details of the matter in your letter of explanation. Your letter can include up to 100 words.
3. *Use the strategies in this book to cut expenses, and apply those savings to outstanding balances.* Reducing the loan balances that are reflected on your report will improve your score the most and in the shortest period of time. By the time you have finished with this book, you should be in a position to pay down an extra $300 to $500 per month on outstanding debts.

Follow the suggestions and steps outlined in this chapter to begin building a powerful credit profile, and repeat the worksheet process once
every six months in order to continuously maintain and improve your
overall score.

Day 10

Individual Retirement Plans

It will happen one day, you know. One day you will wake up and realize that your working days are done. Finally, you have reached retirement!

Before you begin daydreaming about all the things you want to do during your retirement, we need to focus on today's lessons so that you have the ability to fulfill all those dreams.

On Day 10 of your *30-Day Money Makeover*, we will examine individual retirement plans.

Throughout your days of employment, you want to make sure that you structure your financial life in a way that allows you to retire and live the lifestyle of your choice. An Individual Retirement Account (IRA) happens to be one of the simplest and most effective financial tools for accumulating wealth.

IRAs are available to almost everyone. They are easy to establish, provide access to a variety of investment choices, and may be free through certain trustees. Best of all, they can be easily habit forming!

The only negative feedback I receive from investors regarding IRAs is the fear concerning the penalties imposed for a premature distribution (which would be withdrawals taken before age 59½, typically).

Nevertheless, it is this very feature that makes IRAs such effective savings plans for most people. The severe penalties actually work to deter investors from "stealing" from their own retirements. Dollars that go into an IRA should stay in an IRA until you reach retirement. Do not avoid contributing to an IRA because of the potential penalties. Instead, make the investment because there is a good chance that you *will* follow a strict "hands off" policy.

There are several different types of IRAs available—11 types in all.

Today we will focus on the two most popular IRAs simply because these two types, the traditional IRA and the Roth IRA, are available to almost all working Americans.

IRA Basics

An IRA is a personal retirement account available to many people who receive taxable income. Taxable income includes wages, salaries, commissions, tips, profits from your business, alimony, and payments from a separate maintenance agreement.

Married couples may have separate IRA accounts, even if one spouse is not employed. A person's maximum annual contribution is 100% of total **taxable income** not to exceed $5,000 starting in 2008. Thereafter, the number rises and is indexed to inflation in $500 increments.

The contributions made to your IRA are voluntary, and you are not required to continue placing funds into the account after you have initiated the plan. So you can make a contribution one year and pass the next year, if you so desire.

The main attraction and advantage of an IRA is the tax-deferred accumulation of earnings. Due to the fact that we have a pay-as-you-go tax system, we are normally required to pay tax on everything we make as we earn it. This prevents the possibility of us earning any interest on the money sent to Uncle Sam each pay period.

But the money you put into an IRA has the chance to grow and grow and grow without being taxed as long as you leave that money in the IRA (subject to certain rules).

This tax-deferred treatment can result in a significant difference in net worth. For many, it will mean an increase of tens of thousands of dollars, and for others, hundreds of thousands of dollars! This is due to the compounding effect of earnings that would otherwise be paid to the IRS each year. That is the beauty of tax deferral.

Now that we have established the basic tenets of an IRA, let's explore the specifics for each of the two most popular options: the traditional IRA and the Roth IRA.

Traditional IRA

The benefits of the traditional IRA are that, under certain circumstances, a tax deduction is given off the top of your income, in addition to the previously mentioned tax-deferred accumulation.

The IRS is very specific with regard to which individuals may write off contributions, as Congress has decided it is unfair for the highest-wage earners to benefit to the same degree as the middle-class or upper middle-class taxpayers. To determine your ability to deduct your contribution, you must consider your filing status, adjusted gross income, and the availability of a qualified retirement plan through your employer. If covered under your employer's plan, there is a phase-out on deductibility.

For the year 2012, the phase-out is $58,000 to $68,000 of modified adjusted gross income (AGI) for those filing as "single" or "head of household."

For those of you who file "joint" returns, the phase-out applies for an AGI of $92,000 to $112,000.

And for "married filing separate," the AGI phase-out figures are $0 to $10,000.

The phase-out works on a percentage basis. If you are 50% of the way between the top and bottom phase-out number, then you can deduct 50% of the IRA contribution amount. An example would be a single tax filer with an AGI of $63,000 or a joint filer with an AGI of $102,000. Therefore, even when you are also participating in another qualified retirement plan, you may still write off 100% of your IRA contribution, provided your taxable income does not exceed the lower phase-out figures.

Non-Working Spouse

A non-working spouse can make a tax deductible IRA contribution in 2012 of up to $5,000, provided that the couple's combined adjusted gross income does not exceed $173,000. With an adjusted gross income of $183,000 or more, the contribution may not be deducted at all. Use the phase-out rules for incomes between $173,000 and $183,000.

Making Withdrawals

Money may be withdrawn any time from a traditional IRA. However, withdrawals should be avoided at all costs as the money withdrawn is immediately subject to taxes and potential penalties. With very few exceptions, money withdrawn from your account will be taxed at ordinary income tax rates. The money will be added to your other income and taxed accordingly.

In addition to this taxation, money withdrawn prior to the age of 59½ gets hit with a 10% penalty in addition to being taxed! If you made contributions that were nondeductible, that portion can be withdrawn tax free. If your account represents both deductible and nondeductible contributions, take a look at IRS form 8606. This online worksheet can be used to calculate the tax liability if you were to withdraw funds from your IRA. To get a copy of form 8606, go to www.IRS. gov/pubirs-pdf/8606.pdf. It will populate as a PDF on your computer screen.

There are several exceptions to the 10% penalty that is typically imposed on distributions taken before the age of 59½. These exceptions are disability, death, taking payments over your life expectancy, non-reimbursed medical expenses in excess of 7.5% of your adjusted gross income, first-time home purchase (up to $10,000), qualified higher education expenses, and to pay back-taxes due to the IRS levy. The IRS will give you a free pass on these distributions.

Still with me? Let's keep going then.

This may seem like a lot of information and some unfamiliar jargon, but it is important that you know everything about these retirement options so that you can take full advantage of their benefits without suffering any consequences.

Remember: take each day's lesson at your own pace. Stop and re-read sections that seem confusing. Take the time to check out the Web sites that I include for each topic. It may help to look at a form on your computer screen while you still have the relevant information from the chapter fresh in your mind.

Whenever *you* are ready, move on to the next section.

Roth IRA

The Roth IRA was introduced in 1997. It was intended to give tax-payers an investment vehicle that would allow them to make nonde-ductible contributions in return for a tax-free accumulation. Unlike the traditional IRA where you pay taxes as you make withdrawals, every-thing in the Roth IRA accumulates tax free.

Even so, the Roth IRA comes with its own cautionary stipulations.

You may make nondeductible contributions to your Roth IRA; how-ever, you may not exceed the smaller of either the maximum allowable IRA contribution *or* 100% of your taxable income minus contributions to any other IRAs you may own (excluding educational IRAs).

In other words, you cannot try to increase your maximum IRA con-tributions by investing in both traditional IRA *and* Roth IRA vehicles within the same year. You will need to determine which account is more suitable for your situation. Not sure which IRA best fits your situation?

No worries—we will sort out the choices more in just a moment. You may have already guessed that not everyone can contribute to a Roth IRA. The phase-out figures range from $110,000 to $125,000 for single taxpayers and $173,000 to $183,000 for married filing jointly.

As I mentioned earlier, all qualified distributions from a Roth IRA are excluded from your gross income for tax purposes. It all comes to you tax free.

There are some stipulations, of course. First, in order to avoid taxa-tion, you must be qualified for the distribution. Therefore, you must either reach the age of 59½, become disabled, use the money for a first-time home purchase (up to $10,000), or die. *(I think I'd rather pay the tax, wouldn't you?)* Additionally, the account must be held for at least five years before it can be considered for a tax-free qualification.

The stipulations are not overly restrictive given the tremendous tax advantages available.

I believe that Roth IRAs are one of the most underutilized invest-ment tools available to taxpayers. The underutilization stems from the fact that most people simply have no knowledge of the great benefits provided by IRAs.

Roth versus Traditional

Now that you have information on both types of the most popular IRAs, the big question is: "Which is the best Individual Retirement Account for you?"

Truthfully, that question may not have an immediate, clear-cut answer.

Did you really think it would? Come on, now! This is serious business. It requires some critical analysis on your part. You must factor in your current tax bracket and consider your projected future bracket. You must also estimate how much time you will have before you will start making withdrawals from your IRA.

Let me help with the analysis.

If you are able to take the tax deduction for your contributions, invest in a traditional IRA. It is better to take the certain tax deduction today rather than a potential future tax savings. The IRS has proven to be unpredictable regarding tax policy changes. Take the write-off while you can get it.

In the event that your adjusted gross income and/or participation in another plan prevent you from deducting the contribution from your gross income, then fund the Roth. This is a pretty good rule of thumb regarding IRA contribution decisions.

Setting Up Your Traditional IRA/Roth IRA

There are a number of financial institutions that will gladly provide the documentation needed to set up an IRA. They will ensure that you stay in compliance with IRS guidelines for establishing your account. Banks, credit unions, insurance companies, independent trustees, and brokerage firms provide the necessary account services.

I recommend that you set up a self-directed account with a discount broker. Some discount brokers, like Scottrade (www.scottrade.com), will perform this service free of charge. There is no cost for the initial paperwork and no maintenance fees. They will give you a range of options in which to invest your IRA capital. The choices include stocks, bonds, mutual funds, CDs, REITs, and options.

Some independent trustees have accounts that will even allow IRA funds to be invested in real estate.

However, it only makes sense to invest IRA funds in real estate when you have a relatively large balance (above $100,000) as the fees are usually much higher for this kind of investment flexibility.

Funding the Account

The easiest way to ensure your account will get fully funded is to have your contributions automatically deducted from your payroll.

If your goal is to invest $5,000 a year, simply have $416 deducted from your checks each month. If the contribution is deductible, you will more than likely be able to increase the number of allowances you claim on your W-4, thereby increasing your net take-home pay. The net effect is that Uncle Sam will actually be making a portion of the contribution on your behalf. Now *that* is a good strategy!

When the money is automatically deducted (therefore, it never reaches your "pocket"), you will learn to budget without it. Meanwhile, your IRA will be growing every year, creating a nice, comfortable nest egg for you to hatch when you reach retirement!

So...what are you waiting for? The advantages are too great to pass up. Figure out how much you are able to contribute, and start investing in your future...NOW!

My IRA Worksheet

Which IRA is best for you?

It is time to do a self-analysis, and then start investing. Ask yourself the following questions:

1.a) Can you take the tax deduction, following the rules of the traditional IRA and keeping in mind any employer-based programs you might participate in?

If you answered yes to question 1.a, you can take advantage of the traditional IRA benefits and deduct 100% of your contributions.

If you are unsure of the answer to this first question or how to calculate it, try this:

1. b) Do you make more than $58,000 if filing single or more than $92,000 if filing jointly with your spouse?

If the answer to either part of question 1.b is yes, you need to pursue the Roth IRA. You have reached the phase-out tax bracket. Therefore, you would not be able to deduct the contributions made to a traditional IRA.

You are better off taking the tax-free earnings with the Roth IRA.

There! That analysis was not as difficult as you expected it would be, was it?

Now…do not let today's lesson go to waste!

Open an IRA today!

Day 11

Boost Your Income

For the past 10 days, we have talked about eliminating debt, saving money, and preparing for retirement.

Today we will begin to explore a facet of this *30-Day Money Makeover* that you may find even more exciting.

Day 11 will be devoted to a topic that everyone loves. That subject is…

WAYS TO MAKE MORE MONEY!

Just by earning an extra $500 to $1,000 per month, you could enhance your lifestyle while simultaneously reducing the number of years needed to reach your retirement date.

You need to learn how to maximize your potential income.

How, you ask?

Think bigger! Think greater! Think expansion!

Today's lesson will teach you to transform the way you think about your personal potential so that you become more aware of your financial opportunities. In many ways, the mental side of today's lesson will act as a prelude to the lesson found on Day 29, *Minding Your Mind*.

Let's look at each of the possible areas where *you* may be creating roadblocks in your path to success.

Everyone Has a Price

Here, the word *price* refers to your value in the market, essentially.

And…whether you realize it or not, you have your opinion of your personal *market value* firmly fixed in your mind.

There is an old saying that life will produce that which you expect it to produce.

Understand?

If you *believe* you are worth an income of only $35,000 per year, you will naturally look for a job that pays approximately $35,000 per year.

However, if you *believe* that you are worth $35,000 *per month*, you will set your sights on an entirely different set of opportunities.

The person making $35,000 per month is probably no more intelligent and no more talented than the person making $35,000 a year. The person making $35,000 per month is just pursuing a greater level of purpose.

Do not misunderstand my meaning here: even though the person making $35,000 per month is making much more money than the person making $35,000 per year, it does not necessarily mean that the person making $35,000 per month is working *harder* or putting in more hours.

In fact, the person who is making only $35,000 *per year* is likely to be working a second job in order to make ends meet.

A huge part of making more money simply depends upon your willingness to develop a higher self-image and, subsequently, your commitment to create greater self-worth.

When a professional athlete is holding out for a $10-millionper-year contract, most people usually become incensed because they just cannot relate to the individual who would demand that kind of money.

If you are the kind of person who cannot comprehend someone believing that his or her efforts are worth that amount of money, you need to change the way you think.

Athletes have a very high self-image. **They know what they are worth.** At the very least, their agents know what they're worth! Nine times out of ten, a sports team will be willing to pay the best athletes millions and millions of dollars thereby *proving* that these athletes, or their agents, had an accurate understanding of the athlete's true market value.

Not everyone will become a star athlete, but for each of us, there is a personal aspiration with which we can achieve greatness to the same level illustrated by the professional athlete who is able to command millions of dollars.

Learn to raise your personal expectations, and you will elevate your results.

Our first step: it is time to learn *how* to raise your expectations.

First, ask yourself, **"What is my value in today's marketplace?"**

Do you have any idea of your personal value? Do you know what the highest paid people in your field are earning? If not, find out.

The average person has no idea what he or she is worth in terms of marketplace value.

Again, *you* are reading this book because you do not want to think, behave, or live like the *average* person.

You are here to do better.

If you are one of those folks who is still unsure of your marketplace value, today is the day to determine what you are worth.

Your Current Job

If you have been at your current company for more than five years, it is likely that you are underpaid. I can almost guarantee it.

If you have doubts about the fact that you are probably underpaid in your current position, then it is time to open your eyes and discover the truth about the real opportunities that are available to you. To begin, you can check out some of the competitive employers. See what they will offer. I am going to bet that you will find the competitive offer will be *at least 20% more than the amount that you are making with your current employer.*

Why does the business world operate like this?

Think about it.

Within your entry level position with a company, you may bring very little to the table other than potential. You probably do not know their business methods, and you may not know the overall industry very well. In this situation, any company is going to start you at a modest salary with promises of future advancements based on your performance levels. The starting salary might not equal much, but your real priority is to gain valuable experience. With a job well done, you may also create a good reputation within the industry.

In about three to five years, you should become a seasoned professional who can make an immediate impact on any organization in that industry. That ability commands bigger dollars in the workplace. Use it to your advantage. Do not accept stagnation or relatively small advancements.

If you are happy with your current choice of occupation, but you want to know how you can maximize your earnings, review the following list of ideas that could hold the key to achieving a higher income.

1. *Always do more than what is expected.* Decision-makers are well aware of which employees take ownership of any task and which employees simply go through the motions in order to collect a paycheck. Extra effort will pay off with your employer, and developing a personal habit of going "above and beyond" will benefit you whether you are an employee or you own your own business.

2. *Ask what you can do to make yourself an extremely valuable member of the team.* You should meet with your supervisor (or whoever is responsible for your advancement) and ask him or her to give you a blueprint with a plan of moving you forward in the company. During your conference with your supervisor, express your willingness to take on more responsibility or your interest in learning a new skill set. It is hard to impress your superiors if you do not even know what they are looking for or how they judge performance in the workplace.

3. ***Look the part.*** Wearing the proper attire sends a definite message to your colleagues. In almost every business situation, you need to dress appropriately for the position you hold or for the industry in which you are employed. People make superficial judgments about others all the time—it is a fact of life, and it is most certainly relevant to the business world. Those who will judge you include the person responsible for your pay. Dress for the position you would *like to have*, not just for the position in which you are currently employed. Pay close attention to personal hygiene. Clean hair and a sharp haircut are a reflection of your opinion of yourself. Make sure your body odor is not offensive and your breath is fresh. If you stink, so will your income! Your nails should be neat and clean. Stay healthy and fit.

    If these suggestions offend you, perhaps your plan should be to pursue a career in an industry that welcomes alternative or casual manners of dress. If you want to spend your life dressed like a rock star, you better devote every minute of your life to perfecting your music and singing skills. If you prefer a situation in which you can have varying levels of hygiene…good luck. Even when you choose self-employment, you will have to work with others at some point. In all likelihood, you will need to develop great communication skills in order to be successful. How you present yourself *is* a form of communication. Your appearance speaks to others before you can get a single word out of your mouth. When you are your No. 1 product representative, you need to do your best to be professional and presentable.

4. ***Keep a current résumé posted out in the marketplace at all times.*** There are great Web sites that allow you to communicate with prospective employers without risking your current position. Check out the following sites: www.monster.com, www.careerbuilder.com, www.hotjobs.com, www.fedjobs.com, and www.theladders.com (the last site listed contains only jobs that pay above $100,000 annually).

    There is also a comprehensive Web site that has information about all of the sites I just listed (and more!). Make sure to visit the Web site at www.worldprivacyforum.org/jobguide.html.

One note of caution: if you decide to post personal information on the Web, be careful not to provide sensitive information such as your social security number, date of birth, personal address, and so forth. Identity theft is a serious problem, and becoming an identity theft victim is the last thing you need while you are trying to hunt for new opportunities.

Communicating with outside employers will give you a better idea of your market value and will help you when you negotiate your salary with your current employer.

5. *Get into the inner circle.* At every company, there are a group of people who essentially run the show. This could be at a higher corporate level or within your current department. If an "inner circle" exists at your company, *you need to penetrate that group of movers and shakers if you plan on advancing within that organization.*

For example: at one company where I once worked, I noticed that the owner enjoyed riding his motorcycle on the weekend. One day, I asked him who he rode with, and he said that he did not know anyone else with a bike. I told him that I had been thinking about purchasing a motorcycle (which was true) so that I could ride. Next thing you know, I was a riding my new motorcycle...as president of one of the company's divisions.

Does that story rub you the wrong way?

Well, its message illuminates another fact of life: *people promote other people that they like, trust, and with whom they can find common bonds.* As long as you allow someone else to hold your career's success in his or her hands, you need to find *something* in common with each of those folks. You may think this is unfortunate or unfair, but this is reality, and merely doing a *good job* is probably not enough to get you far in the business world today. It does not mean that you have to go out and buy a motorcycle, nor do you need to risk your life or well-being doing some activity for which you are not suited. Just make sure to find some kind of common ground with the decision-makers so that you can build favorable relations with key members of your organization.

Additional Income-Building Ideas

Moonlighting

I am a big believer in creating multiple streams of income. Whenever you rely solely upon one source of income to pay for all of your expenses, you risk becoming an indentured servant to work that you may grow to dislike. Also, you tend to put up with treatment that you should not tolerate, and you put yourself at greater financial risk.

With one source of income, you limit your options. There is always more risk that you will compromise your self-respect and overall satisfaction whenever you participate in any relationship where an unequal level of need is present. People will do just about anything to keep a particular job if they feel like they could not replace that income anywhere else.

I am a business coach and mentor, I own a furniture store, trade the stock market, and dabble in real estate. I am an author, a consultant, and I frequently take part in a variety of media productions including on-camera spots, webinars, and various forms of literature. I am having a ball because I do what I love and derive income from a number of different sources. That is freedom! This is exactly what I want you to experience.

My life is rewarding, always interesting, and profitable.

I've found time to be a husband, a father, a son, a brother, a 10-handicap in golf, play tournament-quality tennis, read, travel, fish, and ride my horses. I do not choose to spend much time watching television, but that is a personal preference.

The point of the previous paragraphs is not to brag about my great life.

The point is to demonstrate to you that most people are capable of much more than they are currently achieving. When you truly understand your origin, the substance with which you were created, and your vast potential, you will be capable of achieving any level of success.

But…you will never become greater than the self-image you hold in your own mind.

Let me remind you of the initial message from today's lesson: the key to manifesting a greater net worth is to first create a greater self-image.

Boosting your current income begins with an examination of the skills that you already possess. I believe that everyone has the same amount of talent. You need to determine how to take advantage of *your* God-given faculties to the fullest extent possible.

Do you like to work with groups of people? Good with computers? Possess organizational skills? Are you multilingual? Love teaching kids? Enjoy gardening, painting or photography, hiking or driving? Are you a natural-born salesperson?

If you feel like you lack any special skills, maybe you should survey the people who know you best. Ask each one of them to list five skills or traits that comprise your areas of excellence or expertise.

What may be difficult for you to see might be readily apparent to those around you.

To move ahead as efficiently as possible, you will want to look for opportunities that make the most of your strengths. I call this taking the path of least resistance. The reason I have found success at great levels is that most of my endeavors involve subject matter that I enjoy or situations that address issues with which I am comfortable or that I find easy to resolve.

I tried playing the piano for a couple of years. I discovered that although I adored the instrument, I just did not like the way it sounded when *I* hit the keys. Clearly, becoming a pianist was not something I felt driven to achieve, so I left piano playing to others and took up the guitar instead. For whatever reason, I found it easy to commit to playing and practicing the guitar and have gradually increased my ability to strum out a few tunes. More importantly, playing the guitar every day 's a major source of enjoyment and relaxation for me.

If you spend most of your time stuck in an occupation that does not highlight your strengths and which does not stir any feelings of passion, *you* are making your life much harder.

It does not mean that you may be able to "quit your day job" tomorrow because you have always dreamt of being a rock star or something. However, no matter what is going on in your life today, you need to determine what really matters to you—what drives you—and then find a way to bring those elements into your life as soon as possible. Maybe you will become a successful musician, or maybe you will be happy just as long as you are involved in the music industry in some capacity. Maybe you want to become an architect, or perhaps acting as managing editor of an architectural magazine would do the trick. You need to figure out where your passions are fueled, and never lose sight of your inspirations.

What Turns You On?

There is no single recipe for converting personal interests into a source of income, but I would suggest beginning by establishing a list of possibilities.

Write down everything you truly enjoy and all the skills you feel you possess. Leave enough space after each item listed so that you can make some notes later.

After you have created your list, begin exploring potential income opportunities that might fit for any of the items that you listed.

For example, if you find yourself looking at residential homes whenever possible, perhaps getting a real estate license and selling property part-time would be an appropriate opportunity. It does not mean, necessarily, that you sell real estate forever or that real estate sales will ever become more than part-time work. However, if you are already spending your *free* time browsing home listings and exploring your community's perks, why not share your knowledge and expertise with others... and get paid for your *free* time!

If you have been a stay-at-home parent for years and feel most comfortable caring for children, you should begin by pursuing work that is connected to kids. For those with a knack for teaching, you could hire yourself out as a tutor or coach. Again, it does not mean that you will remain a tutor or child caregiver forever. You should intend to own your own business at some point. If you start as a tutor, you could set a goal of developing your own teaching center. Someone who begins part-time work as a nanny could use his or her networking skills and contacts to create a successful and safe referral service for families and nannies.

The point is: no matter what you choose to do, you should always continue to grow! If you have special knowledge in any field, consulting would be a natural pursuit for you.

The options and opportunities you have are limitless. If you have not discovered them already, then you just need to think outside the limits of your current occupation or situation.

You are the only person who can determine which opportunities fit your interests and talents. Too many people allow others to steer them in directions that are neither appropriate nor fulfilling in any way. But if you will not make decisions for yourself, then you risk being misguided by someone else. It is not *their* fault. *You* have to take responsibility for each choice that you make or agree to.

For example, there is a ton of money to be made in the real estate business, either as an owner or as a broker. But real estate is not for everyone. Some people are well-suited to dealing with property issues and tenants, while others would do well to stay as far away from these situations as possible. You know your personality better than anyone. What suits you best?

Network marketing has attracted hundreds of thousands of takers with promises of big incomes generated from the efforts of others. There are some marketers who do make a fortune in that industry. On the other hand, if you are not particularly persuasive and do not enjoy recruiting others, it is not likely that you will achieve success in this type of venture.

Do not let others try to sell you on *their* plans...*you need to find a career match that is right for you, and make sure to choose like-minded business partners and associates as well.*

Changing Careers

Simple fact: some occupations provide greater income opportunities than others.

At some point, you may realize that it would be best for you to change careers.

According to the Bureau of Labor Statistics published in August of 2004, the average white-collar position pays $21.85 per hour, blue-collar pays $15.03 an hour, and service industry employees only earn $10.40 an hour.

Obviously, the sector in which you work can be a strong factor in determining how much you can make, ultimately.

According to the Employment Policy Foundation, the nation's 10

Chief Executive	$176,550
Physician	$168,650
Dentist	$161,750
Petroleum Engineer	$138,980
Lawyer	$130,490
Architectural Manager	$129,350
Natural Science Manager	$128,230
Marketing Manager	$126,190
Computer Systems Manger	$125,660
Industrial Psychologist	$124,16

A drastic change of career may require some sacrifice and a significant amount of education or training on your part. As long as you remember the golden financial rule—to pursue only those areas that are, in some way, connected to your core passions and values—the investment in education and use of your time will not be wasted.

I believe that the average American is underemployed. They are engaged in a job (j.o.b. = just over broke) that pays the bills but provides little else in the way of financial and emotional rewards. Begin your move toward *above average* by using the techniques you have learned today to maximize the financial benefits of your current position. If you find yourself at an impasse with your employer, it is time to take your talents elsewhere. Do not let irrational fears keep you from living your best life. Have the courage to accept and embrace CHANGE. That being said—make sure that you secure alternative employment *before* you decide to "pack it up" at your current job.

Do not forget the important objective of producing multiple sources of income. When you start to receive checks from three or four different sources, you will have greater ability to make adjustments in your life without experiencing major financial setbacks.

This is where true financial security is born.

You are going to spend most of your adult life performing some type of work.

I want you to be engaged in work that you love and that provides you with the lifestyle you prefer.

It is time to get started!

My Strengths Worksheet

List your skills and talents, and then try to apply them to either a new career or secondary income stream opportunity (or both!)

My greatest skills at present are:

1. _____

2. _____

3. _____

4. _____

5. _____

I can apply my skills in the following possible income opportunities:

1. _____

2. _____

3. _____

4. _____

5. _____

Day 12

Start Your Own Business

Today, I will explain why it is imperative that you consider starting your own small business.

Owning your own business is the single most powerful vehicle available to launch your financial life.

Small-business owners enjoy the best of both worlds:

- Unlimited income potential
- The best tax shelter available in the U.S.

It also provides an opportunity to build and self-direct your retirement savings program. That opportunity alone could be worth millions of dollars to you and your family.

However, before you turn your dining room table into a work desk or production stand, we need to use today to explore all the business possibilities that are available and, more specifically, narrow down the choices in order to find the business for which you are best suited.

Finding Your Business Idea

The process of formulating a business concept is more the product of self-exploration than economics. The key is to find an opportunity that is aligned with your personal interests and abilities. On Day 11, we discussed the need to focus on those things which you know or do best. That application from Day 11 will give you a sound starting place for today's journey.

No matter which small business you choose, the endeavor will likely take a significant amount of time and energy to operate. Depending on your current reserve of both of those requisite items, you need to be wise about the type of business in which you invest your time, money, and energy.

111

Now the good news: there are literally thousands of incredible small-business opportunities in America. Let's begin by examining how you spend most of your time right now. Is there a special hobby or personal interest that could be translated into a business? Many people successfully turn their love of crafts, music, teaching, care-giving, technology, photography, or sports into full-time or part-time enterprises.

If you have specialized knowledge in a particular subject, you may even want to consider consulting in your area of expertise. I have had clients who have retired from corporate positions only to return to these same firms as consultants. As consultants, they commanded rates that were 50% to 100% greater than their former hourly compensation. In addition to the much-increased earnings, they also had full access to their retirement plans.

To help get you started down the path toward a business concept, the following list will provide some of the hottest business ideas. If you discover that there is nothing in this list that interests you, don't worry. This list is not intended to be comprehensive. It is meant to highlight some great opportunities. To help yourself find the business concept that fits you the best, you may want to try browsing your favorite subject online. Web sites such as www.smallbiztrends.com can also provide useful discovery tips.

Business Coaching

Coaching has grown into a billion-dollar industry. Effective coaches are able to enter any organization, recognize its flaws or inefficiencies, and then provide workable solutions as well as ideas to motivate employees to improve their overall productivity. Coaching may also refer to one-on-one mentoring, which is becoming increasingly prevalent in many different industries.

Business Brokerage

Business brokers match would-be business owners with current owners who are looking to sell a business. It is basically real estate brokering for enterprises as opposed to properties. The average business broker can feasibly earn a solid, six-figure annual income!

Garage Organizer

Look inside the garage of the average American home and you will likely see total chaos. Look closer and you may find an opportunity to make serious money. Whirlpool has entered into this market with a division designed to help homeowners clean up their act. Along these lines, a franchise opportunity is available with an organization named

Garage Tek. To check out their Web site, go to www.garagetek.com/FranchiseOpportunities/.

Specialty Clothes

There is a huge demand for specialty markets like performance clothes, sun protection, or insect-resistant garments. (Cool stuff, huh?) Most of the manufacturing is done overseas, and then the product is marketed and sold in the United States. You can start a business as a distributor of this unique apparel.

Medical Transcription

Doctors create oral reports on everything from physical exams, to operating room procedures, to autopsies. These recordings have to be transcribed and saved. This is the job of the transcription technician. Top earners make around $20 per hour or more and enjoy flexible hours and the ability to work from home. (This might make a great fit for the stay-at-home parent!)

Junk Removal

Americans have been accumulating more and more "stuff" at increasing rates. Much of this "treasure" quickly drops in favor and becomes unwanted garbage that needs to be hauled away. Many people will pay to have someone remove the junk for them, especially in situations where the owner either does not have a suitable vehicle for hauling items or perhaps has such a busy schedule that *junk hauling* never makes it onto any of their "to do" lists. Also, in many regions where retirement populations flourish, the owner may not be willing or able to haul the heavy or bulky unwanted items for long distances. For all of these reasons, junk removal is an increasingly needed service and has actually become a franchised business. Check out www.1800gotjunk.com for information on starting your own junk removal franchise.

Currently, *1-800-Got-Junk?* has more than 300 franchises in Canada, Australia, and the United States with plans to expand in the United Kingdom.

Anti-Aging Spas

Personally, I think that "pro-youth" is a better mantra than "anti-aging" and also makes for a better marketing strategy overall. In my opinion, it is always better to advertise the pro angle (whatever is desired) rather than to push the anti slogan (whatever is not desired). Regardless of the business model, as Americans extend their life expectancies, there will be an increasing demand for products and services that attempt to slow the aging process. The demand for health and rejuvenation facilities and products will continue to grow in popularity as the majority of our population reaches age groups of 50 years old and up. The profit margins in this industry will surge as most of these products and services appeal to the relatively high-net-worth consumer.

College Consultant

The college game gets more difficult and more competitive every year. The crazy maze of college requirements, application deadlines, and entrance testing may seem like a virtually impenetrable jungle to many prospective students and their parents. Many people consider college education choice to be one of the most crucial of life's decisions. They invest countless amounts of blood, sweat, and tears (and cash) into college educations. For all of these reasons, the need for college consultants has increased. The college consultant is able to guide students and parents through the university labyrinth of paperwork and entrance requirements, provide information regarding crucial deadlines or cutoff dates for testing, and also give insider tips concerning all aspects of the college application. Qualified consultants can earn anywhere from $20 to $50 per hour. This could be a highly enjoyable pursuit for anyone with a great appreciation for secondary education and who enjoys working with students.

Real Estate Agent

As we all know, real estate sales are cyclical. In a hot market, even a relatively new agent can generate outstanding commissions. When the market slows, it is the seasoned real estate professional, with an established client base, who will continue to produce relatively steady income. Regardless of the cyclicality of the business, real estate still offers almost anyone an opportunity to get into business for themselves due to its low barrier to entry. Anyone willing to sit through the required class (which is relatively short in duration), and who is able to pass a state real estate exam, will find multiple brokers waiting with open arms. Compared to almost all other businesses, the startup costs for obtaining a realtor's license and the necessary business tools are minimal.

Most brokers will also allow their agents to work in a flexible, part-time capacity

Selecting a Business Structure

Once you have chosen an appropriate business idea for yourself, you may need to decide how it will be structured. There are many different types of business entities from which to choose. As with most things in life, it is best to keep your structure as simple as possible with respect to the sort of business you would like to conduct.

I kept this list of structure types and their descriptions simple as it is meant to provide an informative introduction to the reader. It is often advisable to get the counsel of an attorney when starting a new business. For you *do-it-yourselfers* out there, the Internet has an endless source of information regarding business structures, related requirements and laws, and tax information. Organizations such as *BizFilings* (www. bizfilings.com), *The Company Corporation* (www.incorporate.com), and *LegalZoom* (www.legalzoom.com) provide comprehensive, easy-to-follow instructions which explain how to set up any of the business structures mentioned in this chapter, and they also provide a business comparison chart for a quick-reference guide to choosing the structure that is best for your business.

We will take a brief look at each one of the options.

Sole Proprietor

Of the different types of business structure, this is by far the simplest to set up and the easiest to shut down. All that is needed is to file a tax form SE which will be attached to your regular 1040 tax form. The possible downside of the sole proprietorship is that it exposes the owner to unlimited personal liability and also subjects the owner to self-employment tax.

Partnership

A partnership is a useful structure for dividing up business interests between a few individuals. Partners can also receive unequal distributions of profits as agreed upon in the partnership documents. However, be aware that you can be personally liable for the actions of your partners! It is important to be extremely cautious when choosing your business partners. With respect to taxes, partnerships may be favored over corporations because, in general, a partnership usually is not taxed on profits before the profits are distributed to the partners. You will still be subject to self-employment taxes.

Incorporation Types

S Corporation

The main advantage to an S Corporation is that you can eliminate self-employment or Medicare taxes on profits or dividends. Any losses incurred by the business can be passed through to the individual shareholder (you) and can be taken as a loss on a personal tax return. This structure may fit well when a new business is expected to lose money in its early years. One note, however: choosing an S Corporation structure may negate your ability to take a home-office deduction, even if you are conducting your business from home.

C Corporation

The C Corporation allows for 100% of health insurance premiums and 100% of your contributions to your retirement plan to be deducted from the gross income of the company. Retained profits of up to $50,000 are taxed at a rate of just 15%. Typically, there is some level of liability protection for the shareholders. However, the paperwork and account-ing tasks for a C Corporation are more complicated and costly than those in other structures.

Limited Liability Corporations

LLCs are considered to be the ultimate business structure for several different reasons. Owners have the protection of the limited liability fea-ture (as seen is the C Corporation structure) combined with the income-splitting flexibility of a partnership. However, you will be required to pay self-employment tax.

Writing a Business Plan

Now that you have some potential business ideas and have re-searched information that explains how to structure that business, it is time to put some of your goals and strategies on paper. You cannot skip this part. Writing a business plan is one of the most crucial steps to cre-ating a successful business.

Hate to write?

Try using crayon. The cheerful colors will keep you going through-out the process!

A business plan is basically a detailed description of what you in-tend to do to make your business operate and how you propose to make a profit. If you find that you cannot formulate a detailed plan, chances are that you are not prepared to move forward with your business idea. For those of you who are ready to complete the task at hand, grab your laptop or a writing tool and paper and read on.

Your plan needs to answer the following five core questions:

1. What service or product does your business provide?
2. What need does it fill in the marketplace?
3. Who are the potential customers, and how extensive is the pro-spective patron base?
4. How do you intend to market your products and services?

5. What are the capital requirements, and what are the probable sources of funding?

To help you structure your business plan correctly, I would suggest considering a document-creation software product such as Business Plan Pro (www.paloalto.com/ps/bp/) or some similar comprehensive product. Small investments like this (about $99) can save incredible amounts of valuable time and energy. Business Plan Pro provides more than 500 sample business plans along with built-in market research data and other valuable business references. Alternatively, if you use

Microsoft Office software, you will find free business plan templates in the Microsoft Word program. Once the Word program is open, click on **File**, then **New**, then type in "**business plan**" in the search box under **Search online for:**. Obviously, you must be online in order to use this function.

After you have completed this entire task, you will have a better understanding of how your enterprise will function, and you will have a document that can help you understand how and where you can raise startup capital. A bonus: if you do purchase the Business Plan Pro software, the money spent on the purchase may be tax-deductible, depending on your business structure.

Marketing Your Product or Service

Marketing is a major component for any business, regardless of the company size and structure. Begin your marketing plan by answering the following questions:

1. Who are your target consumers?
2. What is the most cost-effective method of reaching them?
3. Who is your competition, and how are they delivering their message?
4. What is your unique selling proposition in the marketplace? (How are you different or better than the competition?)
5. How much money do you plan to invest in your marketing campaign?

The answers to these five questions may not come easily. However, just as I stressed the criticalness of the business plan, I will stress to you the importance of answering these five questions instead of blindly beginning your marketing efforts.

There is a marketing method called *guerilla marketing*. It asserts the idea of getting valuable advertising without paying the typical rates charged by conventional marketing mediums like radio and television. I would strongly suggest using your favorite search engine to get all the information on this creative and cost-effective approach to advertising.

Accounting

The accounting that is required for any business may be considered, by many, to be the most challenging or frightening of all of the aspects of running a business. To make your life easy and to avoid letting this step prevent you from realizing your business dreams, let me suggest purchasing accounting software. It will do the toughest work for you.

The software product *QuickBooks* is an excellent place to start. It will track business expenses automatically as you pay your bills. Quick-Books software can create invoices and can calculate taxes automatically. Their Web site (www.quickbooks.intuit.com/) offers a tremendous amount of useful information for any entrepreneur. You can shop for any number of similar products at your local office supply store, or use your search engine to search for similar products. It is always a good idea to have a hard copy of your accounting software, and also make sure you familiarize yourself with and utilize a recommended file-backup routine to ensure that you always have a copy of all of your accounting records. The Quick-Books support Web pages explain backup processes and options in detail.

Building Your Team

Assuming that you do not plan on being your organization's chief cook and bottle washer forever, you *will* need to begin building your business team. Every team needs a leader. The leader should be a visionary who can articulate his or her ideas in a concise and inspirational manner. The leader is the soul of the organization. As the owner, you have two choices: BE the leader, or hire a strong leader for your team.

Once you have made the decision on leadership, the next task is to find a disciplined, capable individual who can manage the day-to-day operations of your company. Oftentimes, the leader is not a suitable type to fulfill the role as operations manager. An inspiring personality cannot replace organization skills and excellent time-management ability. The latter qualities are necessary for an effective operations manager.

You will also need someone to manage and oversee the financial aspects of your company. You might decide that you prefer to fill this role yourself. Ideally, this task would also be part of your operation manager's job description. It is always prudent for you to keep up-to-date with your company's financial standing and any financial decisions. However, having someone else manage the day-to-day inputting and processes will provide you with the freedom to spend more time on business development.

Beyond these key functions, the company will likely only require "foot soldiers" who will follow instructions and execute the basic tasks of your business.

CAUTION: Beware of growing your personnel ranks too rapidly. First, you want to make sure that you only hire high-quality employees. Secondly, you want to make sure that you can balance the amount of revenue being produced with your ability to cover your employees' salaries. One sure way to kill an otherwise successful business startup is to encumber it with unnecessary overhead.

Retirement Plans

Here we go talking about retirement again.

Owning your own business gives you access to several retirement plans which allow for immediate tax deductions and the deferral of interest and capital gains to a future date.

Let's take a look at some plans.

SEP-IRA: If your company employs only a small staff and you are looking for a plan that has low cost and very little maintenance, consider establishing a SEP-IRA. There is no plan document required, and you do not need to file annual reports with the IRS. Contributions are made exclusively by the employer as employee contributions are not allowed. The employer can vary the amount that is contributed from year to year. All eligible employees must be covered under this plan.

Simple IRA: These plans are great for employees, but they are not as advantageous for the business owner as the SEP-IRA. Employees are able to make contributions, and the employer must match contributions. Contributions are generally limited to $10,000 a year plus 3% of the employee's contribution. Simple IRAs may be worthwhile if your company has less than 10 employees.

Profit-Sharing Plans: These plans give the employee an opportunity to share the wealth and give employees an incentive to maximize company profits. They are normally set at a percentage of profits with a maximum contribution limit. **401(k)**: If your business has more than 25 employees, you may want to investigate the benefits of a 401(k). These plans are among the most popular retirement plans for both employers and employees. As of 2012, employees can contribute up to $17,00 per year.

Retirement plans can make your company more attractive to potential employees, which will give you some leveraging power during the hiring process. What could be more attractive than an account that allows tax-deductible contributions and allows funds to grow tax deferred? Retirement plans also allow your employees to be fully integrated into the success of the business. If your employees believe that they can actually retire after a career with your enterprise, they will be more likely to give their best effort during their employment.

In relation to your company's reputation, a retirement plan also adds to the appearance of stability. Brokerage firms such as Fidelity Investments can provide the resources you will need to establish any of the previously mentioned plans.

Get Real-World Business Experience

How would someone without the time or money needed to obtain his or her MBA learn the practical skills that are required in order to be competitive in a business environment? The answer is easy: join a network-marketing or direct-selling organization. They will teach you how to market, how to sell, how to deal with the public, and how to manage a small business. The best part is that you will receive your business education for free! Some of the highest-paid people in the country work for network-marketing organizations. Find a company that offers products that you would be proud to represent, identify a sponsor who would be willing to mentor you, and get started! Many of these companies will allow a new affiliate to join for less than $100. The business experience you obtain could be worth as much or more, in practical terms, than an advanced business education.

Fun, exciting, stressful, taxing, challenging—owning your own business can be any or all of these things. Most of all, if you take the time and make the effort to do things the correct way, owning your own business may bring you endless rewards, both emotional and financial. It may take a lot of work, but when you are working for yourself, with all of the freedom and satisfaction that comes from self-employment, you are more likely to stay motivated and more likely to motivate those around you. Have fun! Get started!

Launching My Business

Step 1: List favorite business ideas.

Step 2: Write a mission statement.

Step 3: Choose a business structure.

Step 4: Build a business plan.

Step 5: Create a marketing plan.

Step 6: Set up a retirement plan.

Step 7: Identify your teammates.

Day 13

Making Life Less Taxing

Although our forefathers fought vehemently for freedom from the tyranny of the British Empire and its oppressive taxes, we Americans eventually accepted the necessity of creating an income tax.

In 1913, the Sixteenth Amendment was added to the U.S. Constitution, and, essentially, we, the taxpayer, have been at war with ourselves, namely, the IRS, ever since.

From that moment on, income taxes became a permanent part of every wage earner's life. Although the tax provision has been around for nearly 100 years, the rules and regulations that govern income taxes remain a seemingly indecipherable puzzle to most of us.

With regard to your current plan to make over your financial life, you do not have the option of remaining ignorant about the tax system. Make a commitment to yourself, right now, to learn what you need to know in order for you to benefit as much as possible from any advantages afforded to you by our tax system. Look at it this way: an education on tax planning and strategizing will produce financial rewards that will last a lifetime. I believe that most taxpayers could reduce their tax burden by 25% to 50% by using the correct approach.

Today, you will take the first step toward achieving those results by learning how the tax code operates.

An Overview

The United States' progressive tax system takes a larger percentage of income from high-wage earners and a smaller percentage from low-income earners.

Basically, the more income you make, the more money you are going to dish out in taxes each year.

Surprised?

You see, it is a very common misconception that the wealthy in this country "get away with" paying little or nothing in the way of income taxes. This is not reality. In fact, the top 1% of taxpayers in the United States pays almost 35% of the total tax burden. Seeing how your goal is to become wealthy, these statistics should be of interest to you.

Current tax rates range from 10% to 35% of taxable income, but do not despair! Taxes are calculated on taxable, not gross, income. If you learn to spend your money in a certain way, you may be able to benefit from particular types of deductions that can reduce the amount of your taxable income.

OK, prepare yourself. The first thing we need to do is look at how the tax liability is computed.

The 1040 Tax Return

The Form 1040 might seem like a very imposing document until you take the time to break down each section and examine the information that is recorded. Once you understand the purpose for each section, it will be easier for you to determine how you might take advantage of any available deductions. On the following pages, you will find a sample 1040 tax return. The subsequent pages are divided into brief segments that explain the different sections of Form 1040. It is a good idea to refer back to the form as you read each segment so that you can really familiarize yourself with each portion of the 1040 tax return.

1040

Department of the Treasury—Internal Revenue Service
U.S. Individual Income Tax Return 2008 | (99) IRS Use Only—Do not write or staple in this space.

For the year Jan. 1–Dec. 31, 2008, or other tax year beginning , 2008, ending , 20 | OMB No. 1545-0074

Label
(See instructions on page 14.)
Use the IRS label. Otherwise, please print or type.

| Your first name and initial | Last name | Your social security number |
| If a joint return, spouse's first name and initial | Last name | Spouse's social security number |

Home address (number and street). If you have a P.O. box, see page 14. | Apt. no.
City, town or post office, state, and ZIP code. If you have a foreign address, see page 14.

▲ You must enter your SSN(s) above. ▲

Checking a box below will not change your tax or refund.

Presidential Election Campaign ▶ Check here if you, or your spouse if filing jointly, want $3 to go to this fund (see page 14) ▶ ☐ You ☐ Spouse

Filing Status
Check only one box.

1 ☐ Single
2 ☐ Married filing jointly (even if only one had income)
3 ☐ Married filing separately. Enter spouse's SSN above and full name here. ▶
4 ☐ Head of household (with qualifying person). (See page 15.) If the qualifying person is a child but not your dependent, enter this child's name here. ▶
5 ☐ Qualifying widow(er) with dependent child (see page 16)

Exemptions

6a ☐ Yourself. If someone can claim you as a dependent, do not check box 6a . . . . }
b ☐ Spouse

Boxes checked on 6a and 6b

c Dependents:

| (1) First name Last name | (2) Dependent's social security number | (3) Dependent's relationship to you | (4) ✓ if qualifying child for child tax credit |

No. of children on 6c who:
• lived with you
• did not live with you due to divorce or separation (see page 18)

If more than four dependents, see page 17.

Dependents on 6c not entered above

d Total number of exemptions claimed

Add numbers on lines above ▶

Income

Attach Form(s) W-2 here. Also attach Forms W-2G and 1099-R if tax was withheld.

If you did not get a W-2, see page 21.

Enclose, but do not attach, any payment. Also, please use Form 1040-V.

7 Wages, salaries, tips, etc. Attach Form(s) W-2 . . . . | 7
8a Taxable interest. Attach Schedule B if required . . . . | 8a
b Tax-exempt interest. Do not include on line 8a . . . | 8b |
9a Ordinary dividends. Attach Schedule B if required . . . . | 9a
b Qualified dividends (see page 21) . . . . | 9b |
10 Taxable refunds, credits, or offsets of state and local income taxes (see page 22) . . | 10
11 Alimony received . . . . | 11
12 Business income or (loss). Attach Schedule C or C-EZ . . . . . . | 12
13 Capital gain or (loss). Attach Schedule D if required. If not required, check here ▶ ☐ | 13
14 Other gains or (losses). Attach Form 4797 . . . . | 14
15a IRA distributions . . | 15a | b Taxable amount (see page 23) | 15b
16a Pensions and annuities | 16a | b Taxable amount (see page 24) | 16b
17 Rental real estate, royalties, partnerships, S corporations, trusts, etc. Attach Schedule E | 17
18 Farm income or (loss). Attach Schedule F . . . . | 18
19 Unemployment compensation . . . . | 19
20a Social security benefits | 20a | b Taxable amount (see page 26) | 20b
21 Other income. List type and amount (see page 28) | 21
22 Add the amounts in the far right column for lines 7 through 21. This is your total income ▶ | 22

Adjusted Gross Income

23 Educator expenses (see page 28) . . . . | 23
24 Certain business expenses of reservists, performing artists, and fee-basis government officials. Attach Form 2106 or 2106-EZ | 24
25 Health savings account deduction. Attach Form 8889 . . | 25
26 Moving expenses. Attach Form 3903 . . . . . . | 26
27 One-half of self-employment tax. Attach Schedule SE . . | 27
28 Self-employed SEP, SIMPLE, and qualified plans . . . | 28
29 Self-employed health insurance deduction (see page 29) | 29
30 Penalty on early withdrawal of savings . . . . . . | 30
31a Alimony paid b Recipient's SSN ▶ | 31a
32 IRA deduction (see page 30) . . . . | 32
33 Student loan interest deduction (see page 33) . . . . | 33
34 Tuition and fees deduction. Attach Form 8917 . . . . | 34
35 Domestic production activities deduction. Attach Form 8903 | 35
36 Add lines 23 through 31a and 32 through 35 . . . . | 36
37 Subtract line 36 from line 22. This is your adjusted gross income . . . . ▶ | 37

For Disclosure, Privacy Act, and Paperwork Reduction Act Notice, see page 86. Cat. No. 11320B Form **1040** (2008)

Form 1040 (2008)

Tax and Credits	38	Amount from line 37 (adjusted gross income)	38
	39a	Check { □ You were born before January 2, 1944, □ Blind. □ Spouse was born before January 2, 1944, □ Blind. } Total boxes checked ► 39a	
	b	If your spouse itemizes on a separate return or you were a dual-status alien, see page 34 and check here ► 39b □	
Standard Deduction for—	c	Check if standard deduction includes real estate taxes or disaster loss (see page 34) ► 39c □	
	40	Itemized deductions (from Schedule A) or your standard deduction (see left margin)	40
• People who checked any box on line 39a, 39b, or 39c or who can be claimed as a dependent, see page 34.	41	Subtract line 40 from line 38	41
	42	If line 38 is over $119,975, or you provided housing to a Midwestern displaced individual, see page 36. Otherwise, multiply $3,500 by the total number of exemptions claimed on line 6d	42
• All others: Single or Married filing separately, $5,450	43	Taxable income. Subtract line 42 from line 41. If line 42 is more than line 41, enter -0-	43
	44	Tax (see page 36). Check if any tax is from: a □ Form(s) 8814 b □ Form 4972	44
Married filing jointly or Qualifying widow(er), $10,900	45	Alternative minimum tax (see page 39). Attach Form 6251	45
	46	Add lines 44 and 45 ►	46
Head of household, $8,000	47	Foreign tax credit. Attach Form 1116 if required	47
	48	Credit for child and dependent care expenses. Attach Form 2441	48
	49	Credit for the elderly or the disabled. Attach Schedule R	49
	50	Education credits. Attach Form 8863	50
	51	Retirement savings contributions credit. Attach Form 8880	51
	52	Child tax credit (see page 42). Attach Form 8901 if required	52
	53	Credits from Form: a □ 8396 b □ 8839 c □ 5695	53
	54	Other credits from Form: a □ 3800 b □ 8801 c □	54
	55	Add lines 47 through 54. These are your total credits	55
	56	Subtract line 55 from line 46. If line 55 is more than line 46, enter -0- ►	56
Other Taxes	57	Self-employment tax. Attach Schedule SE	57
	58	Unreported social security and Medicare tax from Form: a □ 4137 b □ 8919	58
	59	Additional tax on IRAs, other qualified retirement plans, etc. Attach Form 5329 if required	59
	60	Additional taxes: a □ AEIC payments b □ Household employment taxes. Attach Schedule H	60
	61	Add lines 55 through 60. This is your total tax ►	61
Payments	62	Federal income tax withheld from Forms W-2 and 1099	62
	63	2008 estimated tax payments and amount applied from 2007 return	63
If you have a qualifying child, attach Schedule EIC.	64a	Earned income credit (EIC)	64a
	b	Nontaxable combat pay election	64b
	65	Excess social security and tier 1 RRTA tax withheld (see page 61)	65
	66	Additional child tax credit. Attach Form 8812	66
	67	Amount paid with request for extension to file (see page 61)	67
	68	Credits from Form: a □ 2439 b □ 4136 c □ 8801 d □ 8885	68
	69	First-time homebuyer credit. Attach Form 5405	69
	70	Recovery rebate credit (see worksheet on pages 62 and 63)	70
	71	Add lines 62 through 70. These are your total payments ►	71
Refund Direct deposit? See page 63 and fill in 73b, 73c, and 73d, or Form 8888.	72	If line 71 is more than line 61, subtract line 61 from line 71. This is the amount you overpaid	72
	73a	Amount of line 72 you want refunded to you. If Form 8888 is attached, check here ► □	73a
	b	Routing number	► c Type: □ Checking □ Savings
	d	Account number	
	74	Amount of line 72 you want applied to your 2009 estimated tax ►	74
Amount You Owe	75	Amount you owe. Subtract line 71 from line 61. For details on how to pay, see page 63	75
	76	Estimated tax penalty (see page 63)	76
Third Party Designee		Do you want to allow another person to discuss this return with the IRS (see page 64)? □ Yes. Complete the following. □ No	
		Designee's name ►	Phone no. ► ( )	Personal identification number (PIN) ►
Sign Here Joint return? See page 15. Keep a copy for your records.		Under penalties of perjury, I declare that I have examined this return and accompanying schedules and statements, and to the best of my knowledge and belief, they are true, correct, and complete. Declaration of preparer (other than taxpayer) is based on all information of which preparer has any knowledge.	
		Your signature	Date	Your occupation	Daytime phone number ( )
		Spouse's signature. If a joint return, both must sign.	Date	Spouse's occupation	
Paid Preparer's Use Only		Preparer's signature ►	Date	Check if self-employed □	Preparer's SSN or PTIN
		Firm's name (or yours if self-employed), address, and ZIP code ►		EIN Phone no. ( )	

Form 1040 (2008)

The Label: This displays your personal identification information. The key component is your social security number. If you do not provide the correct number, your return will not be processed, and you may face penalties for filing a tax return after the deadline.

Your Filing Status: This is fairly straightforward. Normally, the biggest question is whether a married couple should file separately or prepare a joint return. There are really two issues that must be considered when deciding to file jointly or separately. The first consideration is the tax liability. That one is simple. Run the calculations both ways and see which filing status produces the smallest tax bill. The second issue deals with personal liability. If you file a joint tax return, the IRS will see the couple as one entity. For example, the two of you have a tax refund due, but your spouse owes outstanding child support. That check will automatically be diverted to the legal obligation. If your spouse does not claim all of his or her income, the two of you could be held jointly liable for the taxes, penalties, and interest. Carefully consider how well you know the other party's tax situation before signing a joint tax return.

Exemptions: These are deductions you receive for the support of yourself and others. The idea is that large families should pay less in taxes than smaller families with the same income. Each exemption was worth $3,800 in 2012.

Income: In this section you must account for all income earned during the year. This includes wages, interest, qualified retirement plan distributions, alimony, and so forth. With very few exceptions, anything you earn must be disclosed.

Your Adjusted Gross Income (AGI): This is income minus certain expenses, such as IRA contributions, medical expenses, alimony paid, and so forth. This number is particularly important because many deductions are only available *if* they exceed a percentage of your AGI.

Tax and Credits: In this section you determine your taxable income and liability for the year. Itemized deductions or standard deductions (whichever is greater) are subtracted from your AGI to determine taxable income. Then use the appropriate chart to determine the taxes due.

From your gross tax liability, you can subtract any tax credits that apply to your situation.

Other Taxes: This may include self-employment taxes for the small-business owner or social security taxes on tip income that is not reported to the employer.

Payments: This section gives you credit for taxes already withheld or paid during the year.

Refund: This shows the amount due to be paid to you (if any).

Amount You Owe: This shows the outstanding balance (if any) that you still owe the IRS.

Tip: Be sure to **sign your return**, or it will not be accepted!

OK, you can let out your breath.

That really wasn't that bad, was it?

Just like most seemingly insurmountable tasks in life, breaking up the larger whole into doable sections will keep you from hyperventilating or threatening to pack up in the middle of the night to sneak off to some remote island in the middle of the Pacific Ocean. If you are going to head off to some remote island, it should be for a dream vacation, where you can lie on the beach, smiling about your newly developed financial prowess (while you are reading my latest book, of course).

Do not start drifting off to Tahiti just yet.

Let's spend the rest of Day 13 learning some crucial techniques for minimizing your taxable income.

Optimal Tax Strategies

To ensure that you come out on top, so to speak, in the tax game, it is necessary to have a good plan in place. The basic idea of tax planning is to convert ordinary expenses into tax deductions, defer income where possible, accelerate or bunch deductions, and take advantage of long-term capital gains rates.

To accomplish these objectives, we need to look at the following concepts.

1. ***Convert Your Lifestyle into Tax Deductions***. Whenever you turn any expense into a tax-deductible event, you are basically discounting the expense by your marginal tax bracket. For example, let's say that you are in the 25% tax bracket. When you deduct a dollar on your tax return, the IRS kicks back 25 cents. Therefore, a $2,000 computer written off through your home business now has a net sticker price of $1,500. (The $2,000 computer purchase deduction reduces your taxes by $500 because 25% of $2,000 equals $500). Follow me? Good. Just checking. Let's keep finding more money.

   With this knowledge, you will now want to arrange your financial affairs in such a way as to be able to write off as much as possible. You will notice that I mention the following more than once in this book: the very best vehicle for converting everyday expenditures into deductible expenses, recognized by the Internal Revenue Service, is to set up some kind of small-business venture. Remember, this enterprise can be run as either a full-time or part-time operation. It is worth your time and energy to explore this option. The tax benefits can be enormous. Potentially, you could be writing off cell phone costs, Internet service, salaries to children, automobiles, and travel, just to name a few potential deductions. I consider a small-business enterprise to be the single best tax shelter available today.

2. ***Income Deferral.*** Use qualified retirement plans like 401(k)s, IRAs, 403(b)s, and so forth, to defer income until retirement age. These plans allow you to forego current income in favor of taking it at a later date. There is a two-fold benefit to this strategy. First, you are able to compound earnings on dollars that would have normally ended up in Uncle Sam's pocket. Secondly, you will more than likely find yourself in a lower tax bracket when you are retired than during your working years.

   You should also consider deferring bonuses or any other earned income until January of the following year. This will give you additional months to use the money before you need to send a percentage to the IRS. For example, if the boss offered you a $10,000 bonus in October of 2012, you would owe the tax by April 15th of 2013. By taking the bonus in January of 2013, you will have deferred the taxes by one full year, even though you only waited three months for the money.

3. ***Accelerate or Bunch Deductions.*** This strategy is the flip side of the one just covered. Now we want to move potential deductions into the current year, instead of the next, so that we might enjoy the tax write-off *sooner*. In addition, we will want to bunch certain deductions to overcome certain thresholds for purposes of deductibility.

OK, what do you say to us making this simpler to follow?

With certain deductible expenses, you have a choice to pay them this year or next. Those expenses would include your last state income tax estimated payment, property taxes, and medical expenses such as elective surgery or therapeutic equipment. Pay for them this year, and you can write them off this year, even if the payment was made in December.

Considering the fact that you are only able to itemize your deductions or write off things like medical expenses once they exceed a certain dollar amount, it may benefit you to bunch expenses every other year. You will have one lean year with few writeoffs, but then you will have one fat year with lots of deductions that will help you to break through minimum-dollar thresholds.

4. ***Long-Term Capital Gains.*** As most of you know, long-term capital gains rates are lower than ordinary tax rates. In order for a gain to be considered long-term, the owner must have held the asset for a minimum of 366 days. Your capital gains rate will depend upon a number of factors, most especially your personal tax bracket.

If you are in the 10% to 15% tax bracket, your capital gains tax would be tax free on the profits you earned on property held for at least one year. If you are in the 25% or higher tax brackets, your long-term capital gains tax would be 15% of the profited amount, subject to what congress ultimately decides with respect to the Bush tax cuts.

Summary

Today we reviewed a tax return and explored the best ways to minimize your tax life. The IRS forms are pretty clear if you analyze them carefully, one line at a time. The tax-reduction strategies are fairly straightforward, but they do require some attention to detail on your part.

My Tax Strategies

Review last year's tax return and consider the lessons learned today. Start finding ways to implement the four basic tax strategies into your tax life. The financial rewards for doing so could be worth hundreds of thousand of dollars during your working years.

Day 14

Capitalizing on the Stock Market

Almost every wealthy person in this country keeps a significant portion of his or her net worth invested in equities, and for good reason. The stock market has provided the highest historical rate of return over any other investment in the history of this country. During the last 75 years, the stock market has created an average total return (dividends plus price appreciation) of about 10% per annum. That means that money in the market will double every seven years. Those are just the results achieved by the *average* investor. What if you were smarter than the average bear? (Pardon the pun.) Would it be possible to double your money approximately every five years? I believe the answer to that question is a resounding YES!

Let me show you how to trade stocks like the pros.

A Brief History of the Stock Market

No grumbling. This stuff is actually very interesting, and, as Americans, we are talking about OUR history here! Whether you were born and raised in the United States or you are currently reading this book while going through the naturalization process, the reality is that the stock market has played an integral role in the development of this country. This may come as a surprise, but the stock market as we know it actually dates back to 1792. In those early days, when you wanted to buy or sell shares of stock, an ad would have to be placed in a local newspaper.

As I am sure you have already guessed—this system was not very efficient.

Skip ahead to 1817. Twenty-four gentlemen decided it was time to do something about the system. They created rules and regulations to govern the buying and selling of stocks. So, they set up shop at 22 Wall Street in New York, New York. Stocks and bonds were auctioned every business day at noon and sold to the highest bidder. The exchange was paid a commission for its services. This organization was called The

Stock Exchange Office, and it represented the birth of the modern-day stock market.

OK, now that you are officially a history buff, let's discuss some terminology.

What Is a Stock?

A stock, by definition, represents an ownership interest in a company.

A company will sell stock through what is called an initial public offering (IPO) in order to raise money for the operational expenses and expansion of its enterprise. Investors who are willing to accept the risk of possible failure are entitled to share in the financial benefits should the company succeed. The investor's gain comes in the form of dividends, appreciation, or both. The stockholder or investor is taking a calculated risk on the future viability of the corporation.

Basically, when you buy stock in a company, you are betting that the company will be profitable. If you have bet incorrectly, you will share in the company's misfortune with a deflated stock price. That is why it is important that you research the financial viability of the company whose stock you are considering. Guessing randomly about a stock's future is not how you win in the market. We will explore stock choices more intently a little later in this chapter.

The Exchanges

One of the primary benefits of owning stock is that your investment is considered to be *liquid*, meaning that it can be readily converted to cash. This is mostly because of the stock exchanges that exist around the world and the market makers and specialists who ensure that investors can cash out whenever they desire.

The best way to visualize a stock exchange is to picture a super-market where stocks are gathered at one giant location, like your local mega-mart.

However, *these* markets are used for buying or selling shares of stocks. Stock exchanges make it possible for anyone in the world to

Day 14: Capitalizing on the Stock Market purchase and sell securities. In the old days, an investor would have had to conduct business in person. Today, of course, you can have a broker do your bidding for you.

The New York Stock Exchange (NYSE) is the oldest and largest of the exchanges in the United States. Unlike some of the newer exchanges, the NYSE still uses a large trading floor to conduct its transactions. It is home to some 2,800 companies with a combined market value of more than $18 trillion. The NYSE uses specialists who agree to buy or sell shares of specific companies if no other investors stand ready. This is what provides the liquidity investors cherish.

You may have heard of the American Stock Exchange (AMEX). The AMEX was started as an alternative to the NYSE. It originated when brokers began meeting on the curb outside the NYSE to trade stocks that did not meet the Big Board's stringent listing requirements. In fact, up until the 1950s, the AMEX was referred to as *The Curb*. The AMEX is the second largest exchange in the United States, is known for more lenient listing requirements, and prides itself on being a bit more progressive than the NYSE. It has gained recognition as a leader in exchange-traded funds and has branded the iShares products, which are gaining popularity among the investing community.

The National Association of Securities Dealers Automated Quotation System, otherwise know by its more familiar name, Nasdaq, is different than the NYSE and the AMEX because Nasdaq does not have a physical trading floor for bringing together buyers and sellers. Instead, it uses a sophisticated network of computers and telephones. Nasdaq began when brokers started trading informally over the phones. The network was formalized and linked by computers in the 1970s. Instead of using specialists to buy unfilled orders (like those which are used in the NYSE), Nasdaq uses market makers who list their bid- and-ask prices. Nasdaq is known as the exchange for finding technology-oriented stocks. The Over the Counter Exchanges (OTC) was originally named to signify any exchange that did not have a trading floor. This has changed over the years. Today the OTC is the home for lower-priced and lower-volume trading stocks. Although there have been some great success stories, stocks traded here are considered to be riskier and less liquid than those traded on the NYSE, AMEX, or Nasdaq. You better have a high level of investment experience before venturing into these uncertain waters.

Now that you have a good overview of the stock market, let's move on to the "how to" section of today's topic.

Setting Up a Brokerage Account

There are several options you can choose from when you are ready to establish an account at a brokerage firm.

First, you will need to consider whether you want to do business with a full-service firm, or if you would rather find a discount broker who will allow you to execute trades online for a fraction of the costs found at the full-service outfits.

Let's explore each option.

Full-Service Brokers

Full-service firms, such as Bank of America Securities, Morgan Stanley, and Raymond James, primarily cater to high-net-worth individuals. They provide investment advice and research in exchange for the relatively high commissions and management fees charged to their clients.

Lately, more and more investors have been questioning the quality of their full-service broker's advice. The number of firms who have been exposed as being *in bed* with analysts has caused serious concern. These firms' objectives have nothing to do with the financial welfare of their clients. Before you decide on a full-service broker, be sure to research them thoroughly on the Internet. Review any information and feedback you can find about them. It will be worth your time and effort.

I am not saying that all full-service brokers behave contrary to the financial interests of their clients. My primary concern is in regard to the very nature of the relationship between the broker and the customer.

There is an obvious conflict of interest.

The broker gets paid for making money for the firm. The broker does not get paid for making money for the customer. Therefore, what might be best for the broker may not be best for the customer.

For example, if a broker makes more money selling a proprietary mutual fund than a fund from an outside provider, this may tempt him or her to do what is best in self-interest, no matter what the consequences may be for a client's portfolio.

In addition, the more frequently the customer makes trades, the greater the commissions the broker generates for the brokerage firm. This is good news for the broker but counterproductive for the customer. These potential conflicts have been the basis for the bad reputations that are often tied to some full-service brokers. With these things in mind, I would suggest using the services of a full-service retail firm only under the umbrella of a managed account. In this case, you pay a fee based upon a percentage of assets under management and not on a per-trade schedule. You will not be pressured into buying the stock-of-the-day, nor will you be pushed into purchasing your broker's in-house funds. If you do not have enough money to warrant professional management yet—then learn to manage your money yourself!

Online Brokers

Online discount brokers are growing in popularity for a number of reasons. You can establish an account with a very modest initial investment ($500 to $1,000 at most firms). Also, their commissions are very inexpensive, ranging from $5 to $30 per trade, and there are no high- pressure brokers trying to steer you in any particular direction. You will be expected to make your own investment decisions as most of these brokerage firms offer little to no investment advice. To date, my favorite online brokerage firm has been Scottrade (www.scottrade.com) because they are consistently ranked among the top firms for customer satisfaction. Other firms to consider include Charles Schwab, OptionsXpress, TD Ameritrade, E*Trade, and Fidelity.

To set up your online trading account, you need to be…online! (Go figure.) The brokerage firm of your choice will want you to sign a *new customer account form* for their records. You can print this form at your home or office and send a hard copy to the brokerage firm. Once they have your application and the initial check deposit clears, you can begin trading. Trades that are executed online are not only cost-efficient, they are fast—most trades require only a few seconds for confirmation. Just like with any important decision, make sure that you do sufficient research before you begin a relationship with a broker. Find out what other people have experienced using a particular broker. You can do your own research online by going to www.finra.org/InvestorInformation/InvestorProtection/index.htm and refer to the "Before You Invest" section. Click on the **BrokerCheck** link. You can read about your prospective broker's professional history and any complaints contained in their file.

How a Trade Is Routed

So how, exactly, does your trade order get from your computer to the exchange? Well, on the New York Stock Exchange, for example, it works like this: You instruct your broker to buy 100 shares of *AAPL* stock at the market (for the best available price at the time). The firm's order department sends the order to its floor clerk on the exchange. The clerk alerts one of the floor traders, who, in turn, finds a trader willing to sell 100 shares of AAPL. The two agree on a price and complete the transaction. Your broker then reports back to you, or the firm sends you a confirmation notice.

On Nasdaq, everything is done electronically through a vast network of computers that matches up the buyers and the sellers. The most powerful advancement of the Nasdaq system is the establishment of the Electronic Communication Networks (ECNs) in the market.

ECNs give institutions, investors (big and small), and traders a tool with which they can electronically transmit their current best buying and selling prices. These prices are very competitive with market maker quotes and recently have been used as the standard. This system has given investors the opportunity to trade among themselves, bypassing the market makers entirely—and eliminating the market makers' spreads. A spread is the difference between the bid and the ask price. It is truly free-market economics at its finest.

Overcoming Your Fear of the Market

Most people have been convinced that the stock market is a scary and intimidating place. The same might be said for anything that is new or unfamiliar. Can you remember when you were learning how to drive a car? Your worries of the unknown probably scared you half to death! *What if someone suddenly pulls into my lane? What if the car in front of me loses control?* With time, you learned that you were capable of handling just about any driving situation by using caution and good judgment. The fears began to subside, and you could get behind the wheel of a vehicle without giving it a second thought. Learning to drive is an important accomplishment for most of us as it provides a much faster and more reliable way for us to get where we want or need to go.

Now relate this process to learning to invest in the stock market, which, currently, may be a totally unfamiliar environment for many of you. The more you understand and the more effort you make to learn the facts, the better you will feel about the whole process. If you put in a little effort each day, I promise you that one day you will look back and laugh at how nervous you felt about managing your own money.

You now know the basics facts about the stock market and how it works. Tomorrow, we will take the next step and begin to learn about actual trading strategies.

One day at a time. One step at a time. That is all that it takes to turn your financial life around and start preparing for your new life—a life free of debt and full of promise.

Your Homework

Your assignment for today is to begin researching brokerage firms so that you are able to set up a brokerage account with the firm of your choice. Whether you select a full-service or a discount broker, you need to get the research process started. Once you have chosen a firm, you can open an account with an amount of capital that you consider to be reasonable for your situation. Some of you may start with $1,000 while others may be able to begin with $100,000 of capital. As you gain experience, you will become more comfortable with the idea of trading stocks. Still, it is usually better to start with a conservative bankroll. You can always increase the stakes further down the road.

My Stock Market Research Plan

Short-Term Plan: Purchase and read today's issue of *Investors Business Daily.*

Long-Term Plan: Purchase and read Jim Cramer's book: *Sane Investing in an Insane World.*

Long-Term Plan: Purchase and read Phil Town's book: Rule #1

❖ ❖ ❖

Day 15

Building Your Stock Portfolio

We will spend today discussing stock market investment strategies.

On Day 14 we discussed the history of the stock market, brokerage types, and how transactions are actually processed. Today, we will take this topic to the next level. You will begin to learn strategies that will enable you to make successful trades on your own.

In my opinion, there are few things more exciting and rewarding in the world of personal finance than investing in the stock market. The stock market, when used correctly, can be a great source of profits which can accumulate significantly over time. It is always a thrill to watch your money grow exponentially whenever you make a great trade.

As you read in the previous chapter, the stock market has provided total returns at a rate of approximately 10% per year during the last 75 years.

That does not mean that stock market investing is free from risk. Like every investment opportunity, the stock market holds its own share of potential pitfalls. To make the statement that the stock market, in general, has increased 10% during the last 75 years is not to say that this performance level has been the experience of everyone who has invested in the market.

Finding Your Correct Trading Strategy

To be successful in the stock market, you need to learn to take advantage of the market environment. When the market is going up, it is probably a good time to buy. When the market is going down, it is probably a good time to sell. Knowledgeable investors call that behavior *trading with the trend*. But…hold that thought for a moment. In reality, there are many different ways to invest in the stock market. It is best that we explore specific strategies that have been tested by professionals who eat, breathe, and sleep the stock market.

As you might imagine, due to the complexities of the market, many moneymaking theories have been developed and then fine-tuned over the decades.

The important thing to understand is that no single strategy has proven superior under *all* market conditions.

If a magic formula existed that consistently beat the market, everyone would use it all the time, right? You will need to learn how to assess the market and how to figure out which strategy is best to apply to the *current* market conditions. That is the key to success.

No quitting now! Keep reading!

Let's take a look at some of the more popular strategies. For starters, virtually every approach identified by market strategists can be put into one of two categories: **fundamental** or **technical** analysis. Fundamental analysis focuses on the financial integrity of the company whereas technical analysis identifies the up or down momentum of an individual stock. In other words, fundamental analysis determines what to buy. Technical analysis indicates when to buy.

Fundamental Analysis

The underlying goal of fundamental analysis is to determine the true value of a particular company. Fundamentalists believe that a company should be valued based upon its anticipated future profits and discounted for time value of money plus the value of the business assets. Investors who subscribe to this type of analysis will review balance sheets, income and expense statements, credit ratings (as provided by firms such as Standard and Poor's), and P/E ratios. Basically the analysts want to know the financial stability of the company, and they will spend hours pouring over the numbers of the company in an effort to make an accurate determination. These analysts approach the investment as if they were actually buying the business. Other details taken into consideration include net income, free cash flow, and EBITA (earnings before interest, taxes, depreciation, and amortization).

There are two primary challenges to the fundamental approach.

First, there is a need for timeliness in regard to the company information. Second, there must be an ability to understand the data. The investor is making buy and sell decisions based upon dated information (balance sheets are not current; they are historical). Furthermore, most investors lack the educational background necessary to interpret the financials of a publicly traded company.

If you are fairly conservative in your stock selections and find comfort in owning *good companies* as opposed to *hot stocks*, then fundamental analysis is the appropriate path for you.

Let's see if we can narrow things down just a little bit in order to come up with a practical application of the fundamental approach. Although there are other theories in the marketplace for those who want to engage in fundamental analysis, these three, GARP, Quality, and CAN SLIM, seem to be the most realistic for an investor to comprehend and apply.

GARP

GARP is an acronym for "growth at reasonable prices." Perhaps the most famous practitioner of this approach was Peter Lynch, former manager of the Fidelity Magellan Fund. Mr. Lynch looked for companies that combined future growth prospects and current share prices that did not reflect the intrinsic value of the stock. The calculation for this strategy is pretty simple: buy stocks when their P/E ratio is lower than the anticipated growth rate of the earnings per share. Future growth drives down the P/E ratio, making the stock more desirable, thereby driving up the price down the road.

Quality

When you talk stock quality, the first name that comes to mind is Warren Buffett. Mr. Buffett is always in the market for high-quality businesses that are selling at realistic and sustainable prices. The key statistic of quality is the company's return on equity. This quantifies the effectiveness with which corporate assets are utilized.

CAN SLIM

My favorite fundamental approach was pioneered by William O'Neil of *Investors Business Daily*. Mr. O'Neil coined the acronym CAN SLIM.

This approach considers seven critical factors:

1. **C**urrent earnings per share should be up 10% and should have a pattern of accelerating over recent quarters; sales should also be up 10% or increasing.
2. **A**nnual earnings should be up 10% or more for each of the last three years, and the return on equity should be 10% or more.
3. The company should have a **N**ew product or service that is fueling its growth.
4. **S**upply and demand should show increasing volume as the stock price moves up.
5. **L**eaders in the industry are a particularly good target.
6. **I**nstitutional ownership should be on the uptrend; this would include mutual funds, pension funds, and major players in the market.
7. **M**arket indexes such as the Dow, the S&P 500, and Nasdaq should be in an uptrend as three out of four stocks follow the markets' overall trend.

All of this information is readily available with a subscription to *Investors Business Daily*. *IBD* recommends investing only in stocks that have an earnings-per-share rating of 80 or higher, relative price strength of 80 or higher, industry group rating of A, sales + profit margins + return on equity of 80 or higher, and accumulation/distribution rating of B or higher. If you stick with this criteria and follow the general trend of the marketplace (invested in a bull market, out in a bear market), you should produce profits like the pros!

Technical Analysis

Technical analysis is a method of evaluating securities by analyzing statistics generated by market activity, past prices, and volume.

Technicians believe that the future can be foretold by examining the past and that stock patterns tend to repeat themselves. There are many instances of investors successfully trading the market with no knowledge of the company represented by the stock.

In many ways, this approach is the opposite of fundamental analysis. Fundamentalists study the *corporation* while technicians primarily study *history* and *momentum.*

There are a number of approaches to technical analysis, and each has merit.

We will explore some of the simpler approaches. A novice investor should use a simple approach until he or she has had a significant amount of practice (and success) in the stock market.

Moving Averages

A moving average is one of the easiest indicators to understand, and for years this was the most popular form of technical analysis. The moving average shows the average value of a stock's price over a certain period of time.

The most commonly used moving averages are 20, 50, and 200 days.

When a stock is trading above its moving average, the trend is *up,* and this represents a good time to purchase a stock. When a stock is trading below its moving average, this is seen as *bearish* (negative), and this triggers a sell signal.

MACD (pronounced "mack-dee")

The MACD (moving average convergence divergence) is a momentum indicator that shows the relationship between two moving averages of prices. You can find MACD charts online at www.stockcharts.com.

To calculate the MACD, the 26-day EMA (exponential moving average) is subtracted from the 12-day EMA. You will probably never perform this calculation yourself as it is already built into the chart.

A 9-day dotted EMA of the MACD, called the signal line, is then plotted on top of the MACD. Please view the chart for illustration of this concept.

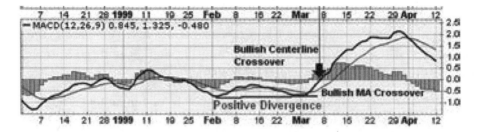

There are three common signals followed by those employing this tool:

1. When the MACD falls below the signal line, it is time to sell. When the MACD moves above the signal line, it is time to buy.
2. When the security diverges from the MACD, it represents the end of a current trend.
3. When the MACD rises dramatically and the shorter-term moving average pulls away from the longer-term moving average, the stock is overbought and should return to its more customary levels.

This may sound complicated, but it is a learnable strategy for most investors. You will need either a Web-based or otherwise installable software tool and access to the Internet in order to receive the moving averages and/or MACD profiles.

Support and Resistance

The support and resistance levels for a stock represent the floor and the ceiling for that stock's traditional price range. For example, if you were looking at a two-year chart for Coca Cola,

Inc., and noticed that each time the stock fell to a price of $40 per share it started to climb back up in price, you could establish $40 as the *support* level for Coca Cola.

This would represent a buying opportunity.

If each time the price of Coca Cola climbed to $50 its stock price began to retreat, it could be stated that it *hit resistance* at $50.

This would indicate the proper time to sell.

Be aware that no stock will maintain a consistent support/resistance price structure forever. The structure will change after some time, and you must keep an eye out for these new patterns as they emerge. Quite often, when a stock drops below its previous support level, the new low price becomes the new resistance number and vice versa. You can establish any stock's support/resistance prices by looking at a one-year or two-year price chart. You can view these charts for free at www. big-charts.com.

This is a relatively easy concept to master.

Other Charting Patterns

Trying to read charts can be as vague an exercise as attempting to interpret tea leaves in a cup. However, many investors are quite successful at chart reading.

The following three approaches presume that history repeats itself, which is a common occurrence in the stock market.

Unless you plan to spend considerable time reviewing charts, the following concepts might be a bit much. However, assuming that some of you will be interested in acquiring these particular skills, I wanted to include the following information for your learning pleasure.

(Author's note: Dear Reader, if you have reached your boiling point already, you can skip this next section and begin reading the following section titled *Summary*.)

Charting Patterns

Cup and Handle: This strategy requires a bar chart for any stock (I prefer one that shows 52 weeks). If you see the chart form a large U-shape (the cup) followed by a period of a downward drift in the price (the handle) followed by an upward spike, it is time to climb aboard. This is what happens: The price rose to a point of resistance and then moved down ever so slightly due to profit-taking from investors who believed that the price of their stock had hit its peak. But then new investors moved in and began accumulating shares, believing that the stock price deserved to be higher. The new investors' participation drives the

149

price through the previous resistance number and sends it on to greater heights.

Head and Shoulders: This is a chart formation that resembles the letter M. This occurs due to the stock price rising to a peak, then ebbing, then rising above the former peak, and then once again declining in price. The third time the stock price rises, it does not reach the level of the second peak, and the price of the stock is likely to break down from there.

The Double Bottom: This chart formation looks like the letter W. The price of a stock drops to a certain level and then rises. The stock does the same thing within a period of a few weeks or months. The time for you to purchase this stock is when the price of the stock passes the highest point in the handle. It is particularly bullish when the second decline stops at a point higher than the previous decline.

Putting It All Together

Now I will share a technique that I use in order to "cheat," so to speak, when it comes to technical analysis. Go to the Web site at www. stockta.com. Click on *Bullish Technical Analysis Screens*. Then click on *Bullish Stocks; Overall*. You will be provided a list of stocks that technicians would regard as bullish using a variety of screens. Using this, I then impose a couple of rules to these stocks:

1. I only purchase stocks that trade 500,000 shares per day or more.
2. I use a trailing-stop-loss order that is placed 10% below my original purchase price. A trailing-stop-loss is triggered if the price of the stock falls 10% or more from its highest price during the time you own the stock. This method limits your downside while not restricting your potential gain. I use this type of order on all of my stocks that I am holding in my portfolio.

Summary

New strategies and approaches to stock investing are always popping up. Some of the strategies really do work...*if* you apply them correctly.

However, allow me to let you in on a little secret. When it is all said and done, the one factor that will govern the price of a stock is a very simple principle: **supply and demand**.

Supply and demand is one of the oldest economic concepts, and this concept still applies to today's stock market. Whenever there are more investors buying a stock than selling it, the demand is up and the supply is down. This means that the price is going to increase. Whenever there are more people selling the stock than buying it, the demand is going down and the supply is up. This devalues the stock.

To put it all into practical perspective, think about the last holiday season and the latest video game system that was released for sale. The supply was limited, and the demand was high. What would have been a $500 purchase, normally, instead turned into a $3,000 purchase (for shoppers who just could not wait!).

The same situation occurs in the stock market. The hard part: knowing which stocks are going to become a hot commodity in the future.

That is enough for today. If you are feeling a little fuzzy-headed, do not worry about it. In life, no matter what the pursuit, you have to go at your own pace. I would not expect you to become an expert investor overnight and wake up tomorrow morning and start applying the "Cup and Handle" strategy. Maybe the only cup and handle you will be ready for tomorrow morning is your coffee mug. No problem. If at any point you feel that you need to reread a chapter or pause to take time to do more research about something you have read—do it! You are the only one who should be keeping tabs on your progression. It took me a span of 20 years in the stock market to learn all that I know now, including the lessons contained in this chapter. It is OK if it takes you more than one day to fully comprehend the various techniques contained in today's chapter.

The important thing is to keep learning. Investing in stocks is an important part of your portfolio, and if you have not considered stock investing in the past, well…I want you to start thinking about it now.

If I lost some of you with all the technical talk today, take heart!

In the next chapter I will share one of the simplest approaches to making money in the stock market—without having to become a stock market expert.

Take a break! No chapter exercises or worksheets today. We will review more stock strategies in tomorrow's lessons.

Day 16

Autopilot Investing

Welcome to our last lesson day on investing in the stock market.

I hope you have already gained some useful tools and valuable insights. The stock market is an incredible source from which to draw power for your financial portfolio. It can give you a jump-start toward achieving your goals for retirement.

There are many benefits to stock investing, so hang in here for just one more lesson day about the market.

In yesterday's lesson, I told you that I would let you in on another secret that I use for trading the stock market. With this tool, I can successfully invest in the market without delving into all of its complex intricacies. There is no need to try to wrap our minds around thousands of company statistics.

The strategy is simple enough that it can be implemented by almost anyone. I know that the lessons from the past two days may have scared some of you away from the idea of investing in the market. If you are having any concerns, today's lesson will most likely calm your fears.

Dollar-Cost Averaging

Dollar-cost averaging is a powerful approach that takes all the emotion out of investing. The principle is pretty simple. The investor places a fixed amount of money into a designated vehicle (we will use a mutual fund). This is done on a regular basis over a long period of time. This is a particularly advantageous strategy when you are dealing with assets like equities which experience price fluctuations. Your regular contributions will purchase more shares when the stock price is low and acquire fewer shares as the stock price rises.

For example: $100 buys 50 shares at $2 per share but only 25 shares when the price rises to $4 per share for that same stock.

That is all there is to it.

The buy-low/sell-high technique requires no analysis or research on your part. As long as the market rises over time, *as it has done for the past 100 years*, the investor wins.

Average Share Price vs. Price Share Cost			
Quarter	Amount Invested	Share Price	Shares Purchased	Cumulative Average Share Cost
1	$300	$15	20	$15.00
2	$300	$10	30 $	12.00
3	$300	$ 5	60	$ 8.18
4	$300	$20	15 $	9.60
	$1,200 (total)	**$12.50** (average)	**125** (total)	**$ 9.60** (average)

Selecting the Right Security

Before you run off and buy 10,000 shares of IBM, we need to analyze which investment will prove most effective for *you*, assuming you were to use the dollar-cost averaging strategy.

First, it would not be a smart investment if you allocated your dollars to the same company each month by buying the same stock over and over again. Unless you bought the shares directly from the company, you would be charged a brokerage commission for each trade, not to mention the fact that you would end up with all of your money tied to the performance of just one investment instrument. This would result in no diversification, which makes it a risky maneuver.

Here is what I would suggest: couple your dollar-cost averaging strategy with an index mutual fund or an ETF. A mutual fund is a relatively simple financial intermediary that allows a group of investors to pool their money together and invest in a manner that has been predetermined by the fund manager. The advantage of the mutual fund vehicle comes from economies of scale. If a thousand people each invested $1,000, the fund would have $1,000,000 to employ. Theoretically, this would result in lower overall expenses and sufficient funds to achieve the proper level of diversification.

An ETF is a security that tracks an index and represents a basket of stocks like an index fund, but it trades like a stock. The largest ETF is the SPDR (symbol SPY) which tracks the S&P 500 index. This is the ETF that I would recommend for the novice investor as its returns will largely mirror the overall return of the stock market.

Today, mutual funds are almost as numerous as the number of stocks being traded on the various exchanges. You must choose wisely. Although each mutual fund creates a track record over time, it is impossible to determine which fund will out-produce the rest from year to year. That is why I recommend that you select an index fund for your regular deposits.

An index fund is a passively managed account that tries to mirror the performance of a specific index, such as the S&P 500 or Nasdaq. There are hundreds of such funds available to investors.

Seeing how this is **my** book, I get the opportunity to be somewhat subjective in my communications with my readers. I will now narrow down the field and discuss the mutual fund that is my personal favorite. Like every investment, you should do your own research and make your own choices, just as I have done. But from my perspective, utilizing the dollar-cost averaging technique, you will be hard pressed to find a better fund than the Vanguard 500 Index Fund.

Vanguard 500 Index Fund

The Vanguard Group was founded in 1975 and has more than 200 unique mutual funds with combined assets under management equaling more than $1.7 trillion. Vanguard is known in the industry for offering investors a wide selection of low-cost mutual funds. According to Lipper Analytical Services, Vanguard's expense ratio is 75% lower than the average mutual fund. Additionally, their no-load funds carry no front end and no back-end commissions as they are offered to the customer without requiring a broker's participation.

The Vanguard 500 Index Fund seeks to track the performance of the S&P 500, which is an index consisting of 500 stocks chosen for market size, liquidity, and industry group representation.

It is a market value–weighted index with each stock's weight in the index proportionate to its market value.

In other words, this investment should provide a return that mirrors the general market trends. The concept has become wildly successful, and this particular fund is the largest in the world.

Getting Started with Vanguard

It is pretty simple.

I am going to attempt to give you instructions on how to navigate the Vanguard Web site. Keep in mind that Web sites are often updated or redesigned. (What you find on Vanguard's Web site today may vary from the date upon which I wrote these instructions.)

1. Go online and visit The Vanguard Group's Web site homepage at www.vanguard.com.
2. Click on the **Personal Investors** label, or click on **Go to the site>>** which appears in blue font just below the **Personal Investors** label.
3. Under **What we offer**, click on **Vanguard mutual funds and ETFs**.
4. Next, on the left-hand side of the page, click on **index funds only** and scroll down until you come to **500 Index Fund Inv** listed under the **Domestic Stock-General** chart.
5. Click on the **500 Index Fund Inv** in blue font. In the right-hand column, you will see a section that reads: *I want to…* You will notice that just below there is an option to **Buy this fund**; click on **Buy this fund**.
6. On this page you will see a light blue box marked **Invest Now**. Click on this box.
7. The final page will ask whether you are an existing client. It will prompt you to either *log on* if you are already a client, or, if you are ready to create an account, you just click on the blue font that reads: **sign up for access.** This will return the Web page to

Day 16: Autopilot Investing

Open an account where you can complete the application process. The minimum initial investment is $3,000. After that, you can add as little as $100 at a time.

The key to dollar-cost averaging in a mutual fund is to continue making regular periodic payments. Whenever it is possible (and safe), it is best to automate any periodic payments whether for any regular bills that you pay or for regular contributions to investment accounts. This way you can focus on other issues, and you will not have to worry about missing any critical due dates.

You might want to consider giving the mutual fund company the authority to automatically withdraw the monthly contributions directly from your paycheck or checking account. This would also be a good practice for your annual IRA investments. Most people wait until the end of the year and then find themselves scrambling to come up with the needed investment funds. If the money is being automatically deducted, you will never see it and will not be tempted to use the funds elsewhere.

Pay Yourself First

When it comes to putting money aside for the future, most of us tend to have our priorities in the reverse order of what they ought to be. We take our paycheck, deposit it into a non-interest-bearing checking account, and then proceed to pay everyone but ourselves.

We cover the mortgage company, credit card firms, the notes on our vehicles, and so forth. If anything is left over, we try to set a few dollars aside for a rainy day. The problem is that there never seems to be anything left over! The vultures at the front of the line end up with the spoils, right?

Here is the key: you need to pay yourself first!

Instead of trying to invest with some meager amount of funds that may remain after you have paid your bills, you should reverse the order. From this point forward, I want you to invest for your future before you pay any other obligation. You can take either a percentage of your net check (10% is a good place to start) or a stated dollar amount, and automatically have the money flow into the investment vehicle of your choice. (A good option would be the mutual fund you are about to open.)

Now, I already know what you are thinking. You are thinking, "I cannot afford to invest 10% of my salary; I barely make ends meet as it is."

Was I right? Here is the truth of the matter: **you will adjust**.

Fewer dollars in your hands will require that you make better buying decisions, and trust me, after reading this book, you will make better decisions.

How do I know this? Because you will not have any choice! You will need to become more resourceful, and so you will become more resourceful. We are a species that is amazingly adaptable when faced with a challenge.

The payoff for the strategy you learned today is a $1,000,000 investment portfolio down the road. Money compounding over time is like a sticky snowball rolling down a snow-covered hill. It will gather more and more momentum the longer you allow it to roll along.

Why are you sitting there with that look on your face? You don't believe that this can work for you?

Let me remind you that money in the stock market has historically doubled every seven years.

If you make intelligent investing a habit the way most people make spending a habit, the world will be yours.

Please, do not delay in getting started.

It is time you put your financial future on autopilot.

I am sure that you have enough to do already—tons of things that you have to take care of or that you would rather focus on during your regular day-to-day activities.

Investing may take some sacrifice on your part, but in the end… it will change your life and, in turn, will change the lives of those who depend upon you or who interact with you.

What a great day this was. See you tomorrow.

My Autopilot Investing Plan

Step 1: Determine how much money you want to invest each month.

Step 2: Go to the Vanguard Web site at www.vanguard. com.

Step 3: Follow the instructions listed in the Day 16 chapter for setting up your Vanguard account so that you can make automatic monthly or bi-monthly investments into the Vanguard 500 investment fund.

❖ ❖ ❖

Day 17

Smart Car Buying

So it is time to buy a new car, huh? Excited? Happy?

Or...are you dreading the thought of dealing with those sweet-talking (and pushy) salespeople?

Unfortunately, most people report that buying a car is a shopping excursion that they absolutely hate. Many are afraid that a car salesperson will take advantage of them and that they will end up getting locked into a bad purchase and financing contract for years.

Today, on Day 17, you are going to learn how to buy your next car and every other car for the rest of your life. Buying a car can be a wonderful experience. You should never have to feel as though shopping for a car is a chore to be dreaded.

It can be exciting and fun—as long as you go into the buying process prepared because you have done your homework and you have confidence that you know what you are doing and know how to defend yourself from those who will try and manipulate your purchasing decision.

The trick is that you need to know everything that the car salesperson knows. Otherwise, you risk getting pushed into a deal that is not good for you. Getting yourself well-prepared to buy a car is not difficult, and it will most likely save you years of grief by preventing you from being cheated on this major purchase.

New Cars vs. Pre-Owned Cars

You need to decide whether you are in the market for a new vehicle or one that has been pre-owned. We will discuss the specific pros and cons for each in a bit, but first let me tell you why I think buying a used, eh-hem, I mean, *pre-owned* car is the best option.

You have probably heard this before, but the worst financial concern with owning a car is the rapid depreciation that occurs. The value of the car always goes down over time, unless of course, the car is a collectible, and I am guessing that most of you are not in the market for that type of vehicle at this time.

When does your new car depreciate the most?

The first five minutes you own it!

That is not an exaggeration. If you have somehow missed out on learning this fact, I am here to tell you, the immediate loss in value of a brand-new car is a financial killer.

The moment your front tires leave the car lot and hit the open road, you can kiss 20% of the purchase price goodbye!

On a $30,000 vehicle, that immediate depreciation equals approximately $6,000. It takes the average family two months to earn that amount of money and more than a year to save it.

Think about that for a second.

For an enlightening exercise, read this paragraph and then do the simple math required in the instruction. Take the estimated price on the new car that you are dying to own, multiply that number by 0.20, and then study the answer you get…and then THINK. Think about the fact that this is the amount of money you will instantly lose. Then think about all the other things you could do with that $5,000, $6,000, $7,000. (The amount may be more when considering the inflated costs of a new, luxury-grade vehicle.) By the way, the first alternative choice to pop into your thoughts should have been that you could open a very solid investment account with all that money!

Can you really afford that kind of a drain on your net worth? If you are already wealthy, go ahead and indulge, with "wealthy" meaning that you are able to buy any car you want with cash. Maybe automobiles are your passion and your hobby. Good for you. You are keeping people with specialized skills gainfully employed. If you are not wealthy yet, think twice before selecting a brand-new car, especially if you cannot afford to buy it for cash.

Day 17: Smart Car Buying

Let's compare some figures.

According to NADA (the National Automobile Dealers Association), a 2012 Chevy Tahoe carries a sticker price of $39,000, whereas a 2010 version of the same model sells for around $29,000 at a dealership and for about $25,000 through a private party.

By purchasing the slightly older model vehicle, you save about

$10,000 to $15,000 right away. You could buy an entire extra car with those savings. You must also consider the interest savings if you are going to finance. For example: $39,000 financed over five years at 8% interest means **total payments of $47,400** for a vehicle that will be worth **less than $15,000** by the time the note has been satisfied.

On the other hand, $25,000 financed over three years will have almost the identical monthly payment, but it will remove two years of car payments for a total amount of about $28,200. Which is better, the new-car smell or no car payments?

Not sure?

Try this: take a giant wad of new, crisp $100 bills into your hands and inhale. In fact, maybe that is exactly what you need to do when you go out car shopping! If you get suckered into taking a seat in a brand-new vehicle at some dealership and you feel yourself start to succumb to that new-car aroma, you can quickly pull out your giant wad of cash, begin to inhale, and safely remove yourself from the vehicle before that new-car aroma sends you into a mindless new-car coma. In the finance examples I just mentioned, the difference in total payments is nearly $20,000. We are talking about the same make and model vehicle! Remember that your new car will only feel new for a very short period. After that short period, it will be just another car that gets you from point A to point B. If you shop around, you can find that many pre-owned (but recent model) vehicles look nearly brand-new and have most of the bells and whistles as the current year's models. (Important note: as far as the money-sniffing idea goes, maybe you should not take it literally. I am fairly certain that, after reading this last paragraph, some concerned reader will contact me to let me know that inhaling ink is not a healthy pastime. Which is kind of ironic because I recently heard concerns have arisen regarding the fact that the "new-car smell" that we love so much may actually not be a healthy scent for us to inhale.) Regardless, make sure you arm yourself with an effective defense that will prevent you from making any impulse automobile buys.

In spite of the case I just made concerning the advantages of purchasing a used vehicle, I know that some of you will not resist buying a new car. If there is no way to talk you out of buying that brand-new vehicle, let me, at least, give you some pointers on how to minimize your financial pain, both at the point of purchase and later down the road. For you money-smart folks, skip this next section and begin reading the section titled *Purchasing a Used Vehicle*—**just kidding!** Much of what will be discussed in this next section still applies when buying a pre-owned vehicle. Please make sure to read it carefully. You can save yourself, your family, and your friends thousands of dollars simply by becoming an informed consumer.

Purchasing a New (Unused) Vehicle

First, determine which kind of vehicle will serve your particular needs. If you are single with no children, a sports car may be a fine consideration. If you are married with a family, you are probably looking for something roomy, like an SUV or wagon. Identify your vehicle type before you shop so that you will be less likely to make an emotional decision and less likely to get talked into a car that does not fit your lifestyle at all.

Now determine the amount that you think you can afford and that you are willing to pay. It seems to me that most people drive the most expensive vehicle they can possibly manage to get under contract. This is not financially sound thinking.

Please keep some things in mind when deciding on the amount to spend on a car. A car is a depreciating asset which means it is a guaranteed money pit. My question to you: "Would you rather drive a car that makes you *look* rich but *keeps* you poor, or drive a car that might *not* make others believe that you are rich, but which will still allow you to actually *become* wealthy?" If you think I am trying to be humorous here, think again. Forget all the kidding around. No fancy vehicle is worth jeopardizing your financial well-being. If you have talked yourself into believing that driving some ultra-ritzy car around town (after you just pulled away from your rented apartment) will somehow get you ahead in life, in ANY way...YOU ARE FOOLING YOURSELF. You do not want to be your own worst enemy. By the time you are ready to purchase your own first car, you should have attained the emotional maturity needed to make an appropriate purchase for your situation. If not, I hope the information in today's lesson will help you make the right financial decisions.

Remember Sam Walton, the billionaire founder of Wal-Mart, who drove around in his old pick-up truck? I believe things turned out OK for him. Truly wealthy people usually have a different attitude about money than the rest of the population. You have to learn the difference between thinking and behaving like someone who ACTUALLY wants to be wealthy compared to the "wanna-be" who just puts on a show, hoping to fool other people into believing that he or she has already "made it." This "wanna-be" affliction is widespread and seems to affect the young-adult crowd more than other age groups. If you know that you are this type of person, or have been this type up to this point, make a commitment to QUIT that behavior today. When you finally achieve real wealth, the personal sense of satisfaction will be incredible!

Still going to buy that new car?

Well then, if you allow for some flexibility in the timing of the purchase, there are periods during the year in which you can negotiate a better deal than during other periods. One of the optimal buying periods occurs during the major holiday season. With everyone out shopping for presents, the car lots are empty of customers. Salespeople are starving for a sale so that they, too, can purchase their holiday gifts. You can cut a very skinny deal at this time of year. Also, July through October is the period when dealers are able to cut their prices due to factory incentive rebates provided by the car manufacturers. The price cuts can range from $1,000 to $5,000. Have you ever wondered why dealers' advertisements sometimes say, "We will sell you a car at under factory invoice?" This is because their profits come from the factory subsidies. Oftentimes, you can purchase a new car for thousands of dollars below invoice if you catch the dealers at the right time of year. You can find out exactly how much a dealer paid for a car by accessing one of several outstanding Web sites. These Web sites include www.invoicedealers. com, www.edmunds.com, www.nadaguides.com, and www.cars.com.

The information on these sites will give you good reference points to use during your negotiations. Understand that the dealer needs to make a profit to stay in business, but you want him to make the lion's share of his profit off the *other* guy—the person who did not read my book!

To get the lowest price possible, there is no substitute for shopping around. In the days of yore (whenever that was), you had to kill an entire weekend driving from dealer to dealer.

Today, you can do your preliminary shopping online through sites such as www.autoweb.com, www.carsdirect.com, www.cars.com, www. edmunds.com, and, of course, www.ebay.com. If you are interested in purchasing a Ford product, visit www.forddirect.com. After you have obtained information on the lowest price available for the vehicle of your choice, make a call to your local dealer and see if they will meet or beat the deal for the opportunity to service the vehicle while you own it. The dealer gets the benefit of servicing your car, and you have the convenience of purchasing your vehicle through a local dealer.

The days of sitting under a heat lamp in the general manager's office while the two of you haggle over an already overpriced vehicle are over!

There is another angle to buying a new car of which you need to be aware. The dealer can give you a very attractive price on a vehicle but still take advantage of you through other tricky offers. If you are not wise and very careful, this is how they will get you: look at the following add-ons that can boost the price of your car by hundreds, maybe even thousands of dollars.

- *Dealer Prep Fee.* This is a charge for getting the car ready for the purchaser. This fee is ridiculous. This is pure profit for a dealer.
- *Extended Warranties.* These are insurance policies that cover the owner in the event of expensive car repair bills. It sounds good in theory but is statistically disadvantageous to the vehicle owner.

For every dollar that is collected by these warranty companies, only a fraction gets paid out for actual repairs. That is precisely why dealers try to shove these warranties down your throat. I have even heard customers say that a salesman told them that they could not get financing without buying a warranty. *That is a complete lie.*

- *Rust-Proofing Treatment.* Most vehicles come directly from the factory with some kind of rust protection. There is no reason to pay a dealer extra money for this feature.
- *Interest Rate Bump.* Dealers will try to finance most customers
- through the dealer's own group of lenders. Why? Because the dealers can bump the interest rate on the loan. The dealer will acquire the funds at one rate, say 6%, and then write a loan for you at another rate, like 9%. Solution to this problem: find your own financing. (We will discuss how to shop for car financing in the next section.)
- *Credit Life & Disability.* When your car salesperson tries to don the hat of an insurance agent, you know trouble is coming. Credit life and disability are both overpriced insurance policies, and neither makes any sense. Credit life pays off your car loan in the event of your death. Why would a dead person need a free-andclear car anyway? The disability coverage makes more sense, but it is much less expensive if purchased directly through an insurance company.
- *Trade-In Value.* Dealers can give you a whale of a deal on a car if they short you a few thousand dollars on the vehicle you intend to trade in. The advantage of trading in your old car instead of selling it on your own (besides the convenience factor) is that you will only pay sales tax on the difference between the value of your trade and the cost of the new car. Regardless, you should have a good idea of what your car is worth before you visit the
- dealer. The easiest way to find the trade-in value of your car is to visit the Kelly Blue Book site at www.kbb.com. Fill in the relevant information about your car, and you will get the dollar figure for your car's trade-in value. This service is free and is a must-do task if you are going to trade in your vehicle.

Financing Your New Vehicle

Car financing is something you do in advance of car shopping. The easiest way to get financing is online. Check out www.capitaloneauto-finance. com, www.eloan.com, www.autocreditfinders.com, and www. lendingtree. com. In a matter of minutes, you will know the loan amount for which you qualify and the best available rate and terms. Absolutely do not hit the car lot before doing your financing homework.

Auto Leasing

Let me go on record right now and tell you that I do not like the idea of leasing vehicles. In my opinion, it is nothing more than a financing ploy that entices consumers to drive vehicles that they could not otherwise afford to own. In the end, a lease guarantees that you will never end up owning a free-and-clear car. (Owning your car, free and clear, should be your goal.) Leasing forces you to obtain a new car every three years or so, which is exactly what the dealer wants. Do not act like the simpleton who goes into a dealership and only asks, "How much money down, and how much per month?" Remember, leasing deals are like financial quicksand designed to suck in the customer and then forever bury him or her in the lease-cycle trap. Dealers know that if they make it easy to *sign and drive*, many consumers will take this path of least resistance. Laziness will always cost you in life, and in this case, laziness could cost you thousands, and thousands, and thousands of dollars.

On a positive note: I read recently that more shoppers are opting to buy their cars rather than lease. That definitely puts a smile on my face!

Purchasing a Used Vehicle

Like I stated before, many points of advice mentioned in the previous, new-car section still apply when buying a pre-owned vehicle. However, there is some additional consideration to be made when buying a used vehicle with regard to the condition of the automobile. What you see on the outside of a vehicle might not represent that car's complete life story. Let me show you how to protect yourself from making a major car-buying blunder.

Before taking the title to any used car or truck, you should ask for a *CARFAX* vehicle history report. This report will tell you whether the vehicle's history is being accurately represented by the seller. The first part of the description displays whether the car has been salvaged, stolen, flooded, rebuilt, or deemed a "lemon" (as per the lemon laws). Next, the report will substantiate or discredit the odometer reading.

The report will also show whether the car has been in any accidents or has been otherwise damaged. Finally, the report displays the history of the car's ownership. It should cause some concern if the report shows that a car was repeatedly sold every year without an iron-clad explanation for these sales. There might be some hidden mechanical problems that only become obvious once you drive the car for a while. To pull a *CARFAX* report, simply go to www.carfax.com and follow the easy instructions.

In addition to getting the *CARFAX* history report, I will give you another bit of good advice. Once you have struck a deal with the seller, you should take sufficient time to test-drive the car and have it checked out by a mechanic. Have the seller agree to escrow the funds with a lawyer while you do your due diligence. Agree to drive the car no more than 50 miles. What about liability? What if you are financing the whole deal? Take the car directly to your mechanic, and have the car or truck thoroughly inspected. Have your mechanic take it for a test-drive. It is always better when you can get a credible mechanic to confirm that the car seems mechanically sound. When the seller claims that a car is in perfect shape, he or she should have no problem allowing you to verify this claim. If you run into resistance, ask the seller to consider the fact that if the roles were reversed he or she would demand that the vehicle be inspected first. If the seller does not want any buyers driving the car for more than a short test-drive, try to make arrangements for the seller to drive the car to your mechanic's lot.

The same Web site sources that I gave to you to attain loans for new cars will also work when financing pre-owned vehicles. You should expect to pay a slightly higher interest rate for a used vehicle loan. Also, you may find it difficult to finance any vehicle that is more than five years old. If a vehicle is more than five years old, you better be able to afford to pay cash for it. You may need to plan for some additional maintenance costs on these older vehicles also, depending on the make and model. Personally, I like cars that have been slightly driven and are not more than two years old. They often represent the best value and typically are covered under the manufacturer's warranty for another couple of years.

I would also suggest that you make one more stop on the Internet at www.intellichoice.com. You will find information on vehicles that have the best retained value, which vehicles have the lowest maintenance costs, which get the best fuel economy, and so forth. You should know exactly what you are buying before you even think of starting the shopping process.

Outside of the investment you make in purchasing your own home, your automobile might be your biggest expenditure. For years, consumers had been at the mercy of slick-talking, well-trained salespeople who could claim just about anything with virtual impunity.

Thankfully for the consumer, car buying has changed. If you follow the techniques in today's lesson, you will give yourself a great advantage.

My Car-Buying Worksheet

For those of you who are in the market for a car, use the following chart to help organize your car-buying research information.

My Top Three Car Choices	Average Price	Insurance Costs	Fuel Costs	Annual Depreciation	Average Maintenance Costs
1					
2					
3					

❖ ❖ ❖

Day 18

Make Social Security Work for You

We are now more than halfway through this 30-day journey to financial success.

It is only fitting that we use today to talk about your plans for retirement or, maybe more accurately, the United States government's plan for your retirement. Long ago the government gave this plan a cozy sounding name: Social Security. It is that little hole in your paycheck every month that gets spirited away to who knows where. We only know it is supposed to have something to do with our retirement.

Today you will learn why any ignorance or ambivalence you have about Social Security is not acceptable beyond this lesson. It is your money! You need to understand exactly where it is going, why it is going there, and what you can do to get the most out of it when it becomes your turn to become a recipient.

The more you know about how the system works, the more able you are to work the system.

Social Security Programs

When most people hear the phrase *social security*, they usually think of a kind of supplement to their company retirement plan that it is managed by the government.

In essence, it is much more than just an income source for your retirement years. It is, in fact, three programs in one.

Retirement

Social Security provides a lifetime monthly income for qualified workers once they reach retirement age (the minimum age is 62 for workers, 60 for widows or widowers). The amount of the monthly income will depend upon the employee's lifetime wages. This is based on a formula that we will discuss later. Depending upon your date of birth, maximum benefits begin at either age 65 or 57.

Survivors

This program provides a lifetime monthly income to the surviving spouse of a deceased worker who had attained retirement age. The amount of the monthly benefit is based on the recipient and survivor's combined incomes while they were working. The Survivors Program also pays a benefit to children under the age of 18 and to the spouse who is caring for that minor. When the children reach the age of 18, the benefit is terminated.

Disability

Social Security also pays a monthly benefit for those who are disabled. This may also include benefits to children under the age of 18 or a spouse.

Qualifications

Contrary to popular belief, not everyone is entitled to receive a social security benefit.

You must first meet certain qualifications to be eligible to receive benefits.

To qualify, an employee must have worked and been paid for at least 40 quarters of social security taxes (which is the equivalent of about 10 years). These quarters do not need to be consecutive. Once the 40-quarter requirement has been met, the employee is considered to be fully vested and is entitled to each of the three plans covered by the Social Security Administration.

To qualify for the Social Security Disability Program, you must meet a very stringent set of requirements. First, the definition of disability means that you are unable to perform any type of work (not just your chosen profession) due to physical or mental impairment. Second, you must have been disabled for more than a year and have paid social security taxes within the recent past.

As previously mentioned, not everyone qualifies.

The Supplemental Security Income

The Supplemental Security Income program is not a part of Social Security. SSI helps aged, blind, or disabled people who have little or no income. In order to be eligible, the worker must be at least 65 years old, blind, or disabled. Although the program is administered through the Social Security Administration, it is not funded by social security taxes. This program is paid for out of the general budget created through income tax dollars.

FICA

Every worker pays a social security tax on their earnings. If you receive W-2 wages, the tax is known as FICA (which also includes Medicare), and it is itemized on your pay stub each pay period. Employers also contribute a matching dollar figure.

Self-employed individuals pay a self-employment tax that covers both the employee's and employer's portion of the total social security tax. The amount you pay will be based upon a percentage of your income with an earnings cap, or ceiling, on your taxable earnings.

For 2012, the social security tax was 10.4% of the first $110,100 earned. Earnings above the $110,00 were not subject to the tax. The money that is collected can be used to pay Social Security benefits only. It cannot be used for general governmental expenses (theoretically).

The Trust Fund

Many people believe that the money withheld from their paychecks is being deposited into the Social Security Trust Fund for their retirement years. Not true. This phantom account only contains IOUs, or the government's promise to pay you when it is your turn to transition from payer to payee. This is the crux of all the controversy that surrounds the Social Security program presently. With the cost of living continually increasing and life expectancies on the rise through better medical care and nutrition, there will be an ever-increasing strain on the working people to shoulder the burgeoning future Social Security burden. As one extrapolates into the future, there appears to be a definite breaking point and a potential meltdown for the system. At some point, the working people of this country will be too few to support the retired population.

To compensate, the existing workers could see upwards of 50% of their salaries being diverted to pay recipients.

Retirement Benefits

Retirement benefits are calculated by considering your 35 years of highest earnings during which you paid into Social Security.

For instance, if you earned $150,000 in 2012, only $110,100 would be considered for purposes of this calculation as you only paid social security tax on the first $110,100 you earned for that year. Previous years' earnings are indexed to inflation and therefore computed in present-value dollars. Once the 35 years have been indexed, they are added together and divided by 420 (35 years × 12 months).

The result is the average indexed monthly earnings (AIME) which is used to calculate your monthly benefit.

If a worker has not been employed for at least 35 years, his or her combined compensation will still be divided by 420 and therefore result in a lower monthly benefit.

Once the AIME has been calculated, the Social Security Administration (SSA) uses a formula that pays lower wage earners a higher percentage of their past income than is paid to the more affluent worker. The income division in this scale is known as *bend points*. The idea is to make certain that every person has enough money when he or she finally retires.

COLA

Monthly benefits are increased each year equal to the inflation rate. This is known as the Cost of Living Adjustment (COLA), and it is designed to preserve the recipient's purchasing power. The amount of the increase is announced each October and goes into effect the following January. It is based on inflation from the third quarter of the previous year to the third quarter of the current year.

Working Recipients

Until a few of years ago, those under the age of 70 who were currently receiving a benefit but decided to go back to work were severely penalized.

Things have changed. The government soon caught on to the fact that it benefits the economy when retired folks go back to work. The government reversed its former decision to penalize the retired persons who chose to regain employment.

However, if full retirement age (62 to 67 years of age) has not been reached, and you are working while receiving a partial benefit, you will still be penalized.

Checking Earnings and Benefits

The Social Security Administration keeps track of your earnings record and work credits through your social security number. The administration mails out this information annually to everyone over the age of 25 who is not currently receiving a Social Security benefit. The estimates will give you an approximation of what you will receive at retirement age, enabling you to engage in some long-term planning. If you are over the age of 40 and have not received a copy of the statement, you can request one by following the instructions on the SSA Web site located at www.ssa.gov.

If you would prefer to make your request in writing, you may fill out a simple form, SSA 7004, called a Request for Social Security Statement, available at your local Social Security office or by calling 800 772-1213.

Checking the Math

Be sure to check the information that the SSA has on record for your case. It is estimated that more then 3% of all statements contain errors. It is your responsibility to catch any of these errors. These miscalculations could cost you money throughout your entire retirement years! Also, when you check your record, make sure that your social security number is correct. You do not want someone else to be credited for your work. Then check to make sure that your earnings numbers are accurate. Remember that your benefit will be based upon the history of your income.

If you discover that a mistake has been made, you need to take prompt and appropriate action. Call the Social Security helpline at 800772-1213. Do not be surprised if the line is busy or if you are placed on hold for a while. Their busiest times are early in the week and early in the morning.

If you prefer face-to-face meetings as I do, call your local Social

Security office and make an appointment to visit with a counselor. Be sure to bring a copy of your statement and evidence supporting your claim. Getting an appointment can be tough, so make sure you are fully prepared with all necessary documentation for your appointment. Also, if the representative agrees with your position, do not be surprised if it takes several months before you see the agreed-upon changes implemented.

Filing for Benefits

All claims for Social Security benefits can be made through your local Social Security office. In addition, claims can be initiated by phone or through the Social Security Web site. Most benefit claims will require at least one visit to your local office. Be prepared to produce your Social Security card, birth certificate, military discharge papers if applicable, and your latest pay stub. Be prepared! There is nothing worse than waiting in long lines only to discover that you are missing the proper documentation needed to proceed.

Finding an Office

Most major cities have at least one Social Security office. You can find addresses and telephone numbers in your phone book under government office, Social Security, or sometimes under Department of Health and Human Services. However, the most comprehensive directory source can be found on the Social Security Web site. You might have to do a little searching on the Web site, but it does provide a *local office search* feature. If you have trouble finding an office, you can call the Administration directly at 800-772-1213 and simply ask for your nearest location's address and phone number.

Timing

Now on to the big question: *when is the right time to kick up your feet and begin enjoying the fruits of your labor?*

There are some very serious issues you must consider before making the decision to retire. You do not want to leave too early and end up with insufficient financial resources.

If you have put in your 40 quarters, you can begin receiving Social

Security retirement benefits beginning at the age of 62. Starting this process early might sound attractive, but there is a catch. If you take early retirement, your benefits will be permanently reduced based on the number of months you will receive checks during the period before you reach full retirement age.

If your scheduled retirement age is 65 and you opt to start at the age of 62, your monthly benefit will be reduced by approximately 20%. Of course, you will collect benefits for a longer period of time. If you live to your anticipated life expectancy, your total income received should balance out in the end.

For those of you who want to keep working, the government rewards you by giving you an extra benefit. Your Social Security benefits will increase on a percentage basis for each month you work past your full retirement age. The following table illustrates the way that the full retirement age is determined.

Year of Birth	Full Retirement Age
1937 or earlier	65
1938	65 and 2 months
1939	65 and 4 months
1940	65 and 6 months

1941	65 and 8 months
1942	65 and 10 months
1943–1954	66
1955	66 and 2 months
1956	66 and 4 months
1957	66 and 6 months
1958	66 and 8 months
1959	66 and 10 months
1960 and beyond	67

How Secure Is Social Security?

The Social Security system faces some (very well-publicized) challenges in the years ahead. The primary threat to the long-term viability of the program rests within the changing demographics of our population base. The good news/bad news scenario is that we are living healthier, longer lives…but that means that we have longer lives that need funding.

In 1935, a 65-year-old retiree was projected to live an additional 12.5 years.

Today, the expectation is that a retiree will collect benefits for another 17.5 years after retiring at age 65. Pretty soon that expected collection period will rise to 20 years. In addition, 80 million baby boomers began retiring in 2012, and in 30 years there will be about double the number of retired Americans as there are today. At the same time, the number of workers paying into the system will not keep pace with the number of new retirees.

Social Security currently takes in more than it pays out with the overage being credited to a trust fund. By 2018, the administration will be forced to begin tapping this fund to make up for deficits. By 2042, the system is projected to go broke, assuming we maintain the status quo.

Future Plans

Several proposals are being bandied about in an attempt to overhaul the system and guarantee benefits for future generations of retirees.

Each option has serious trade-offs. You need to know the elements of each option. The sooner the changes are made, the less the likelihood will be that you will incur negative impacts.

One of the most popular proposals is to keep increasing the age at which a worker can receive a full retirement benefit. Currently, the age is between 65 and 67 years of age, depending upon the year in which you were born. Some have proposed that we move the number up to age 70.

Some suggest that we raise the social security tax from its current 10.4% rate. Critics of this plan will tell you that the tax has already been increased 20 times over the years and that about 80% of Americans pay

Day 18: Make Social Security Work for You more in social security tax than in regular income tax. Increasing taxes always seems to be the easy way out. Let's just punish the working people in order to make up for government shortfalls! It's become the

American way of doing business.

Another faction believes that the system would be vastly improved by allowing younger workers an opportunity to manage their own social security funds so that they could invest those funds in stocks, bonds, and mutual funds, much like the options available under most retirement plans.

I hope to see this option happen in my lifetime!

I have always believed that the person making the money should have the right to determine where that money goes. I have confidence that the average American can do a better job than the government when it comes to allocating his or her income. Of course, critics would argue that if people mismanaged their funds and lost all their money, the government would have to step in and subsidize their retirement income anyway. As you can see, there is no easy answer. Perhaps we should start toward finding a solution by making sure that every American is required to read my book! That would help better prepare them to take responsibility for their own financial well-being.

Conclusion on Social Security

Social Security should only represent one-third of your retirement game plan. The other two portions include your pension plans and personal savings and investments.

Social Security does represent the guaranteed portion and should be tracked and monitored so as to ensure that you receive your due. Remember, this is your hard-earned money that we are talking about! If you think there are errors on your social security statement, let your local SSA office know immediately!

My Social Security Statement

1. Go to www.ssa.com and request a copy of your social security statement.

2. Check to make certain that your Social Security number is correct.

3. Check to make sure that the Social Security Administration has your earnings calculated accurately. If you find errors, contact the **Social Security Hotline at 800-772-1213.**

❖ ❖ ❖

Day 19

Home Ownership Done Right

There is no dream more worthy of being called **"The American Dream"** than that of home ownership.

The level of satisfaction that most feel from owning their own home is hard to replicate. There must be something imbedded in our DNA that makes us want to have our own cave, so to speak.

Having a place to call our own gives us the sense of being grounded. It gives us a place to relax, to raise our families, and to feel comfortable after a long day's work.

Beyond these provisions, home ownership can provide great financial benefits. Owning a home can represent one of the simplest and best investments you may ever make during your lifetime.

Today, on Day 19, we are going to explore the great advantages of owning your own home and then look at some techniques you can use to make the home-buying process fun and profitable.

The Advantages of Ownership

To begin with, an owner can have a fixed monthly payment that, unlike rent, is locked in for 15 to 30 years, depending on your mortgage plan. As time goes on, that payment may actually become comparably cheap due to inflation, pay raises, and the increase in average mortgage costs in your neighborhood. When you are renting the place you call home, your landlord has the right to periodically increase your rent. Your current $1,000 per month rent could become $1,300 per month when the time comes to renew your lease. If you talk to someone who has had the chance to own the same home for around 20 years, you will often hear that person say that he or she could not afford to rent, let alone buy, that same house at the current market prices.

The second advantage to home ownership is the tax benefit. Most homeowners are able to deduct the interest on their mortgage and the amount they pay in property taxes every year. For instance, if the monthly mortgage payment is around $1,500 PITI (principal, interest, taxes, and insurance), the owner will be able to deduct about $1,000 of the payment at tax filing time. Assuming a 25% tax bracket, this will save the owner around $250 a month in federal income taxes, and it may also reduce a state income tax payment. Note: New homeowners, do not forget to adjust the allowance on your W-4 as soon as you can! (Refer to Day 5 for help on this matter.)

As you continue to make the monthly mortgage payments, more of each payment will begin to go toward the principal portion of the mortgage balance. We discussed the advantages of a 15-year mortgage versus a 30-year mortgage on Day 8. If you stay in the property long enough, you may eventually retire the mortgage entirely and will enjoy living without a mortgage payment! If you do decide to sell, the equity you have built up in the house can be used to purchase another home.

For the most part, real estate appreciates over time. How much a particular piece appreciates depends on several factors. The key determining factor is the demand for housing in the market. A *seller's market* means that there are more potential buyers than there are available properties. It is often hard to find a good deal on a house during this time, but it is a great time to sell. During a *buyer's market* there are more houses on the market at good prices, and the homes might actually decline in price if the supply is high and the demand for homes is relatively low.

Low interest rates can also affect the market because people may be able to afford to sign for a larger mortgage without increasing their payments. Thirty-year fixed loans of less than 7.5% normally stimulate an increased demand for housing because people can afford to move into a nicer home while maintaining an affordable payment.

Other factors that can impact the rate of appreciation include the availability of property for development and the homebuilding costs in an area. With a limited supply, the prices will increase more rapidly.

Once you begin to notice that resale properties are selling for equal or greater prices than new construction, the market is typically reaching its high-water mark. This tends to indicate that home prices are becoming over-inflated because of the large demand and low supply of available housing. Over time, the market will eventually balance out, and home prices will become more realistic. You want to try to avoid purchasing a home during an over-inflated market period.

Home ownership has another great benefit. Creditors love customers who own their residence. Not only is it a sign of stability, ownership also represents an excellent source of collateral for the lender. This is the reason we have seen an explosion in the number of home equity lines of credit in recent years. The lender knows that in a worst-case scenario, they can foreclose on the home and sell it to repay your obligation.

Unless you plan on moving more than once every five years, it is a good idea to own your own home. Between the money you will make with the appreciation and the tax benefits, there is a good chance that your home will more than pay for itself.

That's right! When you sell, it is likely that you will recoup all the money you put into the property and then some. Renters (like people who lease vehicles) get a zero return on their investments!

Shopping for a Home

Searching for your new home can be a fun and exciting process, but it can also be stressful. I have outlined eight steps that will help you cut through the stress and help keep you organized and efficient as you search for your new home.

Step 1: Determine Your Price Range

One of the most important questions a buyer asks is, "How much house can I afford?"

Most lenders will tell you that if you have reasonably good credit and a 10% down payment, you will qualify for a payment that falls in the range of 25% to 33% of your net monthly income. This is just a quick rule of thumb, and there will be other factors in the equation (e.g., your age, time on your job, other debt, etc.).

It is a really good idea to get pre-qualified for your loan before you begin looking at properties. That way, you will know, without a doubt, the home prices that fall within your price range. To get pre-qualified, go to the online services I mentioned on Day 8 (www.bankrate.com, www.eloan.com, www.quickenloans.com, www.lendingtree.com, and mycountrywide.com.). In just a few minutes, a loan representative can give you the price range that is right for your budget.

Step 2: Location, Location, Location

Now that you know how much you can afford, it is time to decide where you would like to live. Location is extremely important. Which conveniences are most important to you? Is it important that you live close to your workplace? Shorter commutes save money on gas and avoid wear and tear on your car, not to mention how they may save your sanity. Do you have children? Do you need to be near a particular school? Is it important to have entertainment nearby? Prioritize your preferences before you begin your search.

I once purchased a wonderful home. It was 5,500 square feet of custom craftsmanship built on a 1.3-acre lot in a gated community. I could watch the deer nibbling on my plants when I drove home late at night. Paradise, right?

Wrong. My kids' school was 45 minutes away, so the two boys practically lived in the family vehicle. In the end, I ended up selling the home to move closer to my family's most important activities. When you think location, consider all the aspects of your preferred lifestyle. If possible, narrow your search area to a few square miles.

Once you have determined the appropriate location options that meet your needs and you have begun looking at specific properties, look for features that are unique. (Caution: *unique* in this case, does not mean bizarre or strangely unusual. If you ever plan to resell your home, you may not want to buy the only egg-shaped, UFO-looking house in a neighborhood of otherwise coastal style cottages.) Value-adding factors to consider include the following: waterfront, golf front, water view or other attractive vistas, above-average size, cul-de-sac lot, quiet area, pristine neighborhood, mature trees, community amenities, and low turnover. These criteria should help you narrow the scope even further—hopefully, down to just several blocks.

Step 3: Determine Your Criteria

Finding the home that fits you best is a very personal choice and can depend upon your personal circumstance and family needs. However, when it comes to certain aspects of choosing your new home, there are several criteria that should remain absolute.

When times get tough and the real estate market nears a standstill, it can sometimes be all but impossible to unload a condo. That is why I prefer single-family residences over condos and townhouses. Single-family homes represent a smarter investment in most regions because they tend to sell quicker whenever there is a soft real estate market. I know there are exceptions in some rare U.S. city locations, but typically, it is tough to beat the value of a stand-alone property.

When you buy your new home, you should always think about the investment opportunity, regardless of your other motives. For resale purposes, you should try to avoid homes with fewer than three bedrooms and avoid homes with only one bathroom. Sure, you may be able to sell a two-bedroom, one-bath home to a single person or a young, childless couple, but why take on the risk of restricting your potential resale market? I only want to own property that possesses broad market appeal.

Typically, a better investment can be made in buying the cheapest house in a neighborhood. More specifically, it is best to buy a less expensive home in a nicer neighborhood, rather than the nicest house in a bad neighborhood. The greater appreciation (which occurs in the more desirable neighborhoods) will boost the value of your relatively modest home. This is generally solid advice. The only word of caution I would mention is that you must make sure, before you buy, that the modest house you are considering does not stand out on the street as being the oddball of the entire neighborhood. The basic architecture of the house should complement the rest of the neighborhood. Any simple cosmetic element, like bright pink exterior paint, can be fixed with little trouble and cost.

Fixer-uppers are a great choice IF you can do the bulk of the repair work yourself. Also, if the house needs a lot of work, you should only buy if the home is priced *significantly* under market value. For example, say you can purchase a home in good repair for $200,000 or a fixer-upper for $180,000, but the fixer-upper needs almost $20,000 in remodeling expenses. Make life simple and buy the place that is in move-in condition. If you have never done any home remodeling, just ask someone who has about their experiences. In almost every case the owner will tell you that the remodeling or repairs cost more than they originally estimated and took longer to complete than expected.

On the other hand, there might be a solid opportunity if the same fixer-upper property could be acquired for $150,000 instead of $180,000, and if you could complete most of the work yourself. However, just because a listing claims that the home is a *handyman's special* does not make it a good deal. How "handy" are you, really? Also, make sure to carefully compare the savings you are supposed to be getting with ALL the costs you will incur with remodeling, including the costs tied to your time, energy, and well-being.

Step 4: Go Online

Before the advent of the Internet, shopping for a home was a pretty labor-intensive task. A prospective buyer would have to meet with a real estate agent every weekend or so in order to look at available houses until the right house was found. In those days, I believe that many people used to settle on a home just to avoid getting back into their real estate agent's car. Thank goodness those days are over. While it is still most common that an agent will accompany you on your home tours, more often than not, your search begins online, and the prospective property list is narrowed down to only a few favorite choices.

Starting your search online can help you eliminate some inappropriate options immediately. There are numerous Web sites that will allow you to search through available homes. The listings usually provide photos of the house, a map of the location, the listing price, property details, and the listing realtor's name. Some listings even provide a virtual tour with 360-degree videos. For example, Realtor.com shows nearly every property that is listed throughout the United States. Their sites give visitors an easy way to search for homes by city and state, ZIP code, price range, and property features.

Bargain.com maintains a database of foreclosures, HUDs, VAs, and for-sale-by-owner properties. Additionally, ForeclosureNet.com specializes in properties that are in distress, and Buyowner.com markets homes that are for-sale-by-owner.

Step 5: Spread the Word

Tell everyone you know that you are actively shopping for a home. Explain your basic minimum needs and requirements. Many great real estate deals are transacted simply by word-of-mouth. You know someone who ends up knowing someone who is interested in selling a home located in the neighborhood you desire. This method is particularly effective when shopping during a hot real estate market. Many of the best properties never even hit the listing pages when the market is experiencing a high turnover rate.

Step 6: Pass Out Flyers

Print several copies of a simple letter that reads something similar to the following paragraph:

"I am interested in finding a home in this neighborhood for my family. We noticed your lovely property and wanted to see if you had any interest in selling. I am not a real estate agent trying to solicit listings; rather, I am shopping for myself. If you have any interest in selling, I would love to talk with you. If you have decided not to move at this time but know of someone in the immediate area who is planning to relocate, please pass along my number as I am a serious buyer actively looking for the right home."

Just drive around and drop off a copy of the flyer at any home that looks like a good prospect. You might be surprised at the response.

Step 7: Use Real Estate Agents

The agents are going to hate me for this, but here is the best way to take advantage of their inventory. Find the most active brokerage firms operating in the area in which you would like to buy. This can be done by noting the real estate agent signs in the neighborhood. Find the agent with the most signs on display.

Contact their offices and ask to speak with an agent who specializes in your targeted zone. Let him or her know that you will not be working with anyone exclusively, but you would be happy to come in for a personal interview to show your sincerity. Inform him or her that you will be represented by the first person who finds a home that meets your criteria.

Your objective is to learn about homes before they hit the Multiple Listing Service (MLS). Agents refer to these properties as *pocket listings*. Because you are dealing with the real estate agent who represents the houses in the neighborhood you prefer, you have a better chance of finding a gem if you can deal directly with the seller's agent. There is also a much better chance of having the broker reduce his or her commissions to make a deal come together when he or she represents both the buyer and the seller.

Step 8: Making an Offer

Once you have found the right house, it is time to make an offer.

First, establish a maximum amount that you are willing to pay for that particular property, and begin negotiations somewhere below that figure.

This task may be a little challenging. The valuation of a home is not an exact science. Technically speaking, fair-market value is the amount that a well-informed buyer is willing to pay and a well-informed seller is willing to accept for any property in an open and competitive market, assuming that all parties are acting without any undue compulsion. If you ask 10 appraisal experts to value a particular home, you are likely to receive 10 different responses. The best you can hope for is that all the values fall within a narrow range. Ultimately, you have to ask yourself what the home is worth *to you*.

Your initial offer will contain a number of elements that must be determined in advance. The most important element is the total consideration, or purchase price. Your initial offer should be a balancing act between your goal of getting the lowest possible price and trying to avoid insulting the seller. Once the seller gets sour on a potential purchaser, mending the communication lines can be very difficult. What is an appropriate starting place? At the risk of sounding nebulous, there is no *one-size-fits-all* answer to this question. It really depends on a combination of factors. The first is the motivation level of the seller, and the second would be the market conditions.

If you are dealing with a property that is bank-owned or that is in foreclosure, you can afford to be much more aggressive in seeking a low price than if you are making an offer to homeowners who have their property listed with an agent. And as a general rule, the longer the property has been on the market, the more anxious the seller becomes.

You must also take into consideration current market conditions. Are properties selling like hotcakes, or have houses been sitting on the market for several months, maybe even a year? Under normal conditions, when I believe a property is reasonably priced, I will make an offer that is 10% below the asking price and expect a counterproposal. On a $500,000 property, I might offer $450,000 and expect a counteroffer in the $475,000 range. I will normally offer to split the difference and hope the seller finds the offer reasonable.

That is assuming that I really want the home in question. If I am a bit indifferent about a home and perhaps only interested if I can buy the property well under market value, my first offer might be 20% below the asking price.

When you finally make an offer on a property, you are expected to put up *earnest money* or a *good-faith* deposit. The amount of the deposit is negotiable and can be a powerful show of strength. I agree to a deposit equal to 5% of the purchase price in order to show the seller that I am serious, even if my offer is relatively low. Many times the 5% deposit keeps me in the game.

It is very important that you make your offer contingent upon a home inspection, to be conducted by a licensed contractor within 10 days of a signed agreement.

Essentially, this gives you a free look at the property and an escape clause should you have a change of heart. You should also state that the deposit is to be returned to you should you fail to procure financing under the terms included in the purchase agreement. The seller must deliver the property in good working order and free of any infestation, such as termites. Have all inspections done by licensed professionals!

Also, it is good to keep in mind that, in most states, real estate agreements can only be enforced when they are made in writing. Be cautious about making any oral arrangements as they may not stand up in a court of law. Make sure everything is included in your purchase contract and counteroffers.

Patience Pays

In order for you to get good value for your real estate dollars, you need to have patience and make sure to keep your emotions in check. You are not buying a trinket or some minor appliance. When shopping for a home, it may take several months to find the right house in the very best neighborhood possible, and then it may take a number of days to conduct the negotiations.

Never give the seller an indication that you are overly eager to buy. Always be willing to walk away if you cannot make a purchase under the price and terms you need or desire. Any deal should make good economic sense.

If a deals falls through, do not get caught up in feeling disappointment. It may not seem like it at the time, but trust me—there will be another great house out there for you to buy. Do not let your emotions get in the way of your better judgment. It does not matter how much you think you may be in love with a particular property. If you let yourself get into a dire financial situation over any property, it will cease being your dream home and feel more like your financial graveyard. Never allow yourself to get in over your head.

Now, go find your American dream home!

Buying your first home can be one of your most memorable experiences of your entire life. It can provide a sense of pride and of great accomplishment on so many levels. That is why it is extremely important that you give the entire process the dedication and commitment it needs.

By following the guidelines provided on Day 19, you can ensure that you will find the house of your dreams *and* make a great financial investment.

If you are in the market for a home now, use the lessons in this book to help make your "American dream" come true. Follow the steps, research the provided Web sites, decide on the neighborhood that is right for you, and begin doing your home search online, on foot, or with an agent who specializes in your favorite area. Follow my guidelines, and you will be reading my next book in the comfort of your new home!

My Dream Home Worksheet

1. Determine price range.
2. Choose preferred neighborhood.
3. Determine source and amount of down payment.
4. Estimate monthly payments (PITI).
5. List preferences: number of bedrooms, number of bathrooms, approximate square footage, access to property, style, and so forth.
6. Pick an approximate move-in date.

Remember: The Internet is a great source to use when shopping for properties!

Day 20

Acquiring Investment Properties

Now that you have learned how to find and purchase a house for yourself, you can apply many portions of that lesson toward buying a property for investment purposes.

The process of purchasing an investment property is very similar to the home-buying process that we discussed on Day 19.

In this case, however, there is one significant difference. When searching for investment properties, we look for real estate that has the potential to yield the most profit. All of the typical attachments or feel-good emotions that might be associated with personal home ownership must be replaced with a businessperson's perspective and motives.

Think: PROFIT.

Types of Investment Real Estate

There are several different types of real estate which can prove to be strong investment properties.

Which are best for your investment dollars?

To answer this question, let's take a look at each class of property and discuss some of the pros and cons associated with their ownership.

Single-Family Residential

Single-family homes, residential condominiums, and townhouses are by far the most common choice for novice or small-venture real estate investors. Most people find these property types easy to understand and manage. On the plus side, single-family residences offer the greatest variety of inventory and are generally the simplest to sell. The biggest downside is that single-family residences typically produce the least amount of income, relative to their price.

A $300,000 home may bring in $2,000 a month as a rental whereas a $300,000, multi-family fourplex might generate $4,000 per month.

People who buy single-family residences as an investment are generally more interested in the annual appreciation than the monthly income potential. It is a more speculative approach to investment real estate and, therefore, more reliant upon market conditions. Only purchase residential investment property when the market is soft.

Multi-Family Residences

Duplexes, triplexes, fourplexes, and large apartment buildings can present outstanding long-term investment propositions. Over time, increases in rental income tend to match the overall rate of inflation. In areas where housing is scarce, rental increases can escalate even faster. The basic premise of owning multiple-unit complexes is to fix a mortgage payment and increase rent annually, thereby producing escalating cash flow. Five to ten years down the road, the owner enjoys a strong positive cash flow that can be used to supplement current income or ultimately provide an inflation-indexed source of revenue for retirement.

Commercial and Industrial Real Estate

Commercial real estate includes shopping centers, strip malls, office buildings, and warehouses. These properties will produce the highest revenue per cost and will provide the owner with the most creditworthy tenants.

If you are wondering why most investors forego this segment of the real estate market, there are three potential roadblocks that may block many investors' entrance.

Reason 1: The most obvious potential roadblock is the amount of capital needed for acquisition. Due to the relatively high price of commercial properties (which can reach into the millions of dollars), the requisite down payment could represent an enormous capital contribution.

Reason 2: The process of finding a tenant may become complicated and time-consuming. It may take months and sometimes even years to find a suitable occupant because commercial property tends to be a much more specialized marketplace.

Reason 3: The required paperwork may dissuade the average investor from pursuing this sector of real estate. Completing these documents usually requires the help of a real estate attorney; therefore, the buyer must consider the additional cost of attorney's fees for document review and drafting.

However, if you are prepared to tackle these three issues, there are fortunes to be made in this sector of the real estate market.

Raw Land

Many people are attracted to the idea of owning vast parcels of land. Maybe this desire can be traced back to the *old days* when a person's wealth was judged by the amount of acreage owned.

In today's market, purchasing raw land constitutes my *least* favorite investment choice among all the real estate opportunities. This is my reasoning: in most cases, raw land does not provide a rental income opportunity to the owner, but the owner is still obligated to cover the annual property taxes. This creates a guaranteed negative cash flow situation. I realize that the raw land may appreciate over time. However, it is just as likely that a property which has already been improved with a building will increase in value over time *while* it also provides the owner with a monthly income stream.

The only time raw land potentially represents the best real estate alternative is when it is purchased for development purposes. If you have the means to turn a 50-acre parcel into 100 building lots, that presents an entirely different investment scenario. Income will be produced through the sale of lots. However, this strategy is more akin to owning a business than to buying and selling real estate. In essence, the lots are really nothing more than inventory to a developer.

Understanding Capitalization Rates

The *cap rate* on an investment property might be the single best method for analyzing the property's value. To calculate the cap rate, you must start by figuring the property's net operating income (NOI).

The NOI is equal to the total rent collected minus all operating expenses such as maintenance, property taxes, management fees, utilities, legal fees, accounting costs, and so forth. It should be noted that the property is assumed to be free and clear; therefore, debt service is not a relevant factor when finding the capitalization rate. When you divide the NOI by the purchase price and multiply by 100, you arrive at the cap rate.

For example, if an apartment building generates $120,000 in gross rental receipts and requires $20,000 per year to maintain and operate, this means that the property has a net operating income (NOI) of $100,000.

If the seller of this apartment building demanded a sales price of $1,000,000, the cap rate would be as follows: $100,000 / $1,000,000 × 100 = 10. The cap rate would be stated as 10, meaning that if you bought the property for cash, you would receive an income return of 10% a year on your investment. This is the most common and effective method for evaluating income-producing real estate.

Finding Potential Deals

Anyone can buy a piece of property at fair market value. It takes specialized knowledge to be able to find a deal that is more than 10% below the current appraisal. The trick to achieving this is to find a property owner who is either tired of owning or who simply can no longer afford the property—in other words, a motivated seller.

Here are several strategies to use when searching for a potential investment property.

Foreclosures

There are hundreds of foreclosures in almost every community across the country. It is unfortunate that someone has lost a home or building, but that part is beyond your control. Once a property has gone into foreclosure, it will be auctioned off to the highest bidder. You can find a list of such properties to be auctioned at your county court house or records office. You can also go to Web sites such as www.foreclosurefreesearch.com, and www.realtytrac.com to obtain a list of foreclosures from anywhere around the country.

Bank-Owned Property

Many times banks will repossess a piece of real estate that has been foreclosed upon if they do not receive a viable offer at the auction. Some

Day 20: Acquiring Investment Properties lenders have a resale division, but many small banks cannot afford to set up a separate department solely devoted to real estate resale. Instead, these banks deal directly with real estate brokers or the general public. Depending upon the circumstances, there may be some potential bargains available. Most banks now list available foreclosure properties on the bank Web site. Simply call the lender and ask how you can get access to these properties.

Tax Liens

The county recorder's office maintains a list of people who are delinquent on their property taxes. The fact that the property taxes are unpaid means that it is likely that the owner is experiencing financial problems. This is one source through which a motivated seller may be found and contacted.

Distressed Properties

Whenever a home is in need of significant and obvious maintenance, it could be another sign that the owner or owners have run into financial problems. Contact the property owner and find out if there is any interest in selling. It is important to remember that you should never tell the owner that you contacted them because of the condition of the home (they could become insulted). Just indicate that you are looking for property in the neighborhood, and you want to see if the owner is interested in discussing a potential sale.

For-Sale-By-Owner Property

Check your local paper once a week for ads that have been posted by property owners who are interested in selling their own real estate. In particular, watch for headings such as *Distressed Owner, Foreclosure,*

Bank-Owned, Handyman Special, or Needs Work. All of these indicate that you might find a highly motivated seller.

Running Advertisements

You can advertise in the newspaper, put up signs, or just use bulletin boards in your local grocery stores. Your ad should state that you are willing to buy property in any condition and that you can close the transaction quickly. This should attract some motivated sellers who need to move quickly and who do not have the time or money to fix up their property.

Direct Mail

Many investors have learned to use a technique that has been employed by real estate agents for years. Solicitations are sent out to a mailing list for a given geographical area. Your solicitation should state that you are actively looking for property in this area and that you would like to be contacted before the owners seek to use a broker to market their homes.

Commuting

You need to learn to develop an eye for opportunity. While you are on your routine driving or cycling routes, keep watch for vacant or run-down properties. You will be surprised at the prospects that you can find by just being observant. Once you have found a property of interest, either pay the owners a personal visit, or send a letter expressing your interest. If the property is vacant, you can locate the mailing address of the owner at the county tax assessor's physical office or on that tax assessor's Web site. Most Web sites are easy to navigate, and phone numbers are usually provided for additional assistance.

Realtors

Frankly, I do not put a lot of faith in real estate agents coming up with bargain properties. Common sense tells us that if the deal was really great, the real estate agents would likely take it for themselves or pass it off to a close friend or relative. I only use real estate agents in a soft market where sellers are routinely taking discounts due to their difficulty in getting their property sold. The agents will know which sellers are most motivated.

Flipping Properties

The term *flipping properties* typically refers to situations where a property is bought and then resold in a short period of time. It was once true that you could buy a run-down piece of real estate, apply a fresh coat of paint, install carpets, and then sell the property at a healthy profit.

That is not the case anymore.

In November of 2003, HUD issued a Final Rule stating that FHA would no longer insure a property that had not been owned for at least six months by its current owner.

Many conventional lenders have taken the position that six months is not sufficient and have raised their minimum to an ownership period of one year. This rule change was the result of lenders "taking it on the chin" whenever an investor flipped a property after only doing cosmetic repairs to a property that actually had structural inadequacies.

The new owners of the problematic property would then find that they could not afford the necessary structural improvements, and so these owners ended up walking away from their properties, leaving the lender in a bad spot. It has been estimated that nearly one in three loan defaults happen this way. Therefore, unless you can afford to pay cash for your investment properties, do not think that you are going to make a fortune by rapidly flipping properties.

Using Options

Learning how to option a property gives you the ability to control a piece of real estate without purchasing it outright. It represents the ultimate form of leverage.

For example: you give a property owner $3,000 for the *right* to purchase his home a year from now at an agreed-upon price of $200,000.

You will need to find an owner who is not interested in moving right now but would like to know that there is a buyer waiting in the wings when the time comes to relocate. The option money is tax free to the seller when received.

This could be an owner who is in the process of building a new home that is not scheduled to be completed for 12 months or perhaps someone who is thinking of retiring and moving south in about a year. During the option period, the owner is responsible for all the payments and maintenance on the property.

Your profit comes from the difference in the agreed-upon option price and the property's value a year down the road. Therefore, after a year, if the property you optioned for $3,000 for the right to purchase it at $200,000 is now worth $230,000, you have just made a big profit.

That is not even the best part! If the property, for some reason, was damaged or is not worth the agreed-upon price of $200,000, you do not need to exercise your option and take title to the home. You can sell the option itself and let the next buyer become the owner or just let the option expire. Pretty cool, huh? Remember, this strategy is called an *option* for a reason!

1031 Exchanges

If you are interested in selling investment property and would then like to reinvest the proceeds into more real estate investments, you need to learn about the provisions under IRS Section 1031. This rule allows you to liquidate a property held for investment purposes and use the net equity from that liquidation to buy like-kind real estate while deferring the capital gains indefinitely.

This strategy is used by investors looking to move up or to diversify without finding the IRS in their pockets. Keep in mind that the property must be held for investment purposes only. Your personal residence does not qualify.

In order to comply with the IRS Code, you will need to find a qualified intermediary who will take possession of the proceeds from your property, use them for the purchase of the replacement property, and transfer the title to you. Do not let this process dissuade you from taking advantage of this resource. Professionals handle all the paperwork. To find a qualified professional, check out www.allstates1031.com. All

States 1031 has been in the business for 60 years and is run by accountants and attorneys.

The Tax Man likes his pound of flesh, so in order for you to stave him off, you must follow the 1031 guidelines to the letter of the law. Otherwise, your deal will become a taxable event. In your contract to sell and subsequent contract to buy, you must clearly state your intention to engage in a 1031 exchange. A real estate attorney or your intermediary can help with the wording. Timing is also crucial. From the date you close on the sale of your original property, you have 45 days to identify up to three replacement properties. Furthermore, you must close on one or more of these properties within 180 days from your original closing

Day 20: Acquiring Investment Properties date. Knowing the mechanics of the exchange transactions can save you a virtual fortune in capital gains taxes.

Ideal Investment Properties

Real estate investors have developed the acronym IDEAL to describe the benefits of owning investment property. The letters of the acronym stand for the following:

I = income

D = depreciation tax deduction

E = equity buildup with each monthly payment

A = appreciation

L = leverage that is achieved through financing This combination of benefits makes real estate investing difficult to beat. All that is required is a little knowledge and some time for researching opportunities.

One of my friends started out by developing a small commercial site with money provided by a lender. He took all the positive cash flow to pay down the mortgage and eventually owned the property free and clear. He repeated the formula again and again and currently owns one million square feet of retail space throughout Florida. Now he spends his time chasing cattle and enjoys being a real-life cowboy, just the thing he dreamed about when he was a young boy.

Any investor can make some mistakes in the beginning, so it is wise to start small. As your experience and knowledge grow, so too will your financial rewards. Can you imagine yourself owning 10 rental houses, free and clear, or a 20-unit apartment building? Now that is true financial independence! You can do this.

My Investment Property Worksheet

1. Name the type of investment properties you would like to acquire:

   _____

   _____

2. Determine how many you would like to own in 10 years:

   _____

   _____

3. How much cash flow would you like to generate on a monthly basis?

   _____

   _____

4. 4. Identify the best sources of prospective deals for you:

   _____

   _____

5. 5. Have a conversation with the most successful real estate investor you know, and pick his/her brain for tips and ideas. Ask him/her how he/she got started in real estate investing!

❖ ❖ ❖

Day 21

Investment Traps

As you begin to build your savings and your net worth climbs, you may become tempted to invest in some opportunities that promise to grow your assets practically overnight.

Today, on Day 21, we will go over some of the more prevalent investment *black holes* that all investors should avoid.

I have encountered many of these along my personal path of investing and wealth building and have learned to discern between the investments that are treasures and the investments that are trash.

Investors, beware: everyone has an agenda.

You have heard the old warning, "There are no free lunches out there."

That fact has not changed. Therefore, you should never accept any sales pitch or financial advice at face value without taking the time to do some research for yourself. It pays to be cautious when dealing with investment capital (i.e., your hard-earned money).

High Return, Low Risk

Let's use some common sense here.

High return, low risk?

If these kinds of investments actually existed, we would all become millionaires or billionaires with little effort. Do not let exaggerated promised returns cloud your judgment. A supposed *can't-lose* deal is most likely a financial disaster waiting to happen. When a promoter claims that investors can make 20% or more with very little risk, I ask myself, "Then why doesn't General Motors' pension fund put their money here?"

There is always a reason that no sensible investor is involved in this offer. Unfortunately for many investors, those reasons are usually revealed through lost dollars.

Lack of Diversification

Investing 101 teaches us that we should never put all our eggs in one basket. This means that diversification is one of the keys to smart investing.

I have seen people take their entire nest egg and bet it all on one investment vehicle or place their entire savings with one investment advisor. You might as well put all your money on 17-black in a roulette game, because there is no telling when your investment vehicle is going to crash.

You should never, ever place more than 10% of your investment capital in any one investment product that is not government guaranteed. Furthermore, never place more than 50% in any one investment class (e.g., stocks, real estate, and bonds).

You should also get investment advice from at least three different and unrelated sources. How do you know which one is more qualified?

Getting your investment advice from three unrelated sources creates your own system of checks and balances. You need to compare each advisor's performance over a period of several years in order to get a fair assessment on which one is best suited to handle your investment affairs.

After a couple of years, you can slowly apportion a greater percentage of your financial assets to the person who has demonstrated the highest level of competency. The last thing you want to do is discover that you trusted the wrong advisor after you lose a majority of your savings!

Now let's look at a few of your investment options along with my assessment of their viability for success.

Limited Partnerships

Limited partnerships are a type of business structure or organization. At first glance, there may seem to be nothing dubious about them.

However, when you investigate a little further, you can begin to see the potential disadvantages of this type of financial entity. In most limited partnership arrangements, the general partner has complete control. He takes a salary, receives up-front incentives, and shares in the back-end profits. In contrast, the limited partners put up all the money and have virtually no vote in the day-to-day operations of the partnership. They are considered passive investors. The limited partners' functions are to fund the project, keep their mouths closed, and hope that the general partner has the talent (and integrity) to create a profitable venture.

The limited partners are presumably protected by the fact that they can vote the general partner out of office; however, in the real business world, this provision usually proves to be of little consolation. Even when the general partner is voted out, the remaining partners would then need to find a new general partner who would be willing to take over a failing business and turn it around.

I give limited partnership investments two big thumbs down!

Private Placement Offerings

Private placements are partnership structures that have many of the inherent disadvantages previously noted with the limited partnerships; however, private placement offerings come with one additional pitfall—they do not need to be registered.

This means that, in addition to the relatively loose structure of this type of arrangement, it also lacks a regulator's scrutiny. There are hundreds of horror stories out there about these kinds of offerings.

Even though shares in a private offering are considered a security, and solicitors are required to hold a securities license to market these investments, I have seen many offered by unlicensed individuals. This is a major violation of the securities law; however, many times the behavior goes undetected because the operation is too small to attract any of the official attention. On many occasions, the general partner is personally raising the needed capital from friends, relatives, and through personal referrals. These kinds of investment situations do not usually end happily for the investors.

Penny Stocks

A penny stock is usually considered to be any stock that trades for under $5 per share. However, my main focus here is on the stocks that trade for less than a dollar—the true penny stocks. Stocks that trade for less than a dollar rarely trade for more than a dollar per share anytime in the future.

I know what you are thinking. The price of a cheap stock cannot fall much lower, and you could afford to buy several thousand shares of a 25-cent stock! If that is what you are thinking, you are only seeing a fraction of the whole picture.

On a percentage basis, you stand to risk *more* by purchasing a penny stock than you would if you purchased a blue-chip security.

For example, there are many more 50-cent stocks that will drop to 25 cents than there are 50-dollar stocks that will plummet to 25 dollars. Also consider that in the vast majority of cases, once a stock drops below a dollar, it is most likely that it will never again trade above that level.

With penny stocks, you should only invest money that you are willing and able to lose. In my opinion, it is the equivalent of playing the lottery. And if you think playing the lottery is a good investment of your money, then you have not checked out the odds of winning a lottery payoff.

Phone Solicitations

What are the chances that a total stranger will call you out of the blue and really have the "opportunity of a lifetime" for you? Come on!

If the deal is such a good one, why are *they* calling *you*? If the deal was so great, they would call their family and close friends. Sometimes a little common sense can keep you from making a major financial blunder. Normally, telemarketing brokers or agents are trying to peddle highly speculative investments, and yes, sometimes those callers are part of unscrupulous or illegal scams. My advice: avoid them like the plague. Thank goodness for caller ID.

Currency Market

The currency market is the blackjack of the financial markets. Trading the currency market has seen a big gain in popularity in the last few years. Sure, it may seem easy to bet whether the value of the dollar will rise or fall against another currency like the yen, the pound, the euro, or some other foreign currency. However, there are some problems with this betting scenario.

First, the markets move extremely fast. So, unless you can sit and watch them all day long, currency markets are not for you. Most people have, you know, little things like their LIVES and CAREERS to think about, which kind of get in the way of watching the rise and fall of the dollar all day long.

Second, trading currencies is a zero-sum game. This means that, unlike trading in the stock market or investing in real estate, in the currency market, if one person wins, some other person totally loses. To continue my blackjack metaphor, the middleman or dealer (i.e., the broker) also takes his cut of the profits as well. So you have the winner, the loser, *and* the house. See why this can be compared to the game blackjack?

In the currency market, it is almost impossible to win in the long run. With those kinds of odds (and plenty of other investment opportunities), I would stay away from this type of investing.

Insurance Products

You should always avoid mixing investing and insurance. These two elements do not make for a good combination, and chances are you will end up with a lackluster return. The incompatibility is due to the compensation structure of the insurance industry.

Agents get spoiled by selling life insurance products that are top-heavy with commissions. It stands to reason, then, that if an insurance company wants to get its representatives to branch out and offer other products, the other products must have adequate commissions embedded in the offering also.

A good example of a great concept ruined by internal costs would be annuities. Annuities give the investor the opportunity to defer the earnings within the investment contract until they withdraw their profits.

Typically, the investor may choose from a variety of mutual funds or accept a guaranteed rate of interest. However, in reading the fine print, the investor may discover that there are prohibitive surrender charges if the money is needed sooner than 10 years from the date of the investment.

The management fees are exorbitant, and if a policy holder is promised a certain payout upon his or her death, there is a good chance that the life insurance portion of the annuity is overpriced. The unwitting investor only hears the benefits and does not understand the drawbacks (which are carefully buried in the policy). If you want tax-deferred accumulation using mutual funds, stick with one of the many retirement plans offered by discount brokerage houses.

Oil and Gas Income Programs

Oil and gas opportunities are usually made via a limited partnership structure, and many times they come with certain tax advantages in addition to promised cash flow. That is because the IRS provides a depletion allowance that is similar to the depreciation deduction provided to real estate investors. This depletion allowance may be used to shelter some of the revenue that is paid to the partners.

Before you throw your money into an investment opportunity like this, there are three things you need to keep in mind.

First, the money will pass through many hands and basically be skimmed before there is a net number to be distributed to the partners. Because most investors will not take the time to inspect the detailed income and expense statements, they never even know how their distribution was calculated.

Second, you are dealing with a commodity whose price can vary either up or down, so the income is difficult to project. As long as energy prices rise, you are in good shape. When energy prices drop or the associated costs to extract the resource rise, investors will see their income decline.

Finally, energy is a depleting resource. At some point, the well runs dry and so does your investment. There is no residual value to the operation. Your quarterly checks, therefore, represent both earnings *and* a return of principal. Sometimes, investors forget this fact. They see a

10% cash flow but fail to realize that a part of that number is their original contribution.

Oil and Gas Exploration

Anytime an organization goes looking for oil or gas, there is significant risk involved. *Depending upon the drilling location*, one expedition is a long shot while another is nearly a sure thing. The outcome is very unpredictable.

For the average person, this is not a very prudent investment, especially when you consider that the driller gets paid whether they find the product or not. The investor is taking on all the risk but must still share in any bonanza. Play it smart and steer away from this type of investment.

Investing with Borrowed Money

Using borrowed funds to make investments is what is known as leverage, and leverage can be a double-edged sword.

On the plus side, if you can borrow money secured by one asset to make additional investments that provide returns in excess of the interest rate on your loan, you can build an empire. This is quite common in the real estate business where properties are refinanced and the equity is used to acquire other real estate.

On the other hand, if you take out a home equity line of credit to invest in your buddy's new enterprise and the enterprise proves unsuccessful, you are stuck making payments with little, or maybe no, revenue to offset the debt service. Yikes!

My advice: be incredibly careful when using borrowed dollars to make a non-guaranteed investment. You are placing the collateral for the loan in harm's way.

Faxed or E-mailed Solicitations

Do you really think the next great opportunity is going to magically arrive in your fax machine tray or in your e-mail inbox from a virtual stranger? More often than not, these supposed opportunities are about a bogus stock from a company that is crumbling. In other words: THESE OFFERS ARE SCAMS. Stay away! I suggest immediately filing them away in your trash can.

Pump-and-Dump

The Securities and Exchange Commission (SEC) and the National Association of Securities Dealers (NASD) have done everything in their power to squelch pump-and-dump schemes. Unfortunately, they still persist.

A pump-and-dump scheme occurs when the owner of a publicly held company goes to a stock promoter or brokerage operation and gives them stock in exchange for promoting the value of the company's shares. These promoters make money if the value of the shares moves up. This is accomplished by creating demand for the security. Demand is generated by getting the company's story out to would-be investors. I use the term "story" because that is what the promoter conjures up: a tale. The promoter makes up a hypothetical scenario and distributes it like the gospel through e-mails and cold calls. Listening to their pitch, you may think it silly not to buy a few shares. As investors begin accumulating stock for their accounts, the price of the shares begins to rise, and investors become hopeful of a big payoff. Here is what looms ahead for the naïve shareholder: unbeknownst to the investor, the promoter and managing shareholders are actually selling shares of their personal inventories to the unsuspecting buyer. Once the "promotion" is over, the share price plummets because there was no *real* intrinsic value in the company. The promoters had only manufactured interest by *pumping up* the company through the story they spun. While they were telling you to buy the stock, they were actually selling you *their* holdings. It is nothing more than a shell game where you will be the one to end up with the empty shell.

Before you purchase any stock, check the trading volume and look for uncharacteristic spikes. If a relatively dormant stock suddenly experiences high volume without any solid news that would normally move the price of the stock in such a way, you should be wary. Something is probably amiss.

Long-Distance Real Estate

Many of us have heard the horror stories about the investor who purchases what he believes is prime real estate in some great (but distant) market only to discover (after the papers have been signed) that the purchased land is right next to a garbage dump, or a swamp, or has some other totally undesirable element.

Buying real estate outside of your area of familiarity can be very risky. You cannot make a good real estate investment when you do not know anything about the area. Furthermore, if you were to buy a distant piece of property, what would you do with it after the purchase? Who is going to manage it, and how much will that management cost?

I have seen cases where a property was marketed for just a few thousand dollars per acre, but in fact, it was in the middle of nowhere and only worth about a couple hundred dollars an acre. This was a very popular scheme for Florida properties years ago. It is tough collecting rent from alligators.

Of course, the selling agent had offered the property with very attractive terms in order to make the buying easy and affordable. One selling angle commonly used is that the available property is advertised as being "in the path of progress." Well, if the real story is that the "progress" they are referring to will not be showing up for another 50 years, it probably will not do you much good for your current investing strategy.

Time-shares

Time-shares are one of the most ingenious systems employed to quickly separate people from their money. They just work on so many levels. The big pitch is that you and your family can fix the future costs of your vacations by purchasing a couple of weeks at some swanky resort. So as the costs of hotel rooms rise, your time-share will allow you to lock in a good rate for the rest of your vacationing years. Better yet, the salesperson will show you how you can finance this purchase with as little as 10% down so that you can pay off the rest over the course of several years. Sound good?

Here are the true economics.

A developer builds a group of condominiums that would normally sell for about $200,000 per unit. However, instead of just selling them outright, the developer sells 50 individual weeks of use for each unit for $10,000 apiece. The developer receives a total payout of $500,000 minus selling expenses. In addition, as the time-share purchaser, you will pay the pro-rata portion of the property taxes, insurance, and maintenance expenses. Then, a management fee is tacked on top of everything else. Does this sound like much of a deal?

And…what happens if you later realize that you do not want to spend every vacation in the exact same place every single year? Sometimes you can trade for another location, for a fee, of course. Should you decide to sell your time-share, be prepared to take at least a 50% discount on the price that you originally paid.

My point is, should you feel that you must own a time-share, pick one up off the Internet on a resale basis and save 50%–90%. Never buy directly from the resort.

Lottery Tickets

It is a shame that I even have to mention lottery tickets, but millions of Americans treat the lottery as if it were a real investment. With each paycheck, they will take five dollars or so and buy lottery tickets that they hope will miraculously turn them into instant millionaires. The people who buy lottery tickets are always the folks who can afford it the least. That is why many states continue to consider lotteries to be against the law and contrary to the welfare of its citizens. Please, do not waste your money. Five dollars per week equals $260 per year. Use this money to buy a few shares of a growth stock or to pay down the balance on a credit card.

Smart investing is not about cashing in on the next get-rich-quick scheme. Smart investing is meant to give you a reasonable opportunity to make a reasonable return on a consistent basis.

Avoid these financial traps and scams, and instead stick with the real investment strategies we have discussed in this book. There are no overnight shortcuts to building wealth. Many desperate (or lazy) individuals find themselves grasping at straws in their pursuit of the brass ring. Not you! You are going to work smart and diligently plan your way to wealth.

But for now, take a break. Tomorrow holds another great lesson!

Day 22

Consumer Scams and Rip-offs

It happens every day.

Thousands of unsuspecting consumers fall prey to the devious schemes of unscrupulous salespeople and con artists.

Personally, it is hard for me to accept the fact that there are people out there who will intentionally go out of their way to harm others. Regardless, my job is to deal with what *is*.

I have been fooled, too. Once, many, many years ago, I was taken for $40,000 when I decided to purchase a vehicle online. Weeks later

(after the car failed to materialize), I attempted to track down my money but could not. The remainder of the tale is long and complicated and involves crooks running scams from far-away foreign countries. In the end, I was given no recourse. I learned my lesson the hard way.

That is why it is extremely important to learn how to spot a scam before you give your money away to a criminal.

Today, on Day 22, I am going to show you how to read warning signs and beware of misleading offers so that we can do our best to ensure that you will not get robbed, cheated, or swindled.

Let's Define a Rip-off

Let's make sure that we are on the same page. First, we need to make sure we share the same definition for a bona fide rip-off. Basically, if a purchaser spends money on something because it has been presented as having a certain value, but it is discovered that the item actually is of no value or if nothing is actually received within a reasonable amount of time, the buyer has likely been conned. It does not matter if the product was an illegal scam or if the deal was originally considered to be perfectly legitimate. If the item did not fulfill its claims…it is a rip-off for the purposes of today's lesson.

For example, let's say an insurance product is sold that historically pays benefits equal to only 10% of the premiums collected by the company. In my opinion, its 90% profit margin creates a rip-off for the consumer even though the product has the blessing of the insurance commissioner. For the purposes of this chapter, it is the value (or lack thereof) of an offering, not the law that governs it, which determines whether or not something is a rip-off. The truth is, sadly, much of what I am about to warn you against buying is sold legally.

General Warning Signs

While this is in no way a comprehensive list of warning signs, this list is still a great place to start. Unfortunately, cons keep coming up with more devious ways to take your money. Just remember, when in doubt, always err on the side of caution, especially when your money is involved.

High-Pressure Sales Tactics

Anytime you are made to feel uncomfortable or are put on the defensive by a salesperson, you probably are the target of a high-pressure sales tactic. Think about it. When you walk into a McDonald's restaurant, you usually do not sense that you are being manipulated by the cashier taking your Big Mac order. No sales wrestling match is necessary. The customer has come in willingly, makes a purchase willingly, and is fairly confident that he or she will receive a reasonable value for the money spent. When someone seems a little too desperate to make a sale, there is usually a good reason for the anxious behavior. Desperate salespeople will force the sale even when they know that the product being sold is garbage, or perhaps they are aware that you are probably not an appropriate candidate for the offering. The salesperson may offer you a discounted price, tell you that the supply is limited and that it may run out of stock, or tell you that the offer is only good if you make an immediate decision. No legitimate offer comes off the table because you have stated that you need a day or two to consider the proposal. When that "super-duper deal" suddenly materializes at the eleventh hour, beware! Reputable organizations do not conduct business in this manner.

Unfamiliar Companies

Be wary anytime you consider dealing with an organization whose reputation is unknown to you. Being new on the scene does not always translate into bad news. However, no matter how new a company is, there should be some way for you to do a little research on its inception and current standing. This information should be available through the Internet, the Better Business Bureau (www.bbb.com), or through reliable client references, if nothing else. If you are unable to find any good feedback or solid information concerning a particular business, this could be a sign that the entity is not well-established and that it lacks ongoing support and the ability to fulfill promised warranty work. It could also mean that it is trying to hide something. Before doing business with an unfamiliar entity, take the time to do a little research. Use a search engine like Google to learn company details such as the date it was established and to find any related articles written on the business. You may also find additional comments by searching chat rooms that provide commentary on an enterprise. If you do not like what you find, it is probably best to go another direction.

No Physical Address

When companies are only willing to provide a PO Box or e-mail address as a form of contact information, this should cause you to be cautious. These tactics usually indicate that the company has no established or permanent business site and may "fold their tent" and leave town without notice.

No Phone Number

Companies that are unwilling to take inbound calls are not prepared to give support to the consumers who buy their products. If you purchase from this type of business and then run into problems with their products or services, you may very well be left to fend for yourself.

No References

If a business is totally unwilling to share any customer or client references with you, I would be suspicious. A lack of references usually means that no one is willing to vouch for its credibility. In addition to the availability of a few client recommendations, other business or professional references are highly valued. I usually feel better when the proprietor's banker or accountant verifies that the businessperson and related company are in good financial standing.

Dodgy Better-Business-Bureau (BBB) Reports

As previously mentioned, referencing the BBB is always a good precaution. You can access a copy of a business's Better Business Bureau report for free by visiting www.bbb.org. The BBB provides reports on more than 2 million organizations. If you see an unreasonable number of complaints registered on a business's report, take your business elsewhere. If a business is not a member of the BBB, this should be considered to be a major negative. It is not an automatic guilty verdict, but you have to ask why a business would not want to participate in a service offered to protect consumers. The reason is usually obvious.

Deeply Discounted Price

I have found that most "too good to be true" sales usually are. Nobody gives away quality merchandise or services at a huge loss. Anytime I see a huge markdown, my internal scam alarm goes off. Some discounts make sense, like markdowns on clothing that is going out of season. You can buy those items all day long at a 50% discount. (There is, at least, a 100% profit margin built in to the retail price.) Basically, the clothing store is liquidating at cost to make room for new inventory. On the other hand, some merchants engage in what I call "perpetual sales." Every time you go by their store, they have a 50% off to 70% off sale. *That* is just false advertising. They are marking up the price of their products and then offering what appears like a tantalizing deep discount sale in order to try to lure in gullible customers.

Up-front Fees

Be careful about giving money to anyone before you receive the promised service or merchandise. (Obviously, I am not talking about credit card orders made by Internet or phone with reputable and well-established institutions.)

Elsewhere, you are taking a huge risk. Long ago, I had a house painter tell me that he needed half the cost of a job up front in order to enable him to purchase the needed materials. After he shook my hand and accepted my check, I never saw or heard from the young con artist again. He will end up in jail one day, but that will not get my house painted or return my money!

Free Giveaways

It happens every day. People believe they have somehow won a fabulous prize from a contest that they never even entered. If you find yourself in this position, ask yourself the following question: "Why would someone want to give me something for free?"

Answer: they wouldn't!

Unless you are a guest on *The Oprah Winfrey Show,* or *Extreme Makeover: Home Edition*, the reality is that these other "gift givers" are looking for something in return. They want your personal information so that it can be used or sold to an organization that will try to get you to purchase something else (lost leader) or a scam to make you pay taxes on some supposed prize.

Lack of Information

Be particularly careful when an offer seems to be missing important details. You should get suspicious when the response to your requests for further information brings only a laconic, "Trust me," from a salesperson. At the risk of sounding cynical, when it comes to your money, trust no one. Meaning. it is your responsibility to do some research on every single offer that you encounter. Any legitimate, well-established organization should have background information, documentation, and a performance record that are relatively easy to research. To begin a business, forms must be filed that become a matter of public record.

Therefore, you should be able to determine when an operation was started and be able to discover the identities of the controlling parties. After you have found this basic information, the next step is to go on-line and use a search engine such as Google to review the principals' backgrounds.

Telemarketing Offers

I am particularly wary of anything that is sold over the phone. There is no accountability on the part of the solicitor because there is no personal interaction between the buyer and the seller. When I was a very young man, I applied for a job that, I believed, involved the sale of an investment opportunity in the oil and gas industry. When the interviewer informed me that the only calls I would be making would be to people who lived out of state, I realized that there must be something wrong with the product. Otherwise, the company would be selling its offer to local consumers. This particular company closed less than a year after my interview date (and probably moved its operation to another state in an attempt to stay one step ahead of the law).

Charities

It is a wonderful thing to donate money to others in need. However, as we are covering all types of scams today, you should also be aware that there are people out there who will try to take advantage of your generous nature and your concern for others. Recently, telemarketers posed as police officers asking for donations (that they ended up pocketing). You need to verify the validity of a supposed charitable organization just as you would with any other business entity. I have never heard a good word uttered about a phone room.

Many times, companies will use a knockoff of a legitimate charity to try to collect money. They may use an organization name that sounds very similar to a legitimate foundation in hopes that you will be easily fooled.

Bogus Credit Cards

Telemarketers call consumers who have a high credit balance and offer them a Gold MasterCard with a 0% interest rate—available for an up-front fee of $200. The salespeople tell their "marks" that the high credit balance can be refinanced so that it will lower monthly payments by 80% because of the interest savings. There is no such credit card in existence.

Sweepstakes

People are led to believe that if they purchase magazines, videos, collectibles, or other items, they are sure to win some fabulous and valuable prize. Sweepstakes use language such as, "You may already be a winner." Seniors are twice as likely to fall for such marketing ploys as any other group and, therefore, are usually the main targets. Sadly, they usually have less financial ability to recover from scams than others.

Cash Awards

In this scam, people are told that they have won a large cash prize or settlement. All that is required to collect the winnings is to pay the tax on the prize. Unaware consumers mail funds to perfect strangers in exchange for...nothing but a false promise. Hard to believe anyone would fall for this trick, but it happens on a regular basis.

Lottery Pools

You are offered membership in a club that buys lottery tickets all over the world and splits the proceeds with its members. Memberships can range in price from a few dollars to thousands of dollars. In truth, less than 10% of the money collected goes to purchase lottery tickets. The rest ends up in the pockets of the promoters. What a deal for them! Do not waste your hard-earned money on this kind of garbage.

Betting Software

People are sold software that is purported to help predict the next winning lottery ticket or the outcome of a horse race. No such predictive software exists. If it worked, why would anyone be trying to sell it to you...they should just be using it to make tons of money off the predictions, right? This software is a total rip-off.

Nigerian Scam

This offer claims that it needs to place millions of dollars into your bank account so they can move the money into the United States. Of course, they need a processing fee in order to complete the transaction. And, you guessed it, after they receive your fee money, they never deposit one cent into your account.

Prime Bank Schemes

Promoters claim that there is a secret international market in "prime bank" instruments. You are invited to put money into a trust account that is backed by a guarantee from one of these institutions. You are told that your money can be highly leveraged, and therefore you will receive an inordinate rate of interest. I was approached by one gentleman who promised me 3% per month and that I could have my money back whenever I desired. Thankfully, I was too smart to give them my money. These types of instruments do not exist.

Pyramid Schemes

Pyramid schemes come in many different varieties, but they all have one thing in common: your compensation is related to the number of people you can recruit into the organization.

Many multilevel marketing companies have been put out of business because the government has determined them to be nothing more than pyramid schemes. This is not to say that all MLMs are pyramid schemes. Only those that require you to purchase a bunch of product up front or recruit others in order for you to make *any* money fall under the definition of pyramid scheme.

Ponzi Schemes

This is a type of illegal pyramid scheme named for Charles Ponzi who duped thousands of New England residents into investing in a postage stamp speculation scheme back in the 1920s. Ponzi promised a 40% return in just 90 days, and he actually delivered...for a while.

This is how it works: the promoter takes money from new investors to pay the returns to the more senior investors. Better yet, instead of giving the original investors money, the promoter sends them a written statement that shows how each account is growing at impressive rates. Of course, when people actually begin to ask for their funds, the promoter heads for a faraway island in the Caribbean!

Legal, but...a Loser

The following offerings may be legal, but chances are, they will not give you good value for your money.

Credit Life

Credit life insurance is a policy that pays off a loan in the event of your death. This is often sold in conjunction with car financing.

I have a question for you: why would a dead person need a free-andclear vehicle?

Think about it. Who gets the most benefit from credit life policies?

Answer: the lender.

Here is a better idea: let the lenders take care of themselves. Credit life is an overpriced, decreasing-term life insurance policy sold to those who do not know any better.

Extended Warranties

Have you noticed that whether you are buying something as large as an automobile or as small as a DVD player, the salesperson will attempt to shove an extended warranty down your throat? They do this because they make a fortune when they succeed in selling these warranties to the consumer. The fact is that warranties are nothing more than overpriced insurance. For every dollar collected from shoppers, less than 25 cents gets paid back to the consumer in the way of repairs or replacement items.

Lottery Tickets

As I have mentioned earlier in this book, I think the lottery is a joke. It preys on the lowest-earning demographic in our society by making them think that they are being given a quick, easy shot at the big time. I realize that no one is forced to play, but desperate people are compelled to do desperate things, especially when they are barraged by marketing that targets their emotions. There is a reason why lotteries were once banned almost everywhere. However, the lure of big profits, which are easily plucked from ignorant people, has proven to be too tempting for many states to disregard.

Credit Card Insurance

Boiler rooms (i.e., a room full of telemarketers) all across the country were selling an insurance policy that was supposed to protect the consumer in the event that a credit card was lost or stolen. This insurance scammed people out of $298 for this service. Under federal law, you are only liable for up to $50 in credit card charges if your card is used in an unauthorized manner. Why pay nearly $300 to insure a $50 potential loss? It never makes sense, any way you look at it. Unbelievably, tens of thousands of folks have fallen prey to this unscrupulous offer.

Modeling Schools/Talent Agencies

Some of these agencies post advertisements that claim to be *looking for new talent in your area* and that you should *come by for an audition* or *free evaluation*. At these "agencies," applicants are sold packages of photographs, and usually they are told that they will be represented by the agency as a way of getting into the industry. Of course, most agencies are successful because they play on the customer's ego by convincing him or her that he or she possesses amazing and unequaled star potential. Many of these so-called agencies have never found work for anyone. If you are considering a modeling or talent agency, get great references first.

The bottom line is this: if you truly have the "stuff" that will land you great jobs in the modeling, advertising, or acting industries, your agent or scout will plan to make plenty of money in commissions from all of your future placements. It may be reasonable to expect that, when you are a complete unknown, you may need to have a professional photographer create a composite card, headshot, or short video for you to use to promote yourself. There are professional photographers who specialize in this style of photography. It is highly unlikely that any reputable photographer would be associated with one of the con-job agencies or so-called modeling schools/talent agencies. Again, when seeking the services of any photographer, get references and expect to pay a reasonable professional-rate sitting fee.

Credit Repair

Companies who promise that they can eliminate negative credit information such as bankruptcies, charge-offs, and late payments are blowing smoke. The only way that negative credit will come off your record is for you to prove that the information was inaccurate. It would be impossible for these credit repair companies to disprove something that is fact.

Credit Counseling

The concern here is that many of the so-called credit counseling companies that claim to help consumers who are in serious debt end up not fulfilling those claims. Most of these organizations pose as non-profit educational entities, but many credit counseling firms are nothing more than giant telemarketing operations that use scare tactics to extract money from people who can least afford to pay. This book provides guidance for those facing credit dilemmas. Be sure and implement those safe strategies.

Double Dipping

Unfortunately, this is not a bonus section on delicious recipe ideas.

To conclude the chapter on scams and rip-offs, I want to mention another of the scam artists' angles referred to as double dipping.

Scammers will target the same victim more than once in an effort to increase the spoils taken from these unwitting victims. Thieves figure if a person was naive enough to fall for a scam the first time, why not hit this easy target again. I urge you to be on guard at all times and use the advice contained in today's lesson.

Become an Informed Consumer

All of these scams and rip-offs can be avoided if the consumer is willing to become properly educated. It is my sincere hope that this chapter will help you avoid being victimized by overzealous salespeople or, worse yet, con artists who prey upon the uneducated and misinformed.

Tomorrow we will discuss a much more positive topic—education.

Until then, just take time to consider today's lesson and its warning about the consumer scams that you need to be sure to avoid.

Day 23

Planning for College

Whether you are planning to attend college or you are making plans for your children to attend, this chapter will provide invaluable information for everyone considering secondary education.

A college degree can be a crucial key to a bright future. Need some convincing? Let's look at the facts.

According to the Census Bureau, a 2009 high school graduate earned only slightly more than $34,980. A college graduate earned an average salary of $62,240. Those with a master's degree did even better, earning $79,340.

College can have a positive effect on your financial future, but let's not discount the effects it can have on your personal development also. College is a precursor to joining the real world. It can act as a worthwhile, transitional step—it still provides some of the safety of a relatively sheltered environment, whereas it also provides an opportunity to be away from home, in most circumstances. The new position of independence teaches people how to acquire the skills needed to make their own decisions. You will discover how to think critically, communicate your thoughts articulately, and make better-informed decisions by learning the skill of research.

Now that we have laid out the great things college can do *for* you or your children, we now need to explore the investment that is required to complete a college degree.

Today, the total cost of a college education at a private university can total more than $100,000! Even state-sponsored educations can approach $50,000 for four years when books and housing costs are factored in. The best approach is to begin planning while your children are still young.

Selecting the Right College

To choose the best, most appropriate college, you will need to do your due diligence, researching as many facts and figures as possible.

The choice will come down to whichever colleges and available programs most closely fit your future goals, your lifestyle, personal aptitude, and, ultimately, your financial situation and options. Based on these factors, I will provide some guidelines that can help narrow down the choices to just a few campuses.

1. *Curriculum*. Look for schools that specialize in the course of study you plan to pursue or the programs in which you have a strong interest. If you have not chosen an area of interest, it is best to choose a school with a broad range of available studies.

2. *Size*. Some students feel intimidated and lost when going from a relatively small high school campus to a large university that might have 50,000 students enrolled at one time. You may decide that you are going to use the experience of attending a large university to help you make a major jump in your personal growth. For some, this will provide enormous opportunities to "spread their wings," so to speak. However, the most important part of attending (and paying for) college is to get an education. If you have serious doubts about your ability to cope with, or stay motivated in, a class that may enroll 500 students per semester, you should consider smaller universities. Decide which student body size will be most effective in helping you reach your education goals.

3. *Location*. If you would like to live at home while attending college, you will need to choose the most appropriate local school. If you plan to leave home to live on campus, consider whether you prefer the "big city" or a cozier small-town environment. If you are from a small town and have never lived in a big city, do not assume that you will love it just because "city life" may look cool on television or in the movies. Relocation is a big decision. If at all possible, visit your prospective city choices in the company of your family or close friends. The reality of day-to-day living in a busy, congested big city can be overwhelming to those who have never had to live in that kind of environment.

4. *Cost.* This will be a major factor. For those who lack the financial resources, the available college choices may be seriously reduced. However, scholarships and financial aid, where applicable, may help broaden the possibilities.

5. *Financial Aid.* Some type of financial aid is available at nearly every school. As you might imagine, some study programs are eligible for more aid than others. If you are depending upon financial aid to pay for most of your college education, it is crucial to do research on the specific rules that govern each college, student type, and your desired course of study. We will explore this more in a moment.

6. *Academic Standards.* Find out the average test scores and grade point averages required for admittance into the schools that you find attractive. It is important that you find a school that adheres to your educational standards.

7. *Visit the Campus*. This is really a must. You can get a pretty good feel for the school's atmosphere by paying a personal visit. Walk around and see how students interact with each other. Sit in on a classroom if permitted. Take a tour. Eat the food. Check out housing, and so forth. However, be careful to time your visit appropriately. For example, if you attend a large university during one of its holiday breaks or perhaps during the summer, you may not get the "real picture" with regard to normal campus activity.

8. *Talk to Students and Alumni*. There is no better available testimony than that of students who are currently attending classes or of alumni who have graduated from your school(s) of choice. It is even better to talk to people who have attended a specific program that you would like to pursue. They can give you the real scoop on the challenges or benefits for a particular school.

9. *Sports and Activities.* A rich social life is usually an important part of the college experience. Find out ahead of time whether the school you are considering has the type of clubs or other organizations that you will want to take part in.

10. ***Religious Affiliation.*** If religious involvement is a priority for you, find a school that offers the types of religious programs, places of worship, or like-mindedness amongst students that coincide with your belief system.

Financial Aid

About two-thirds of all student financial aid comes from U.S. Department of Education grants, work-study programs, and loan programs. These programs are based on financial needs—your grades or class ranking are not considered. Grants are the most attractive as they never need to be repaid. Work-study allows you to earn money for your education. Student loans allow you to borrow money for school tuition and expenses. Loans, of course, must be repaid. In addition to federal aid, the states each have programs of their own. Nationally, there are more than 1.5 million scholarships available representing billions of dollars. To begin your search, check out www.fastweb.com.

Applying for Aid

To apply for financial aid, you need to complete just one form: the Free Application for Federal Student Aid (FAFSA). Many states use this same form for processing and making their awards. You can make an application electronically by going to www.studentaid.ed.gov. If you do not have Internet access at home, it is likely that your local public library or your current school will allow you to use one of their online computers to complete your electronic application. If none of these options are available, you can receive an application by submitting a written request to:

Federal Student Aid Information Center

P.O. Box 84 Washington, D.C. 20044 800-433-3243

Pell Grants

A federal Pell grant, unlike a loan, does not have to be repaid. Pell grants are usually awarded to undergraduate students who have not earned a degree yet. The maximum Pell grant for 2012–2013 was $5,550. The amount a student will receive will be based on financial need, cost to attend school, status as a full-time or part-time student, and whether the student plans to attend school for a full academic year or less. A student can only receive one Pell grant per award year. Schools can apply Pell grants directly to a student's expenses or pay the student directly. The amount of the grant will be provided to the student in writing and will explain how the student is to be paid.

Campus-Based Aid Programs

The Federal Supplemental Educational Opportunity Grant (FSEOG), the Federal Work-Study, and Federal Perkins Loan programs are called campus-based programs because they are administered directly by the financial aid office at each participating school. The amount a student receives will be based on financial needs, on the amount of other aid received, and on the availability of funds at the college or school. Funds are awarded on a first-come, first-served basis. Once the funding is gone, no more awards can be made during that year.

FSEOGs

These grants are for undergraduates with exceptional financial needs. A student can receive $100 to $4000 per year. To qualify, the student must not have already earned a degree.

Federal Work-Study

This program provides part-time jobs to undergraduates and graduate students with financial needs, allowing them to earn money to cover a portion of their educational expenses. The program encourages community service work and work related to the student's course of study. It can be a good way to get an education and work experience at the same time. The student is paid by the hour and must receive at least the federal minimum wage.

Federal Perkins Loan

This is a low-interest-rate loan (5%) that is available to undergraduate and graduate students with financial needs. The school is the lender, and the loans are made with government funds. The school must be repaid for this loan. A student can borrow up to $5,500 each year based upon personal need, as long as he or she is attending school at least part-time. The student is allowed a grace period of nine months after graduation before he or she must begin repayment. The student may have as many as ten years to fully repay the loan.

Stafford Loans

Stafford loans are made either through the Federal Family Education Loan (FFEL) Program or the William D. Ford Federal Direct Loan Program. Some schools participate in both programs. Funds for the FFEL will come from a bank, credit union, or other lender that participates in the program. Repayment begins six months after graduation, and there is a choice of payment options.

Plus Loans (Parent Loans)

PLUS loans to meet students' education costs are available through the FFEL and Direct Loan programs. Parents who have an acceptable credit history can borrow a PLUS loan to pay the education expenses of a child who is a dependent student enrolled at least part-time in an eligible program at an eligible school. You can receive an application through the school's financial aid department. If your credit is substandard, the student can opt to have a relative with a solid credit standing endorse the loan document. The yearly limit on a PLUS loan is equal to the cost of attending school, minus any other financial aid that has been made available. For the 2012–2013 school year, the interest rate was fixed at 7.9%. The first payment is due 60 days after the loan is fully dispersed, so parents will begin making payments while the student is still in school.

The 529 Plan

The 529 Plan is an exciting new college savings plan (established in 2002). Its official title is Qualified State Tuition Program, and it is found in Section 529 of the Internal Revenue Code, hence the name 529 Plan. It was designed to provide a strategy to save for the higher education expenses of a child. Programs are administered by a state agency or an organization designated by the state, such as a for-profit investment company. Plans differ from state to state. Some states have a plan with no specific residency requirement that is available to prospective students from any state. Other state plans are available only to residents. Most states have a 529 Plan in place or are in the process of designing such a plan.

In order to qualify, all contributions must be made in cash or a cash equivalent, and there must be a separate account made for each beneficiary. There is a penalty if funds are not used for educational purposes. Neither the contributor nor the beneficiary can direct the investment of the funds, and the investment cannot be used as security for a loan.

Here are the mechanics of this powerful program. The contributor establishes an account for the beneficiary for the purposes of paying expected college expenses. To establish the account, the contributor may use the 529 Plan in his or her state of residence if that state has a plan or another state if it does not have a residency requirement. The funds will typically be managed by one of the major mutual fund companies. The contributor can choose one of the specific funds offered by the company. Maximum contributions for one beneficiary can total $130,000. Earnings are exempt from state and federal income tax until they are withdrawn.

Tax Credits

Some parents will qualify for a Hope tax credit or Lifetime tax credit. IRS Publication 970, Tax Benefits for Higher Education, explains these credits and other tax benefits. Each borrower can also take a tax deduction for student loan interest. The maximum deduction is $2,500 per year. For more information, you can go to the IRS Web site at www.irs.gov, or call toll free: 800-829-1040.

Educational IRAs (Coverdell ESA)

You are now able to set up IRAs for the purpose of paying college expenses. Contributions are allowed until your child reaches the age of 18 and may not exceed $2,000 per year per child. The $2,000 limit is phased out for joint tax filers with an income above $190,000 and for single filers who make more than $95,000. There is no tax deduction when the account is funded, but all withdrawals are made tax-free, including earnings. The funds must be used for school expenses.

Prepaid Tuition Plans

Certain states offer various types of prepaid tuition plans, typically for students attending a state college. Residents of participating states can buy a contract or bonds at a fixed price based on the present-day cost of tuition. The state, in turn, invests the money to earn the difference between the amount you are paying and the projected cost of tuition at the time your child reaches college age. These programs are attractive to very conservative parents who do not want to explore their own investment strategies. Before signing up, be sure to determine the disposition of your funds should your child elect to attend a private school or enroll out of state. There should be a reimbursement available.

Scholarships

I have found a free scholarship search engine which connects students and parents with financial aid and scholarships. Take a look at www.fafsa.ed.gov and give its service a try. Another trusted Web site is www.fastweb.com. Recently, Fastweb claimed that one out of three college-bound students used its service. Fastweb's database matches student profiles with more than 1,500,000 scholarship awards to find the most relevant and obtainable opportunities. There is more than $3.4 billion in scholarship awards available. These services help you create application letters, view a personalized deadline calendar, and locate applicable scholarships using key words.

Free Resources of College Financing

There are a number of expensive services in the market that promise students financial aid in exchange for a substantial fee. Before you hire any of these for-profit organizations, take advantage of the plethora of free sources and services available to everyone. The list of possible resources includes:

- Financial aid office at a college or career school
- High school counselors
- U.S. Department of Education
- Other federal agencies, including the military
- State education agencies
- Reference section at schools or public libraries

- Online sources
- Foundations, religious organizations, community organizations,
- local businesses, and civic groups
- Organizations related to the student's field of interest
- Ethnicity-based organizations
- Employers
- Free scholarship search services

Be smart. Check out all the information and assistance that you can get for free before you pay someone to do the work for you!

Self-Funding

If you are going to rely on your own financial resources, the key to securing the needed funding for a child (or children's) college education is long-term planning. It will be a much easier task to accomplish if you allow yourself 15 to 18 years to get it all done.

Your best step in funding a college education program is to go back and reread the lesson from Day 16, especially the part about learning the benefits of dollar-cost averaging into a no-load index fund. A couple of hundred dollars per month invested using this strategy will accumulate into a substantial sum over several years and very likely will pay for a student's higher education.

You may also wish to use a *Uniformed Gifts to Minors* account so that all profits earned in the investments are taxed at your student's tax rate instead of your own. Although, keep in mind that when your son or daughter turns 18, the money automatically becomes their property to be used at *his or her* discretion. You need to have a fairly high level of confidence in your child's decision-making ability or in your influence as a parent.

Closing Thoughts

College can be costly, but the money spent on obtaining a higher education may be returned at least tenfold during a lifetime in terms of *financial* benefits. For most, there is no price that can equate to the life experiences gained during college years. Those few years can often represent some of the best days of a young person's life.

This is one expense that can create much more value than the money invested.

As a parent, plan ahead so that you can help your son or daughter take advantage of this enriching experience.

As the student, you can do your part by exploring the grants and scholarships discussed in this chapter. Your dedication may produce a fortune in helpful funds and could get you into the college you most want to attend.

Financial assistance is available to almost anyone. There are many different types of funding—you just have to be willing to do some work and be your own money-sleuth.

If you run into roadblocks, seek the assistance of school guidance counselors or financial aid counselors, or find information on the Internet. Do not quit until you get the answers and assistance that you need. I know of an incident where a good student was turned down for financial aid (the student absolutely was in financial need). The student asked for help from a school advisor. After discussing all the details and issues, a few letters of explanation were supplied along with a letter of reference from the advisor, and the student was given the financial award after all (and was able to attend classes and graduate from a preferred university).

Never give up!

My College Finance Plan

1. Make a list of your preferred colleges and their related tuition costs as well as the cost of room and board for each situation.

2. Set up a 529 Plan (if applicable) through the mutual fund company of your choice.

3. Establish a Coverdell ESA (an education IRA).

4. Research prepaid tuition plans.

5. Make sure to review the list of scholarships, loans, and funding sources in this chapter.

6. For high school students: talk to high school guidance counselors regarding financial aid packages for your preferred colleges.

Day 24

Save Money on Life Insurance Products

I know that there are few who actually want to talk about the need for life insurance.

Consumers mostly guess at the amount of life insurance they think they will need or just follow some rule of thumb originated by the insurance industry. Unfortunately, most consumers understand so little about life insurance that they often purchase a policy that is a poor match for their current budget and which does not meet their true financial needs.

That is why today's topic is very important. I do not want you to become the victim of some overzealous insurance agent. I do not want you to be manipulated by having someone prey upon your greatest fears. Many insurance sales agents will try to sell products for which they will make the most profit without regard to whether those products are the best value for the consumer.

When today's lesson is done, you will know exactly how to handle the issue of life insurance and will be able to purchase a policy that is perfect for you and your family.

What is Life Insurance?

Life insurance is a product that pays a designated beneficiary a cash payment in the event of the death of the insured. This lump-sum payment can be used to retire debts and/or create an income for the survivors of the deceased individual. Some people choose to purchase a policy to help pay funeral costs, future college expenses for children, and to cover estate taxes. At the present time, there are no federal income taxes on life insurance payments, so your beneficiary keeps 100% of the disbursement. Life insurance is a very integral part of a solid financial plan.

How is Life Insurance Marketed?

There is an old saying that "life insurance is always sold, never bought." In other words, a person rarely, willingly, goes out looking for life insurance. Usually, a salesman initiates the approach by offering some great package that will protect your precious loved ones upon your demise. Most of us would rather not contemplate our own passing, so purchasing life insurance is a task that also rarely makes it to the top of the "to do" list. The job of the life insurance agent is to explain the need for coverage, whenever applicable.

Your job is to become well-educated about the various products and options concerning life insurance policies so that you end up with what you need at the lowest possible cost.

Most life insurance agents you encounter are independent contractors. This means that 100% of their income is generated from the commissions paid for selling life insurance products. You also need to know that each product they offer has a different commission structure or payout for the agent. Because of this, it is virtually impossible for agents to be objective during the selling process.

Put yourself in the agent's position for a moment. You are sitting at the kitchen table of a young couple that has agreed to discuss their insurance needs. There are two different policies that would meet their requirements: one pays a commission of $2,500 to you, and the other will pay only $150. As an agent, which policy would you encourage the couple to buy?

I think the answer is obvious.

By the way, the potential commission from either product is not disclosed by the agent, nor is it stated in the policy read by the potential purchaser. As far as I know, the insurance industry is the only business that is not forced to divulge this kind of pertinent information.

It has also been my experience that most agents have been brainwashed by their companies and the sales trainers hired by the insurance organizations. The agents are coached into thinking that the overpriced policies actually create a better value for the insured. The brainwashing may not take much work, as there is a benefit to the agent in believing the misleading information provided by their sales trainers.

The point is that you have to learn how to determine your personal need. Then *you* will be able to tell your agent what you need, not the other way around.

Who Needs Life Insurance?

Generally speaking, life insurance should be purchased by people who have dependents (survivors who would be in financial danger in the event of your death). I used to advise clients to picture themselves as dead (I know, kind of gruesome, but a very effective technique) and then answer the question as to who, if anyone, would be financially burdened by the passing? Obviously, if you are the biggest supporter for your family, chances are you have a major need for life insurance. Also, if you are a caregiver or otherwise provide services that your survivors would require but could not afford on their own, you should consider purchasing a policy. Assuming your survivors will have a difficult time dealing with the emotional aspects of your passing, I will also assume that you would not want to compound their grief by creating unbearable financial liabilities as well.

Who Does Not Need Life Insurance?

If you have no dependents, you have no need for life insurance.

Additionally, if you provide nothing of economic value, buying life insurance is a waste of money. Some people are led to believe that they should carry enough insurance to pay off their debts in the event of their death. Others are told to buy life insurance to cover funeral expenses. This is nonsense. When you die, your estate will be liquidated, and the proceeds will be used to cover outstanding debts and the cost of burial or cremation. In the event that there are insufficient monies to satisfy these debts...so what! You are dead! Should you have concerns about your nearest relatives being encumbered with the costs of any parting ceremonies, you could set aside a modest amount to handle those issues, and make sure that none of your kin have adopted the notion that some elaborate service would be necessary.

Insurance agents will try to convince you that if you buy a policy at a relatively young age that you will lock in a lower cost. This advice is absolute garbage. Using that logic, I should buy a car when I am 10 years old in order to avoid being subjected to the higher auto prices when I turn 16 years of age. With life insurance, there is no economic foundation for this approach. Agents are just looking for a sale. Likewise, you do not want to purchase life insurance on your children. Children do not provide any economic value to the family, and to be blunt, they create a drain on current resources. Why would you carry insurance on their lives? I think some agents know that they will be successful if they prey on the parents' instinctive desire to "do the right thing" for their children. Buying life insurance coverage on your children is a waste of money. Only insure lives that provide an economic benefit to a dependant.

How Much Life Insurance Should You Purchase?

Remember, you are buying life insurance in order to fill the financial void that will be created by your death. To determine your need, you have to ask yourself how much money will be required in order for your dependents to make a smooth transition into life without you and your income. I remember counseling a client who told me that he wanted enough insurance for his family to be comfortable, but not so much for them to be rooting for him to croak! Seems like good logic.

So how do you determine that magic number?

Review the following steps:

Step 1: Add up all the short-term needs. These would include final expenses, the amount of outstanding debts, and immediate emergency expenses. Final expenses are any uncovered medical, hospital, funeral, attorney fees, probate costs, and outstanding taxes. Outstanding debts would be those loans you would want to retire immediately, such as credit cards, student loans, car loans, and outstanding bills. Emergency expenses should include a cash reserve that will cover some possible unforeseen expenditures and regular expenses during any administrative delays or transitional period. This number will obviously be very personal to your specific situation.

Step 2: Add together the total of your long-term debts, which include mortgages and the future cost of providing a college education, if applicable, for any of your beneficiaries. You will need to calculate

Day 24: Save Money on Life Insurance Products the future cost of a college education, but a reasonable estimation is approximately $50,000 to $150,000 per student.

Step 3: Determine your family's annual expenses, minus the income provided by employment (of the survivor), investments, interest, and so forth. You need to determine if there is any cash flow deficiency. If so, take the amount of that deficiency and multiply it by the number of years you wish to make up for the shortfall.

Step 4: Look at your existing resources to determine which might help meet the financial needs of survivors. This would include savings, stocks, bonds, retirement plans, and Social Security benefits.

Step 5: Subtract your resources from the calculated needs to determine how much life insurance you should purchase. If you follow this plan, your survivors will be able to maintain their current standard of living for the number of years you have predetermined. After that chosen period, they will be on their own for support but will be free from any debt. Most people are surprised to find out how much capital is required to insure their loved ones' financial security.

How Are Premiums Calculated?

Life insurers price their policies in a way that will allow them to collect enough in premiums to pay the requisite death benefit and make a reasonable profit after commissions and expenses. In order to determine how much the company must collect in premiums, they estimate your life expectancy. The insurance companies have the benefit of historical data on which to base their decision. They have statistics that state how many 45-year-old males (out of 1,000) will die this year and data that pinpoints how long the average 60-year-old woman will continue to live.

Insurance companies basically look at four factors to determine the premiums necessary to cover their risk. These factors are age, gender, health, and lifestyle. The insurer employs underwriters who review the information given by the applicant and analyze the potential risk to the insurance company. Sometimes a person will live longer than expected, and other times the opposite outcome occurs. As long as insurance companies are able to find accurate probabilities and balance the scales, the companies will remain profitable.

Statistics and common sense have shown that young people usually have more years to live than older folks, women live longer than men, healthy people outlive those who are in poor health, and certain hobbies are more likely to lead to premature death. For this reason, an insurance company will ascertain this type of information from prospective clients before providing a firm quote.

How to Save Money on Life Insurance

The single best way to save money on your life insurance premiums is to shop around. As with most purchases these days, the easiest way to receive multiple quotes for insurance is to go online. Take a look at the following Web sites:

- Accuterm.com
  This site was rated the top online term insurance system by *Consumer Advocate.*
- ExamFirst.com
  This site is known for its highly accurate quoting, selection of competitive companies, and its superior brokerage service.
- 4BestQuotes.com
  This site was founded in 1996 for interested consumers and agents across the United States. After conducting an extensive screening process, which is designed to benefit both parties, this site matches consumers and agents.
- NetQuote.com
  This site has provided consumers with a free, simple, and effective method of shopping for insurance since 1989. This online service works with hundreds of partner companies that provide insurance quotes based on information that you supply.
- SelectQuote.com

Since 1985, this company has helped hundreds of thousands of people get the coverage they need at the right price. By combing the marketplace, they are able to find policies that match the individual circumstances of the consumer with the proper insurer.

Aside from shopping around, there are a few other methods you can employ to save big dollars on your insurance policies.

If you are a smoker, quit smoking now. It is a nasty, mindless habit that shortens your life expectancy and increases your insurance premiums (not to mention, decreases your quality of life while you *are* alive). If you are overweight, get fit by employing an exercise and nutritional regimen. If you engage in high-risk hobbies such as skydiving, scuba diving, or car racing, consider whether the enjoyment is worth the additional cost. Where these recreational activities are concerned, only you can determine their value.

Which Policy Type Is Best?

There are basically two types of life insurance policies offered to consumers: term coverage and policies that accrue cash value. You will find that each type is marketed with different bells and whistles.

Term Insurance Policies Options:

- Annual Renewable Term
- Level Premium Term
- Modified Level Premium Term
- Decreasing Term

Cash-Value Policies Options:

- Whole Life
- Interest-sensitive Whole Life
- Variable Life
- Variable Universal Life
- Universal Life
- Equity-indexed Whole Life

In the end, you need to decide whether you are looking for a pure death benefit or a death benefit with cash accumulation. Confused?

Let's clear things up.

Term insurance covers the risk of your death, period. It is the least expensive type of life insurance product. Its affordability makes it more likely that the policy holder will be able to pay for the amount of coverage that your dependents truly need. For this reason, I recommend term insurance to almost everyone who needs life insurance. The challenge will be that most agents will try to discourage the buyer from making this selection. The agent makes significantly more money selling the cash value variety. Unfortunately, some life insurance companies pressure the agent to choose what is best for the insurance company, rather than what might be best for your family.

Policies that accumulate cash value are sold based on a combination of death benefits and an investment account. The premiums for this type of policy can cost ten times as much as the price of premiums for the same amount of term coverage. Although the idea of building cash value might sound appealing, there is a catch. If you want to take money out of the policy, you must either borrow the funds (pay interest for the use of your own money and have your death benefit reduced by the amount of the loan) or cash it in, lose the death benefit, and pay tax on any deferred accumulation. With most policies, the beneficiaries receive only the death benefit upon your demise as the cash value goes back to the insurance company. This is a fact that is usually not mentioned during the sales pitch.

These policies are no bargain.

Stick with a term insurance product that is guaranteed renewable. This provides the most insurance for the money invested.

Switching Companies

After doing some research and discovering better available insurance options, some policy holders realize that it would be advantageous to move out of an existing life insurance policy and into another. Switching policies could be a prudent move due to one of two reasons. The first possible reason is that, compared to the term insurance policy issued several years ago, current term insurance rates may have dropped due to competition and longer life expectancies. The second possibility is that a cash value policy was purchased, and the policy holder now wants to shift to the less-expensive term product.

If you find yourself in one of these scenarios, I want to give you a word of caution before you flip this switch: *make sure you are still insurable*. If you cancel your current contract and subsequently find out

Day 24: Save Money on Life Insurance Products that you have a previously undiagnosed illness which precludes you from obtaining new coverage—chances are that your old provider will not take you back as you would now be considered a high risk.

If you own a universal life or whole life policy, first find out how much money you will forfeit by cashing in the policy. These polices are front-end-loaded, meaning you overpay initially to compensate for the heavy commissions earned by the agencies when the policy is sold. For this reason, switching may be too cost-prohibitive and would be more advantageous at a later date.

You also need to realize that the *two-year incontestable period* will begin anew. This period refers to the fact that, once you have owned a policy for two years, the insurance company must pay the death benefit, even if you were not totally forthright in your application. Switching policies starts the two-year clock all over again. Of course, this issue will not matter if you were completely truthful on your application.

Today's Conclusion

Purchasing life insurance is a significant consideration within the big picture of your overall financial fitness. You need to consider all the aspects of your personal life and any future plans so that you can establish the adequate amount of insurance you will need in order to take care of your dependents. By comparison shopping and purchasing a low-cost term product, you should be able to afford the right amount of death benefit without compromise. Be sure to recalculate your needs every few years. They usually change over time, especially if the number of your dependents changes for one reason or another. My hope is that someday you become "self-insured"—meaning that you have accumulated sufficient resources so that you can provide for your survivors without the need of an insurance policy. Make that your ultimate financial goal.

Use the following *needs analysis* form to make sure that you are adequately covered, and then begin the process of shopping for a renewable term product that fits your financial profile.

My Needs Analysis

Use Steps 1–5 from the Day 24 chapter as your outline to create a framework of your life insurance coverage needs.

Day 25

Asset Protection

For most of us, at least for those of us who are goal oriented and who plan to achieve a certain amount of financial security, a good portion of our lives are spent trying to increase our assets. This accumulation of assets can help to build a solid financial future upon which we can support ourselves and provide support to others. It is scary to consider that, without the proper protection, a single event could jeopardize a lifetime of hard work. Many people are paralyzed by fear when unpleasant possibility crosses their minds.

Ignoring the problem will not make it go away.

Like most difficult things in life, it is best to face this topic head on and find the best solution available.

Today, on Day 25, we will do just that.

To get started, answer the following questions:

- Do you own a car?
- Do you have children?
- Do you own your own home?
- Do you have any rental property?
- Do you have any pets?
- Do you own a business?
- Do you ever give any type of advice?
- Do you know any irrational people?

Unless you camp out, alone, inside a cave in some secluded mountain, I am going to bet that you answered one or more of these questions in the affirmative.

Each of these scenarios carries with it a certain amount of liability which could lead to your involvement in a lawsuit. Do you doubt that anyone would bother to sue you? Crazy things happen all the time in our legal system. If you do not spend any time around legal society or read anything about recent case outcomes, you may not be exposed to the wide (and wild) range of lawsuits that are fought in our courts every day.

More than 80 million lawsuits get filed in this country each year. That figure represents nearly one in every three men, women, and children. Think about that statistic. That means that the next time you are standing in line with six or seven other people...two of those folks standing next to you could be involved in some lawsuit—that is, assuming you are not the one implicated. If not, you could be next! This is one instance in which you cannot afford to put your "head in the sand" and pretend like it could never happen to you.

The best plan is to learn how to protect your assets against potential lawsuits and creditors *before* it becomes an issue.

Limited Liability Entities

This news may shock you, but there are many lawyers who love to go after deep pockets—meaning, they are very money conscious with respect to the use of their time and energy and will typically gravitate toward the larger accumulations of money and assets. This is just a fact. When attorneys evaluate a potential case, they consider two aspects:

- Is there merit to the case?
- Are there assets that can be acquired?

No attorney wants to fight to win a judgment against a plaintiff who has no ability to pay up.

Your first asset-preserving tactic: take care to give outsiders the impression that you are someone of modest means (on paper and otherwise).

Whoa! Before you start burying money in the backyard, let's explore the ways in which you can legally and safely accomplish this first protection strategy.

Limited Partnership or Limited Liability Company

First, by moving your assets into limited entities such as a limited partnership or a limited liability company, you effectively shift those assets beyond the reach of creditors and lawsuits and effectively make yourself look pretty worthless on a financial statement. This is accomplished because the entity owns everything, and you own little to nothing. Nice plan, huh? What asset-seeking attorney wants to go after someone who appears to have little net worth?

Family Limited Partnership (FLP)

Another limited liability entity to consider is the family limited partnership. Family limited partnerships allow you to reduce the size of your estate while still controlling the assets of the partnership. FLPs are set up much like traditional limited partnerships. There are two parties involved: the general partner who controls the trust and limited partners who share in the profits of the trust but have no control of the partnership.

Here is how a typical FLP is structured: the parents transfer assets into the trust and have 100% control as the acting general partners. Then they gift shares to the children with a value not exceeding $13,000 per year (indexed to inflation) to avoid any gift-tax ramifications. They share in the profits of the FLP based upon the partners' respective ownership interests.

Limited partnership shares are very undesirable to creditors as they cannot be readily sold. (There is not much of a market for family limited partnership interests.) Additionally, taking ownership could cause income tax issues of which the creditors want no part. This entity provides both estate tax and asset protection advantages.

Offshore Entities

People who possess large estates totaling in the millions of dollars may become tempting targets for creditors and lawyers alike. An offshore foreign trust can be a great way to keep those assets out of harm's way. Common destinations for these trusts, such as the Bahamas, Bermuda, the Turks and Caicos, the Cayman Islands, the Cook Islands, Gibraltar, and the Isle of Mann, have laws which tend to insulate and protect grantors. In establishing a foreign trust, you transfer ownership of your assets to a trust that has only foreign trustees (with no offices or agents residing in the United States). The trustees manage and administer the trust property from the offshore sites. Even if creditors find your assets, they will be forced to deal with an uncooperative foreign trustee. Due to the fact that U.S. courts have limited or no jurisdiction over foreign trustees, those courts do not have the authority to seize your assets except in extreme cases. Furthermore, the geographical distance between the creditor and your assets provides a logistical roadblock.

Let me give a few words of warning about offloading your assets into a foreign trust. You need to be very cautious when pursuing this course of action. The grantor should execute a statement of solvency with a balance sheet showing a positive net worth. This is essential to establish that you are not entering into the transaction to defraud creditors. Furthermore, not all of your assets should be transferred into the trust. You should maintain easy access to a sufficient amount of assets so that you can support your lifestyle. Remember that it could be every bit as challenging for your family to access these foreign trusts as it would be for your creditors.

You must absolutely, positively use a well-established and well-regarded law firm to assist you with your offshore plans. If you fail to follow the proper procedures, you could be subject to governmental scrutiny.

Delaware Trust

Asset-protection trusts, which have many of the same features of the typical offshore trusts, can now be created in the state of Delaware. Effective July 1, 1997, Delaware has enacted new trust legislation which allows individuals to legally shelter assets from potential creditor claims. Compared to an offshore entity, there is less time and expense required to set up a Delaware trust.

The significant benefits afforded by the Delaware trust must be understood in the context of prevailing U.S. law and the asset-protection strategies that are currently available.

For at least the last 500 years, creditor-friendly English and American common law statutes have severely restricted the ability of an individual to shield his or her assets from existing or future creditors. Existing and known future creditors are protected against fraudulent transfers. Future potential creditors have benefited from laws in every state making most trusts inconvenient or useless as vehicles for safeguarding your personal assets.

It was, and still is, common practice for attorneys specializing in asset protection to recommend to their clients that they use offshore trusts to protect their assets. Some countries enacted laws that allowed individuals to serve as both settlor and beneficiary of the trust. These progressive laws made the popularity of offshore trusts grow immensely in the last several years as this kind of arrangement was not permissible in the United States.

The Treasury Department estimates that thousands of offshore entities have been formed and funded with tens of billions of dollars. In response to the outflow of money and recognizing asset protection as a legitimate business planning tool, the state of Delaware enacted laws that make it permissible for individuals to protect assets from future creditors. A number of other states are likely to follow this trend.

The key provisions of the law include the following:

- A trust can be created in which the settlor is also the beneficiary.
- At least one trustee must be a licensed Delaware trust company, financial institution, or individual who resides in the state. The
- trustee must have some responsibility for the preparation of tax returns and trust administration.
- The settlor has the right to veto any distributions made by the trustee.
- Some portion of the assets must be in a bank or other financial institution located in the state of Delaware.
- The power to make distributions to the settlor must be held by a trustee who is independent of the settlor.

The assets of the trust are protected from any claims against the settlor except:

- Fraudulent transfers
- Spousal support and alimony
- Claims for personal injury or property damage that occurred before the transfer to the trust

- Claims by a creditor who relied upon the express written statement by the settlor that the assets of the trust were available to satisfy the debt to such creditor

The Delaware Trust Law produced new opportunities to create various asset protection plans specifically tailored to individual circumstances and objectives. The following three strategies are worth your consideration:

1. One simple technique is to transfer the family's assets into the trust. The clients can serve as co-trustees with a Delaware trust company. Accounts can be maintained at their current financial institutions with the name changed from the client to the name of the trust. Some minimal amount can be deposited with a Delaware institution to comply with the law. This approach is simple and easy to maintain. The trust can be designed so that all the income from the trust is taxed on the settlor's personal return. If properly structured, the trust will never die and will therefore avoid probate and can be used to minimize estate taxes.

2. The second strategy consists of forming an FLP to hold your family's assets. You and your spouse act as the general partners with the limited partnership interest being held by the Delaware trust. This structure allows the client to maintain control over the assets while protecting the limited partnership interests from charging orders or foreclosure. This can provide an excellent level of asset protection.

3. The third and most sophisticated asset protection approach uses an offshore asset-protection trust as a beneficiary of a Delaware trust. The client and family members would be the ultimate beneficiaries along with the offshore trust. The advantage of this strategy is that the offshore trust represents a convenient place to transfer assets should the need arise.

Equity Stripping

Equity stripping is the process of selling equity, or encumbering equity with debt, so that if a creditor attaches an asset, there is effectively little or nothing of value for the creditor to receive in the event that the creditor sold the asset. Most of the time, equity stripping involves borrowing from an asset that can be attached, like a savings account, to invest in something that is insulated from creditors, like a life insurance policy or homestead equity in a residence.

Qualified Retirement Plans

If your retirement plan is qualified under the Federal Employee Retirement Income and Security Act (ERISA), your ownership in the plan is exempt. No third party is able to get funds held in ERISA-qualified plans. This makes an ERISA plan an excellent asset protection vehicle.

ERISA plans allow you to defer current income for present tax savings; accrue interest, dividends, and capital gains to a future date; and offer protection from future creditors. When a retirement plan is subject to ERISA, it is excluded from bankruptcy proceedings and state court proceedings. Most qualified plans are covered by ERISA, but there are a few notable exceptions such as unprotected IRAs and plans failing to meet qualifications.

Should *You* Be Concerned about Asset Protection?

The whole notion of asset protection is only practical for those with assets to lose. If you are still renting an apartment, have only a few dollars in savings, and drive a leased vehicle, asset protection is probably not for you.

However, once you have used some of the strategies in this book and have succeeded in accumulating significant assets, make sure you visit with an asset protection specialist to see which plan would be appropriate for your circumstances. Use the information you learned today as a guideline.

I want to make it very clear that the goal of asset protection is not to avoid paying for obligations you legally assume. The idea is not to swindle anyone. Rather, asset protection should be used as a strategy to guard you and your family against the unknown and against financial predators. The goal today is to avoid becoming a target for creditors and unnecessary lawsuits. You need to be like a stealth aircraft flying in enemy territory: VIRTUALLY INVISIBLE. A person without assets in his or her name presents a challenging or futile target for money-hungry attorneys!

My Asset Protection Plan

1. Consider your personal net worth and assets.

2. Make certain that you fully fund your qualified retirement plans as they are protected against seizure.

3. If you have business interests or investments that cannot be fully protected through insurance, set up a limited liability company. Suggestion: Go to www.bizfilings.com to establish your LLC.

4. Re-title assets in the name of your LLC.

   IMPORTANT: Have legal counsel review your paperwork.

❖ ❖ ❖

Day 26

Protecting Your Income with Disability Insurance

Ready to start today with a little shock and awe?

How about this: it is an unpleasant statistic, but the fact is that 51 million Americans are currently disabled and 30 million are severely disabled. Did you know that 46% of all foreclosures are caused by the owner's disability, and half of all bankruptcies are attributed to medical reasons? Disability is a major issue in this country, and almost no one is talking about its implications.

Most people understand the need for life, auto, and homeowner's insurance. However, disability insurance is something that most of us never consider.

Today, Day 26, is the day to start thinking about the seriousness of this issue. Unless you can easily support yourself indefinitely with the money and assets that you currently own, you need to read this chapter carefully.

A disability insurance policy insures your ability to produce an income even if you are not able to work. Your insurance company will provide a monthly check based upon the policy you purchased. You insure for a specific dollar amount, and the checks will continue until you reach age 65, or to some point in time as outlined in the contract. The premiums you pay will be based on the amount of coverage you designate, your age, your health, your occupation, the company you select, and other factors that will be discussed in this chapter.

My goal today is to help you decide exactly what you need and how to obtain it in the most cost-effective way.

Determining Your Needs

Many people believe that they do not need disability insurance because they are already covered by their employer or they think that social security will be sufficient. Well, the fact of the matter is that your employer's group policy will only cover a maximum of about 60% of your current gross wages, and the payout is considered fully taxable. How well will you survive with a 40% pay cut?

Worker's compensation laws vary from state to state. They are designed to handle claims from employees who are injured on the job. To be covered by worker's compensation, your injury or illness has to occur while you are on the job and must be a work-related injury or illness. However, if you fall off a ladder at home or contract a disease while on vacation, worker's compensation protection will not provide you with any benefits. The likelihood of getting sick or hurt outside of the workplace is usually much greater than the likelihood of becoming sick or injured on the job. The only time the odds may reverse is when a person's workplace is a relatively hazardous environment.

In order to receive social security disability, you must be completely disabled. No benefits are payable for partial disability or for short-term disability. The Administration considers you to be disabled if you cannot do the kind of work you did before and are deemed unable to adjust to other work situations because of your medical condition. Also, your disability must last (or be expected to last) at least a year or be considered terminal in nature. There is also a five-month waiting period before benefits begin. The Administration can take three to five months to decide whether or not you even qualify. This means that you may have to survive on your own for almost an entire year!

To determine how much disability insurance you need, I would suggest asking the following question: how much income would I need to cover my bare necessities on a monthly basis? Keep in mind that disability payments are tax-free income. How much of that need can I generate from my current savings, investments, or my company's disability insurance? What is the difference each month?

Understanding the Policy

There are many different elements that make up a disability income insurance policy. It is important to understand when and how you would receive the disability income if you became disabled.

For example, it is important to know how a company's policy defines and covers short-term disability, long-term disability, and total disability. It is important to know whether there is a waiting period before income benefits kick in. Also, the income from the disability insurance policy can affect your social security, worker's compensation, or unemployment benefits. There are also different types of policies to consider: short term or long term. Another key element is whether or not the policy covers disabilities from both accidents *and* illnesses.

To help you understand the options, I have listed several important questions that you should pose to your agent.

- What is the definition of disability in my policy?
- What is the renewability?
- How long will I receive benefits?
- How much will I receive?
- Will my benefit amount adjust for inflation?
- How long is the waiting period?
- Can I receive partial benefits if I am able to work part time?
- How will my benefits affect my social security, worker's compensation, or unemployment benefits?
- What is the rating of the issuing company?
- Can I renew my policy without taking another medical exam?

Let's discuss each of these issues in order to tailor a policy that best fits you and your loved ones.

Definition of Disability

Your policy may define disability (and your ability to collect benefits) in one of several ways. The most advantageous definition for the policy holder is known as *"own occupation."* Under this definition, it means the inability to work at your regular occupation. For example, if you had been employed as a dentist but become unable to engage in

267

dentistry (but are still capable of sweeping floors), you would be considered disabled because you have lost the ability to perform in your normal occupation. This is the policy definition of disability that you must insist upon if you hold a highly compensated specialty position.

On the other hand, when disability is defined as *the inability to work at any occupation*, the insurance company can reject your disability claim unless you are virtually bedridden. The company does not have to pay you if you are capable of any gainful employment in any line of work. Therefore, even if you had previously earned a six-figure salary but became sick or injured and could no longer perform your regular job (but remained capable of working in a fast-food restaurant or at some other low-wage occupation), you would not receive compensation from your insurance company.

Scary thought, isn't it?

This could come as a rude awakening for the uninformed disability policy holder. Stay away from this definition unless you are prepared to survive on a minimum-wage paycheck. Something else to look out for: sometimes this definition is softened with the words, *"if unable to perform the duties of any occupation by which the individual is suited by training, education, or experience."* This wording is a little too vague for my comfort zone.

"Modified own occupation" is the third definition of coverage types. In this case, the insured is considered disabled if unable to perform the material and substantial duties of his or her own occupation and is not working in any other occupation. Again, the insurance company has an out for not providing a monthly benefit. I recommend sticking with policies that incorporate the *"own occupation"* definition.

Renewability

Next on the checklist of questions is the *renewability* of the policy, or whether your policy's terms are subject to change over time.

There are three options where renewability is concerned:

- Non-cancelable and guaranteed renewable policy
- Guaranteed renewable policy
- Conditionally renewable policy

The best policy to purchase is a non-cancelable contract as it locks in your rates and benefits. The insurance company cannot make changes unless you request them.

A guaranteed renewable policy is less desirable. After you invest in a policy, your insurer does not have the right to drop you but can reserve the right to raise prices for specific reasons like a change in your health. This is essentially like giving the insurance company a blank check. No, thank you!

Avoid the conditionally renewable policies. An insurer can apply any condition or raise rates at any time.

Length of Benefits

Most policies are considered either short term or long term. Short-term disability policies are designed for employees who are unable to work temporarily due to illness or injury. These policies pay a benefit expressed in the maximum number of weeks that the plan will pay. Short-term disability policies offer a limited amount of protection. They would not be sufficient if you become disabled for an extended period of time.

Long-term disability policies are normally designed to provide a monthly benefit until the retirement age of 65, whereupon social security and other retirement plan benefits kick in. Long-term disability is the type of policy you want to own.

Maximum Monthly Benefits

Typically, long-term disability insurance can be purchased to replace 50% to 70% of your salary. Some employers allow employees to purchase extra insurance from the same company raising the total replacement value to 80% of your current compensation.

The policy's percentage figure is based upon the amount you are making at the time the policy is purchased. Obviously, you will want to modify the policy each time you have an increase in salary. Keep in mind that some plans require that you have a physical check-up before modifications can be made. Check your policy for details. The reason that insurance companies cap their benefits is that they want the policy holder to have an incentive to return to work. If a person could make more money watching afternoon soap operas rather than through employment, no doubt we would experience an overnight increase of illness and injuries in this country!

Inflation Rider

An inflation rider will raise your monthly payout equal to the rate of inflation on an annual basis. This rider is normally offered as an option on disability insurance contracts. This is a critical option as a $3,000-per-month income may buy only $1,500 worth of goods and services in a decade or two.

Inflation riders are generally offered in two forms: simple and compound. You want the compound method as the inflation factor is applied each year to last year's payout. It is the only true calculation that will keep your purchasing power current with the rising costs of living.

Waiting Period

The waiting period is the number of consecutive days that you must be totally disabled before your monthly benefit is payable. Waiting periods range from 30 days to 365 days. Some disability insurance policies restart the waiting period all over again each time you return to work (even when you are employed only part time). Other policies accumulate days of total or partial disability. You need to read your policy carefully.

The longer the waiting period, the more you save on premiums. Generally speaking, it is unwise to select a waiting period of less than 90 days. The premiums would be unaffordable for most people. If you can manage to accrue the financial resources to survive, I would recommend electing a waiting period of 180 days. If you do not think you could survive for six months without financial assistance, then choose a waiting period somewhere between 90 days and 180 days. This represents the best cost-to-benefit ratio.

On a side note: if you are not in a position to support yourself—and any dependents you may have—for a period of several months, make it a priority to become financially solvent to the point that you *are* able to do so. The lessons you are learning in this book will teach you many different ways to achieve that goal!

Partial Disability

Some policies provide a benefit in the event that your disability prevents you from continuing in your current occupation but do not pre

Day 26: Protecting Your Income with Disability Insurance vent you from performing other functions that earn compensation. Let's use the dentist example again. Assume that our dentist could no longer perform dentistry, which earned her a handsome six-figure income. However, she is able to teach at a school of dentistry and earn $40,000 annually. With partial disability coverage, she would receive a monthly check that would help offset the difference in income. Be sure to check whether or not your provider offers this type of coverage.

Effect of Other Benefits

It is very likely that the receipt of other benefits such as worker's compensation, social security, or unemployment could impact the amount the disability insurance your company is willing to pay. Basically, the insurance company wants to make sure that you do not wind up making more money from your injury or illness than you were making when you were able to work. Most insurance companies seem to set a maximum total benefit at 70% of the previously earned salary.

Insurance Company Ratings

At present, there are only about six or seven major insurance companies that still offer disability insurance. There are a number of smaller entities that offer disability insurance, but any potential client needs to be sure that an organization like this will be able to honor the contract. Remember, benefits may be needed for decades. Under the terms of a policy, the client needs to be in business with a company that has the ability to stay in business during strong and weak economic periods. To check an insurance company's rating, go to www.moodys.com, www.standardandpoors.com, or www.ambest.com.

Each site uses a rating system with a series of letters (e.g., AAA on the upper end, down to a lesser grade of C). The Web sites are very user-friendly.

Medical Exams

The type of medical exams and tests required for disability coverage will vary by the amount of coverage requested and by the insurance company's underwriting guidelines. The physical exam can take place in your home or office and is performed by a medical professional at no cost to you. The exam typically requires that blood and urine specimens be taken, blood pressure is measured, height and weight measurements are recorded, and a medical history questionnaire is answered. Test results are available to you from the insurance company, upon request.

Anytime you choose to modify your policy, you can expect that the insurance company will require you to undergo a new examination. The insurance company takes a huge underwriting risk. It is their responsibility to make certain that you are in reasonably good health before agreeing to insure you. They may also reserve the right to reexamine you on a discretionary basis.

Putting It All Together

Now that we have discussed the required steps to getting your disability policy, let me just say a few final words about the importance of this coverage.

Even though the chances of becoming disabled are far greater than the odds of dying prematurely or of having your home burn to the ground, disability insurance remains the most disregarded insurance coverage type. Make the smart choice to investigate disability insurance thoroughly. You can use this insurance to provide for your own wellbeing and for your family's security.

Disability Insurance Checklist:

☐ You will need a monthly benefit that covers your basic obliga-tions, minus other income you could expect from savings, in-vestments, or other sources.

☐ Insist upon an *"own occupation"* definition of disability with a 90-day to 180-day waiting period.

☐ Make certain that your policy is non-cancelable, guaranteed re-newable, and issued by a top-rated insurance company.

☐ Your benefits should extend until you reach retirement age and adjust annually for inflation.

With each of these checklist elements in place, you should rest easy at night knowing that you and your dependents are protected in case of sickness or injury.

Shopping for Disability Insurance

If you are a highly paid professional (the type most likely to be in need of an individual policy), I have found a very impressive Web site: www.protectyourincome.com. This site provides tons of information explaining how to find the best carrier for your particular needs. Just complete an online questionnaire, and you will be directed to an appro-priate provider.

Keep in mind that your employer may have access to additional long-term disability products through their present insurance agent. Be sure to get a quote from them as well!

My Disability Insurance Worksheet

As you work on today's exercise, remember the important points of the disability insurance Checklist:

___ You will need a monthly benefit that covers your basic obligations, minus other income you could expect from savings, investments, or other sources.

___ Insist upon an *"own occupation"* definition of disability with a 90-day to 180-day waiting period.

___ Make certain that your policy is non-cancelable, guaranteed renewable, and issued by a top-rated insurance company.

___ Your benefits should extend until you reach retirement age and adjust annually for inflation.

To begin your research and to shop policies, go to: www.protectyourincome.com

❖ ❖ ❖

Day 27

Affordable Medical Insurance

We have discussed many different kinds of insurance during the last couple of days.

I have saved the most important category for last.

Medical insurance is the one type of insurance that every person in this country absolutely needs. You simply cannot afford to expose yourself to the financial risk or potential ruin that can be caused by becoming sick or injured while lacking adequate coverage. Medical costs are escalating at an alarming rate, and you can bet that they will continue to increase.

I realize that some of you have coverage benefits through your employer. However, according to the U.S. Census Bureau, there are 49.9 million of you out there who lack health insurance coverage. Without insurance, you could find yourself in a critical situation if you were to become seriously incapacitated.

Today we are going to examine the most cost-effective ways to attain health insurance coverage.

Types of Insurance Coverage

Many Americans receive health insurance through their employer or through a spouse's company benefits. This type of coverage is referred to as *group insurance*. Generally speaking, group insurance is typically the least expensive form of medical insurance as the companies are buying this product in bulk, and most employers pay for all, or a portion, of the premiums. If available, this coverage will almost always be less expensive than purchasing coverage on your own.

Many employers offer a variety of policies from which to choose. These include:

- Fee-for-Service Plan
- Health Maintenance Organization (HMO)
- Preferred Provider Organization (PPO)

Let's review the various types and explore the pros and cons of each.

Fee-for-Service

This is the conventional type of health insurance policy and is probably the most well-known plan. When medical care is required, the insurance company pays for the treatment costs, as long as the health care provider is listed in your policy. The advantage of this type of policy is that it gives the greatest amount of flexibility regarding physician choice and eligible treatment facilities. Most people prefer this type of coverage because it allows for the maximum amount of control regarding their health care.

With fee-for-service, you only pay for a part of your doctor and hospital bills. Typically, you are responsible for paying an annual deductible plus a percentage of the medical expenses (generally, around 20%). Also, there is usually a cap on the amount you are required to contribute per calendar year. After that cap number is reached, your insurance picks up 100% of any further bills until the beginning of the next calendar year. Some companies will provide their workers with coverage that requires no annual deductible and no co-payments, but those benefits are becoming increasingly rare. Employers and insurance companies want there to be an incentive for the insured to try to manage his or her personal medical costs.

There are two kinds of fee-for-service coverage: basic and major medical. Basic protection pays for the cost of a hospital room and medical care while you are in the hospital. It covers some hospital services and supplies, such as X-rays and prescribed medicine. Basic coverage also pays toward the cost of surgery, whether performed in or out of the hospital, and any related doctor visits.

Major medical insurance takes over where your basic coverage terminates. Major medical provides for long-term or very costly illnesses.

Some policies combine basic and major medical into one plan. This is sometimes referred to as a *comprehensive plan*. Check your policy to make sure that you have both types of protection.

Many policies will only pay for charges that are considered reasonable and customary. You need to check with your care provider to determine whether certain treatments or tests are covered by your insurance carrier. For certain medical procedures, there may be a particular protocol that you are required to follow in order for the insurance company to pay the full bill.

Health Maintenance Organizations (HMO)

HMOs are prepaid health care plans. As an HMO member you pay a monthly premium. In exchange, the HMO provides comprehensive care for you and your family, including doctor's visits, hospital stays, emergency care, surgery, lab tests, X-rays, and therapy. The HMO arranges for this care either directly (within its own group practice), through doctors and other health care professionals that are under contract with the insurance provider, or through some combination of both. Usually, your choice of doctors and hospitals is limited to those that have agreements with the HMO.

There can be some very negative aspects of HMO plans. Your preferred and trusted physician may not be available to you if he or she is not part of the HMO plan.

In theory, due to the fact that HMOs receive a fixed fee for your covered medical care, it is in their best interest to make certain that you receive basic health care for health issues before they develop into a serious problem. As such, most HMOs provide preventative care such as office visits, immunizations, well-baby checkups, mammograms, and physicals. The range of services covered varies between HMOs, so it is important to compare available plans. Oftentimes, certain services, such as outpatient mental health care, are provided only on a limited basis. Many people enjoy the convenience of HMOs because members are not required to fill out claim forms for office visits or hospital stays. Instead, members present a card, similar to a credit card, upon visiting a doctor's office or hospital. However, members do report that there may be a longer waiting period for service as compared to receiving treatment from their own physician under a fee-for-service plan.

In some HMOs, doctors are salaried and all have offices in an HMO building at one or more locations in your community as part of a pre-paid group practice. In other plans, independent groups of doctors contract with the HMO to take care of patients. These individual groups are called Individual Practice Associations (IPAs) which are made up of private-practice physicians who consent to care for HMO members. The HMO member selects a doctor from a list of participating physicians within the IPA network. When considering a switch into an IPA-type of HMO, first ask your preferred doctor whether he or she participates in the plan.

In almost all HMOs, each member is assigned a primary physician or is permitted to choose one doctor to serve as a primary care provider. This doctor monitors the member's health and provides most medical care. He or she is responsible for referring members to medical specialists and other health care professionals as needed. Typically, an HMO member cannot see a specialist without a referral from a primary care provider. This is another way that HMOs can limit member choices.

Before choosing an HMO program, I recommend talking to members who are already enrolled in the plan. Ask them for feedback on the services and level of care provided.

Preferred Provider Organizations (PPO)

The preferred provider organization is a combination of the conventional fee-for-service plan and an HMO. Similar to an HMO, there are a limited number of doctors and hospitals from which to choose. When those providers are used (which are sometimes called *preferred* or *network* providers), most of the medical bills are covered.

When visiting a doctor in the PPO, an insurance card is presented and patients do not have to fill out claim forms. Usually, there is a small co-payment required for each visit. For some services, a deductible and coinsurance may be required. As with an HMO, a PPO requires you to choose a primary care provider to monitor your health care. Most PPOs cover preventive care such as standard visits to the doctors, well-baby care, immunizations, and mammograms.

In a PPO, the insured can visit doctors who are not part of the plan and still receive some coverage. With this type of visit, the insured will pay a larger portion of the bill (and also must fill out claim forms). Some members appreciate this option because they are not forced to change doctors in order to join a PPO.

Selecting the Right Policy for You

As you begin to explore the various forms of medical coverage, you should begin by determining your priorities regarding your current circumstances. Remember that the staple of any good policy is hospitalization coverage. Without it, you could find yourself dead broke in a matter of weeks. Beyond hospitalization coverage, use the checklist below when comparing policies:

- ✓ Hospital care
- ✓ Surgery (inpatient and outpatient)
- ✓ Office visits to your doctor
- ✓ Maternity care
- ✓ Well-baby care
- ✓ Immunizations
- ✓ Medical tests
- ✓ Dental care, braces, and cleaning
- ✓ Vision care, eyeglasses, and exams
- ✓ Prescription drugs
- ✓ Home health care

Nursing home care Other important questions for you to ask:

- Can I select my own physician?
- How much paperwork will be required?
- How long is the waiting period before the coverage begins?
- What about preexisting conditions?

Financial considerations:

- How much is the annual premium?
- How much is the deductible?

- What is the coinsurance rate, or co-payment?
- Are there annual maximums for coverage?
- What are the maximum out-of-pocket costs each year?
- Is there a lifetime limit on your coverage?

Individual Medical Insurance

Roughly 16 million Americans purchase individual medical insurance. When compared to the estimated 170 million Americans who access their health insurance benefits through an employer-sponsored medical insurance plan, individual medical insurance accounts for a pretty small percentage of the population (about 5%).

The Health Insurance Portability and Accountability Act of 1996 (HIPAA) created the guarantee issue of medical insurance for groups ranging in size from two employees to fifty employees. Furthermore, HIPAA created the guarantee issue portability provision for individual medical insurance in the event individuals exhaust their COBRA coverage or lose their individual coverage as a result of a carrier becoming insolvent. Pilot programs of Medical Savings Accounts (MSAs) were also created for self-employed individuals and small-group employers that have anywhere from two to fifty employees.

Why is it important to mention HIPAA and understand its implications?

Since full implementation of HIPAA, the following has occurred in the individual medical insurance market:

- Premiums are often less than the group medical insurance plan (dependent upon the employer's contribution).
- Adverse selection in the small-group insurance market is now being used.
  There are stricter underwriting guidelines in the individual market. More Americans are uninsured.

When shopping for individual medical insurance, understand that coverage is not guaranteed. In most states, carriers may deny or reject individuals and/or family members based upon a person's medical condition. Currently, 20 states have either mandated, or an insurance carrier voluntarily issues, guaranteed issue individual coverage. In the other 30 states in the country, you may need to qualify with regard to your level of health.

Keep in mind that *guarantee issue* does not mean that *preexisting condition limitations* are not imposed. Individual medical insurance policies can limit payments for prescriptions, mental health, home health care, spinal manipulation, rehabilitation services, and maternity benefits for those who join who have a preexisting condition.

As with any big decision, before purchasing a policy, research more than one carrier and more than one agent or broker. Be very cautious about dealing with a "captured" insurance agent who can only represent one insurance company. Instead, consider talking to a broker who can represent multiple carriers.

And be sure to ask the following questions:

- Is the insurance carrier fully regulated by the state department of insurance?
  Is the insurance carrier marketing its coverage through an association?
  What is the length of the initial rate guarantee, and how often are rate increases assessed after the initial guaranteed period?
- How much has the average rate increased during the past five years?
  What is the projected rate increase for the next year?
  Do I have a *free-look period* after the policy is delivered? This gives you the right for a full refund if you choose to return the policy once you have read its contents.
  How long has the carrier been marketing in the state?

Shopping for Health Insurance Online

Thanks to the Internet, shopping for and comparing medical insurance policies is very convenient. I have researched the following Web sites and have found them to be helpful: **www.ourinsurancebroker. com**

This is a leading online service where individuals, families, and companies can receive quotes from their network of local authorized agents for top insurance companies. **www.affordable-health-coverage.com**

This site serves the individual, family, or small-business owner with free quotes. **www.einsurance.com**

Since 1989, eInsurance has assisted more than 10,000,000 consumers and businesses in researching affordable insurance. They do not sell insurance. Instead, they offer a free consumer service that provides a fast way to shop and compare carriers' quotes and policies. **www.ehealthinsurance.com**

This is one of the better sites on the market—it offers all types of products. Definitely make this site one of your stops as you research insurance.

Wow! We have concluded another day's lesson, already!

To summarize: medical insurance is a "must-have" insurance policy. Without it, you may be one injury or illness away from financial insolvency. Identify your personal priorities for your medical care, do some shopping by speaking with as many brokers and agents as you can, use the checklists I have provided, and get started—right now! What are you waiting for? Go!

Postscript

Let me mention one more thing: if you work for a company that provides health insurance benefits, chances are that the company will pick up most, if not all, of the medical tab. If you are self-employed, you are on your own. I know premiums are high (and getting higher), but so are the costs of medical treatment in this country. Do not procrastinate. Get insurance.

Do not fool yourself by thinking, "I'm healthy. I never get sick. I don't have to worry about this."

No one who reads this book could possibly be a fool.

Even if you were fortunate enough never to become ill, it does not account for the possibility that you could have some sort of accident or become the victim of another person's negligence and need immediate medical attention.

Day 27: Affordable Medical Insurance

Before you move on to read the next chapter, you better make sure you have adequate health protection.

I mean it. Go find the best insurance policy that you can!

My Medical Insurance Action Plan

Determine your medical insurance needs (how much).

Decide which type of policy best suits those needs.

Use the sources outlined in this chapter to shop for the best available coverage and premiums.

Check out which types of policies are available through your employer or through any other associations to which you belong.

If you are currently insured, be sure to shop around to determine whether you are getting the best value in return for your premium dollars.

Day 28

Planning Your Estate

No, the title of today's lesson is not *"Planning Your ESCAPE."*

It's *"Planning Your ESTATE."*

I know, I know…more talk about preparing for life after death.

But we might as well do what we can to ease the stress on the people we will inevitably leave behind.

During our lifetime, we may each build something referred to as an estate. Legally speaking, your estate is the total property owned prior to the distribution of that property under the terms of a will, trust, or inheritance laws. Basically, it is everything you own before you die.

It includes all of the assets and liabilities that were accumulated during your lifetime.

Today, on Day 28, we will look at the ways in which we can protect these assets and, most importantly, how we can protect the inheritance that you intend for your loved ones.

Estate Planning Objectives

Advanced planning will aid your beneficiaries in a number of ways. First and foremost, it provides for the ongoing care and support of your dependents. Without the proper estate planning instruments, the state will decide who raises or cares for any children or dependants you might leave behind. Second, estate planning determines who gets what and when they will get it. Proper estate planning also helps to minimize both the tax implications of death and the amount of time required to settle your estate.

Dying Intestate

Dying *intestate* means to die without having created a will or trust that instructs the court how to distribute your assets to your beneficiaries.

In this event, the court will abide by the laws of intestacy established by the state in which the deceased resided. It is a messy and expensive process. When a person dies without a will, the probate court appoints a person to receive all claims against the estate, pay creditors, and distribute all remaining property in accordance with the laws of the state. The wishes of the deceased are not known and, therefore, cannot be given any consideration during the decision-making process.

Probate

Probate is the process by which legal title of property is transferred from the decedent's estate to his or her beneficiaries. If a person dies with a will (*testate*), the probate court determines if the will is valid, hears any objections to the will, orders that creditors be paid, and supervises the process to ensure that the remaining property is distributed in accordance with the terms and conditions of the will.

If a person dies without a will (*intestate*), the state laws or formulas are followed. Many people do not realize that in most states, in the absence of a will, your property will be divided between your spouse, if one exists, and any surviving children. This could be very disadvantageous for the surviving spouse who is expected to provide full support for your children but may not have the necessary resources to do so.

The cost of probate is either set by state law or by practice and custom in your community. The typical fees range from 3% to 7% of the total value of your estate. This can become a very hefty figure.

Keep reading, and we will explore the ways in which you can mitigate many of these fees.

Estate Taxes

The first step in determining any potential estate tax liability is to inventory everything you own and assign a value to each asset. Here is a list of items to consider:

- Life insurance proceeds
- Retirement plans
- Personal residence
- Other real estate
- Savings
- Investments
- Business interests
- Vehicles
- Jewelry
- Collectibles
- Furniture

Once you have totaled the value of everything you own, subtract any debts and you will arrive at your taxable estate. From your taxable estate, you can subtract the *exclusion amount* (the amount you are allowed to pass along free of estate tax liability). You will be taxed on the balance as outlined below.

Year	Exclusion Amount	Highest Estate Tax Rate
2008	$2,000,000	45%
2009	$3,500,000	45%
2010	$5,000,000	45%
2011	$5,000,000	45%
2012	$5,120,000	45%

As you can see, holders of smaller estates may not be subject to any estate tax implications, but those with larger estates could lose nearly one half of their estates to the federal government. For this reason, you need to consider all available strategies for minimizing this figure. I am going to assume that anyone reading this book has the intention of amassing a sizable estate during his or her lifetime. Therefore, this issue *is* relevant for you, even if you are currently just beginning your financial journey to wealth.

Gift Taxes

Anyone can make a gift to any other person(s) in an amount up to $13,000 per year with no federal gift taxes. A married couple can give $26,000 per year to one person in any given year. A married couple can give $52,000 per year to another married couple or to two children each year. These amounts are indexed to inflation and adjusted annually.

Gifting can be a very effective method of reducing the size of your taxable estate. Of course, you need to be careful that you do not give away everything you own. You still need to provide for yourself and for your own family. Planning is a critical component in gifting.

Building Your Estate Plan (Simple Will)

Under certain circumstances, a simple will is the only estate planning document you may need. This would include cases where the estate is so small that a formal probate will not be required (typically anything less than $50,000), or if there is a situation where it is reasonable or safe to leave all of the property through beneficiary or joint tenancy arrangements. Also, to use a simple will there should be no significant death tax liabilities, no need to hold the heir's share of the estate for deferred distribution, and no mental capacity issues.

Keep in mind that everyone above the age of 18 should have a will drafted. It can be created by an estate planning attorney or you can do it yourself. The basic elements of a will contain the following:

- Your name and place of residence
- A brief description of your assets
- Names of spouse, children, and other beneficiaries
- Alternative beneficiaries in the event that those designated are
- deceased at the time of your death
- Specific gifts
- Establishment of trusts, if desired
- Cancellation of debts owed to you, if desired
- Name of an executor to manage the estate
- Name of a guardian for minor children
- Name of an alternative guardian in case of death of originally
- selected guardian
- Your signature
- Witnesses' signatures

Two of the more critical and thought-provoking elements are naming the guardian(s) and selecting the executor. Let's take a closer look at each of these issues.

Naming the Guardian

Many couples do not consider the possibility of dying simultaneously and assume that one of them could take on 100% of the parenting duties in the event of the other's untimely passing. However, there must be a plan in case something totally unexpected *does* happen and your children are orphaned. By naming a guardian in your will, you are able to nominate who will take over the responsibility of rearing your children. Without a will or designated guardian, the court is forced to make its own determination without any input from the deceased. You owe it to your kids (who, as minors, have little to no power with which to control their own lives) to create a plan that will provide for their wellbeing in your absence.

Naming an Executor

An executor is the person who oversees the distribution of your assets in accordance with your will. Most people will choose their spouse, an adult child, another relative, a trusted friend, advisor, attorney, or a trust company to perform this role. In most cases, the executor will be paid a fee for services rendered. The executor's responsibilities include:

- Paying valid creditors
- Paying taxes
- Notifying Social Security and other agencies and companies of
- the death
- Canceling credit cards, magazine subscriptions, and so forth
- Distributing assets according to the will

Preparing a Will

Start by taking inventory of your assets, your liabilities, family members, and other beneficiaries (including charities). Use the information to carefully determine who gets what. Be sure to take into account any special circumstances: for instance, a disabled child or a dependent with a habitual drug problem. Perhaps a trust should be set up to handle these particular cases.

Any assets not specifically mentioned can be distributed using a catch phrase such as, *"The remainder of my estate will go to..."* However, it is best to make certain that your objectives are clearly stated and that you have left no room for ambiguity.

States require that your will be signed in front of witnesses, the number of which is determined by state law. There are no rules that prevent you from drafting your own document, but I would advise spending the few dollars it will take to have this service provided by an estate planning attorney. The stakes are too high to err due to a technicality.

Storing Your Will

Keep your will in a safe place that is fireproof and waterproof. It is imperative that you disclose the location to a few select individuals so that they know where to look upon your death. Be careful about keeping it in a safety deposit box as many states seal these upon the death of the owner.

A Living Will

A living will is not part of your will at all. It is a separate document that informs family members or caregivers as to the type of treatments you may or may not want in the event that you become terminally ill or permanently unconscious. I realize this is a difficult topic to ponder, but you will make your loved ones' lives much better by giving them specific instructions to use when executing your wishes.

Using Trusts: The Living Trust

More and more Americans are beginning to understand the value of preparing a living trust. Living trusts have skyrocketed in popularity in the past two decades. They have become one of the most common estate planning tools in use today.

This legal arrangement, usually drafted by an estate planning attorney, creates a separate entity called a living trust, which is so named because it is created while you are still alive. Because it does not die even when you do, there are tremendous advantages in creating one.

The living trust document identifies three different parties. The party that establishes the trust is called the *grantor*. The *trustee* is the person named by the trust as the controller of the trust's assets. You can be the trustee of your own trust. The *beneficiaries* are the heirs who will ultimately benefit from the trust once you have passed away.

The primary advantage of a living trust is that it avoids the time delay and expenses associated with probate. Living trusts are also private and therefore much more difficult to contest than a simple will (which is a matter of public record). The trust is essentially controlled by the trustee (you or your designee). Therefore, you can rest easy knowing that your wishes will be carried out, even if you are personally unable to see to them. If you are institutionalized or unable to care for yourself, the trust will carry on and make distributions as needed. The trustee has a fiduciary responsibility to see that your requests are fulfilled exactly as you have instructed.

Once established, almost anything can be placed in a trust: savings accounts, stocks, real estate, life insurance policies, as well as personal property. To fund the trust, you simply change the title of your assets to that of your living trust. You lose control of nothing. The trust is also revocable, meaning that you can amend or terminate it at any time for any reason. The only expense is in drafting the document.

Almost anyone with an estate of more than $100,000 will find it beneficial to use this estate planning tool. Most states will probate an estate larger than this if there is no living trust. Also, those who wish to avoid conservatorship may find that a trust is a good match for their needs. Conservatorship is the legal right given to someone else to manage your affairs should you be deemed incapable.

Using Trusts: A-B Bypass Trust

Let me note that living trusts are not designed to save on estate tax liability. They are primarily used for purposes of privacy and to avoid probate and conservatorship. Those with larger estates (larger than $5 million) should explore the advantages of an A-B trust.

Most people do not need to worry about federal estate taxes thanks to two factors: the marital deduction and the estate tax exemption. The unlimited marital deduction allows you to give an unlimited amount of assets to your spouse, estate-tax-free. The surviving spouse can then bequeath $5,120,000 in 2012 without any estate tax implications.

If you believe your estate could potentially exceed the amounts noted in the previous paragraph, you should look into an A-B trust.

This is how an A-B trust works. Instead of leaving property outright to the surviving spouse, each spouse leaves all or most of his or her property to the trust. When one spouse dies, the surviving spouse can use that property (with certain restrictions) but does not own it outright. Because the surviving spouse technically never owns the property, it is not subject to estate tax. From a practical standpoint, it enables taxpayers to effectively double their exemption from about $5 million to around $10 million in 2012 (after 2012, it's in the hands of congress and the political process). The tax savings could be measured in millions of dollars.

When the trust is established, each spouse names final beneficiaries who will receive the trust's property when the latter of the surviving spouses dies.

Your A-B bypass trust can be created within the context of your living trust providing two valuable benefits. Your estate will avoid the costs and time delays of probate as well as benefit from the significant potential estate tax savings. The two vehicles create a powerful estate planning combination. The following is an example of a bypass trust.

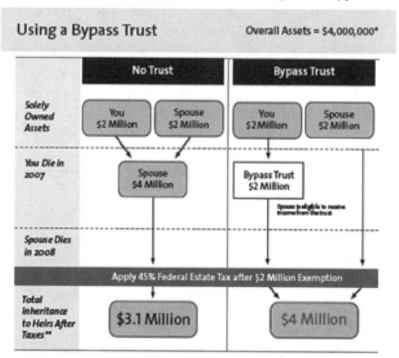

Generation-Skipping Transfer Tax

The federal Generation-Skipping Transfer (GST) tax is imposed on substantial wealth transferred between generations. The GST tax is an extremely complicated system meant to fill what was once a gap between the federal estate tax and the federal gift tax.

Normally, the estate tax would apply to each generation. For example, when a father leaves his son $5 million upon the father's death, estate taxes are due on that amount. When the son passes away and leaves the remaining estate to his son, taxes are due once again. To avoid this double taxation, consider using the GST rules that allow you to leave assets directly to your grandchildren, estate-tax-free, provided the total does not exceed the estate tax exclusion for that year. This strategy should only be considered by the very wealthy.

See, that wasn't so bad now, was it?

Everyone should have at least a simple will to cover the basics.

If your estate equals more than $100,000, consider drafting a living trust.

When your total estate is projected to exceed $2 million, take advantage of the tax savings offered by the A-B bypass trust. Your beneficiaries will thank you when they meet you in heaven!

I know that this subject matter can be difficult to contemplate, but it is absolutely necessary that you consider your situation and all the estate planning options if you care about protecting the people you will leave behind.

So grab the Kleenex, take a deep breath, and start planning!

My Estate Planning Worksheet

1. Review your financial statement that you created during **Day 3.**

2. a) If your net worth is less than $100,000, have a simple will drafted. b) If your net worth exceeds $100,000, draft a living trust document. c) If your net worth exceeds $5,000,000, then use a bypass trust.

❖ ❖ ❖

Day 29

Minding Your Mind

In order to achieve your financial objectives in life, you must first master what goes on in your head. The way you think will determine what you do. Actions are a by-product of thought. Everything you see around you started as a thought before it became anything else. If you can master your thoughts, you can master your life. That is the target of today's lesson.

Like your body, your mind needs to be exercised on a daily basis, and, similar to your body, you should monitor your mind to make sure your thoughts are healthy, as well. Only when you are able to look at the world and your situation in life in an objective way will you be able to plot the best course for *your* life and achieve your financial dreams (and, with those, your personal dreams or missions) to the fullest extent possible.

Unfortunately, the fact is that we are never taught how to think effectively.

Oh sure, any one of us can memorize a list of states or dates or names or facts, but when it comes to conceptualizing the information we are learning, we tend to fall a little short. Why are there relatively few classes offered in school that teach us how to apply the knowledge that we acquire?

I have been researching the mind's relationship to performance for more than 30 years, and you are about to get a crash course on this amazing and critical area of study!

Let's begin with something which each of us suffers from to various degrees:

Mental Illness
Now, do not get offended, slam the book shut, and walk off grumbling to yourself. When I refer to *mental illness*, I am not talking about hallucinations or wearing straight jackets, necessarily. I am referring to

the kind of fundamental mental illness that affects nearly everyone. This kind of mental illness keeps each one of us from achieving our full potential, keeps us from being truly engaged in life, and prevents us from being useful to those around us.

If you have ever felt one or more of the following symptoms, you have allowed a mental illness become part of your makeup:

- Irrational fears
- Self-doubt
- Pessimism
- Inability to make a decision
- Confusion
- Procrastination
- Laziness

What is that? You say that none of these maladies apply to you? Then I am willing to predict that you suffer from another symptom of mental illness, one which is missing from the previous list.

You are D-E-L-U-S-I-O-N-A-L.

Unless you are some super-being (or in total denial), I am going to bet you have been plagued by one or more of the symptoms I have just listed.

As soon as you learn to recognize these symptoms, we can begin to eradicate them. These illnesses are roadblocks to realizing your financial dreams.

Let's discuss how we can get rid of them.

How the Mind Works

When most people picture the mind, they imagine a literal image of the brain.

I am here to tell you that the *mind* and the *brain* are two very different things, and each has very distinct functions. Your brain is a vital organ housed in your cranium. Your mind is something that is a little harder to describe or explain, but, in essence, your mind is your very being.

Conscious and Subconscious

The mind consists of two parts: the conscious and the subconscious. Here again, each one of these parts has very distinct functions. The conscious mind is known as the intellectual mind. This is where we do all of our cognitive thinking. This is the part of your mind that you use to fill out your tax returns or to decide which investment mix would be appropriate for your 401(k) plan. The conscious mind takes in information though the senses, processes data, reasons, comes to conclusions, and makes judgments.

The subconscious mind is like an enormous file cabinet that records everything that happens to you from the moment you are born (and maybe before birth) right up to the moment you die. It is fed by the conscious mind. However, unlike the conscious mind, the subconscious mind must accept whatever information it is supplied. If you conclude that the color black is actually white, the subconscious mind will accept this conclusion as truth. If you decide that all of the good opportunities have already been snatched up by the wealthy, you will get no argument from your subconscious. The subconscious mind is responsible for your attitude, moods, outlook, feelings, habits, and emotional well-being. The subconscious also houses your paradigms…which is a perfect segue to the next section.

What Is a Paradigm?

A paradigm is a set of beliefs, a personal theory, or a world view. It is whatever you deem to be true, whether or not the belief corresponds to actual truth. In the book *Psycho-Cybernetics*, Maxwell Maltz proposed that the mind cannot decipher between that which is real and that which the mind vividly imagines to be true.

Here are some examples of outdated paradigms:

- The world is flat.
- Cigarettes are harmless to your health.
- It is impossible to break the sound barrier.
- Women are not emotionally equipped for the business world.
- If man were meant to fly, he'd have wings.
- I'm not very smart.
- I just don't have a head for business.

- The stock market is too speculative for me.
- It takes money to make money.
- I don't have enough capital to buy an investment property.
- No one will lend me money with my credit history.
- Owning your own business is very risky.

Also, the following list contains some paradigms that may sound familiar:

Every one of the above statements represents a paradigm that holds no truth unless you give it power! Sadly, I know from years of personal experience, in which I coached thousands of people, that many people believe in this garbage as if it is proven fact. This type of faulty thinking creates the obstacles and rough roads that keep many of you from performing at your highest potential. It is not that you lack talent; it is not that you lack intelligence, or ability, or perseverance!

The *only* problem is that you have allowed yourself or others around you to *believe* that you lack these strengths, and that (perceived) lack is the reason for your failures.

Today, on Day 29, you are going to start living in truth. You are not going to make excuses anymore by believing in false paradigms. False paradigms create an easy out for quitters.

Time is up! The excuse-making ends today. (If you still have that box of Kleenex handy from Day 28, you can have yourself one last little pity party, for those who feel the need.)

To start living in truth, you must take control of your mind.

Control Your Thoughts

Let's say that one day you discover that the gasoline you have been using has caused your car's engine to sputter. I am going to bet that, upon this discovery, you would switch brands or grades immediately.

Are you with me so far?

I am telling you that your prevailing thoughts are producing paradigms that are stifling your potential. Negative thoughts cause your mind to sputter and prevent it from operating at the highest performance level possible.

It is time to change the way you think about yourself, your prospects, your environment, and your abilities.

Where do we begin?

Well, the first thing you need to do is listen to your conscious thoughts and try to see if you can identify the kinds of messages you communicate to your subconscious.

For most of us, we internally talk to ourselves in a tone that we would never consider using on a stranger or even on an enemy. Remember, the subconscious mind must accept the messages it receives from the conscious mind. Therefore, if you tell yourself that you are dumb or inept and, therefore, incapable of accomplishing a certain thing, you run the risk that this self-judgment will become an imbedded paradigm, or permanent belief.

It might take some time to truly identify all of the negative messages that you are sending to your subconscious because you have probably been thinking in the same way and have been thinking the same things for a long, long time. These negative thought patterns may be difficult to dispel. The first, very critical step toward change is to become increasingly aware of each thought that you allow into your mind. You will soon learn how you really feel about yourself and how you feel about others.

The next step is to become your own teacher and coach. Immediately begin changing the way that you communicate with yourself. Imagine if you heard your child say, "I'm too stupid to get good grades in school." You would most likely respond with something like, "Honey, that is simply not true. You are very smart. You just need to learn how to get organized and learn how to study more effectively." You would never accept your child's statement as a reasonable excuse for his or her failure. You would certainly never reinforce the child's negative statement, I hope.

The strong stance you might take with your own child is the same perspective that you need in order to combat your own negative thoughts.

You need to begin nurturing your mind the same way that you would support a child's developing mind.

Stop beating yourself up!

It never helps and most certainly can hurt your potential to grow.

Become Your Mind's Sentinel

Throughout the day, your conscious mind is deluged with stimuli which it takes in through the body's senses, most especially that which is heard and seen. Various studies indicate that the average person experiences somewhere between 25,000 and 50,000 stimuli each day. The vast majority of those thoughts are negative. Unfortunately, we live in a world permeated with negative people.

Do you disagree with that assessment? Try watching the news or reading a paper today, and you are sure to discover that most of what is broadcast describes global gloom and doom. Constant exposure to this can be depressing.

These unpleasant thoughts build up like a thick residue on the subconscious mind, leaving an individual mentally impotent.

You cannot control the topics and stories that will be reported on the news, nor can you control the fact that most people have the bad habit of constantly feeling the need to share depressing tales with anyone who will listen. However, you can choose to whom and to what you will listen. You do not want to expose your mind to constant negative and sensationalized reporting.

I am very selective about my sources for information. I am also selective about the amount of time I spend reviewing any headlines. Likewise, I will not spend time with people who try to unload upon me all their stories of woe and self-pity. I simply will not allow this type of negative and worthless communication to become embedded into my subconscious.

The Law of Attraction

The Law of Attraction states that everything that we have in our life, both good and bad, we have subconsciously attracted to us. Through the practice of mental discipline and focused thought, we have the ability to architect the life of our dreams and attract everything we need to become whatever we desire. There seems to be a growing body of evidence as to the veracity of this claim.

The Law of Attraction is not a new concept. Although it was popularized in the 2006 movie *The Secret*, its roots go back thousands of years. In Proverbs 23:7, it is written, "As a man thinketh, so he is." You will also find the idea in the studies of Hinduism and in Theosophy. The most influential English writing on the subject is the book *As a Man Thinketh* by James Allen, published in 1902. There is even a course taught on the subject of the Laws of Attraction offered at UCLA.

This book you currently hold in your hands is all about practical application, rather than theory.

Therefore, we will focus on how you can apply the applying the principles of the Law of Attraction in your daily life in order to get the desired results.

1. ***Know precisely what you want.*** Most people only have a vague notion of their real aspirations. You must take the time to visualize, in great detail, the life you want to live. I recommend making a list of everything you would like to experience, obtain, create, master, and enjoy. Once your list has been committed to paper, it must then be inscribed on your mind so that you can see it with your imagination, down to the smallest component. If this is done properly, it should bring to bear the same emotional response you would feel if you were experiencing these events in real life. By focusing on what you really want, you set in motion a series of universal laws that begin to attract the needed elements required to build the lifestyle you have chosen. Can something this esoteric actually work? Try it. You will be amazed at how things will begin manifesting themselves in seemingly mystifying ways. You must practice visualization by using your imagination.

2. ***Turn your wants into needs.*** There is a very famous verse from a song that reads, "You can't always get what you want, but if you try sometimes, you just might find, you get what you

need!" What is the difference between a *want* and a *need*? Answer: emotional investment. When your emotions are engaged, it sends an alert to your body that says, "Take action! This is serious!" The art of visualization will instinctively employ your emotional reservoir, and that will trigger the required action.

3. ***Act as if you have already received the item or benefit.*** By imagining that the receipt of your goal is a foregone conclusion, it vivifies your beliefs and your expectancy, and it produces an air of gratitude. These powerful emotions put you in the proper frame of mind to obtain nearly anything that your mind can conjure up.

4. ***Be open to receiving.*** There are many people who simply cannot imagine living a prosperous and fulfilling life because they feel unworthy. I am of the belief that each of us is the individualized expression of our Creator, and therefore, we have access to everything in creation. Are you not as valuable in the eyes of God as any other person who occupies Earth? If you think of yourself as a "lesser than"—you will experience scarcity that is consistent with puny thinking. Walk the planet as if you own it. You might be sharing it with 6.65 billion other people, but make no mistake, you are *an* owner!

Here is the way that I begin every day, and I would recommend that you adopt the habit for yourself. I ask myself a series of very important questions and considerations:

1. I ask myself, "What are five things for which I am truly grateful?"
2. Then I spend one minute visualizing my ideal life in detail.
3. Next, I name at least one thing I will do TODAY that will move me closer to this ideal life that I just visualized.

Conclusion

My friend, your mind is the key to your success. If your mind is in need of some major cleaning or reconstruction, then get to work! Executing financial strategies is simple compared with mastering your thoughts. Becoming the chieftain of your mind can only be accomplished through a lifetime of diligence which you must begin today.

Day 29: Minding Your Mind

Mastering your thoughts is much like growing a garden. As the sole gardener, you must continually check for weeds that could choke the life out of your cherished plants and flowers. Your subconscious mind is defenseless against judgments (i.e., paradigms) rendered by the conscious mind. You can convince yourself that the world is filled with unlimited opportunities and that you are capable of getting the best of everything, or...you can accept the opposite notion. What you believe will influence what you do, and those beliefs will ultimately determine your results. When you learn to control your thoughts, you will take control of all of your outcomes.

The road to success begins with **minding your mind!**

What a great lesson to learn and apply to each facet of your life.

Minding My Mind

As a helpful reminder, print out these daily affirmations and put them somewhere that you will see them every day at the beginning of your day. Or create your own reminder!

1. **Name five things for which you are truly grateful.**

2. **Spend one minute visualizing your ideal life in detail.**

3. **Name at least one thing you will do TODAY to move you closer to the ideal life that you just visualized!**

Day 30

Balancing Your Life

This book has been devoted to improving your financial wellbeing.

However, having your finances in order is not the same thing as having your whole life in order.

The whole point of building and fortifying your financial life is so that you will be free to focus your attention on the other matters that are most important to you...like enjoying your life and helping those around you.

I think there is a common misconception that most wealthy people are consumed with monetary pursuits and that they spend all of their time thinking about money. The truth of the matter is that it's the folks who are broke who spend all of *their* time thinking about money. The rich spend more time enjoying life and, for the most part, helping their families, friends, and even total strangers by sharing the wealth. And while both rich and poor are occupied with financial matters, the rich think about them in positive terms while the broke live in fear of what the future might hold.

When I was poor, all my thoughts were consumed with how I could improve my station in life. At church, I would pray for more resources instead of a purer soul. When I played with my children, rather than give them my undivided attention, I worried about my ability to provide them with adequate support. I would watch television mostly to observe people living lives that I could hardly imagine possible for me.

Now that I have lived many, many years with more than sufficient provisions and have acquired the knowledge of how to obtain whatever it is that I need, money seems trivial to me, and I spend very little time thinking about it. The freedom this has given me also provides welcome relief from worry.

That is why (and how) I was able to write this book.

I want to help you achieve those feelings of freedom and relief, too.

Eventually, this achievement will allow you to focus on the things in life that make you happiest, not the pursuit of money alone and not material wealth. Those are things any one of us can have merely by applying the correct strategies and making the appropriate decisions.

There should be balance in all things. I do not want you to become consumed with your financial pursuits to the point that you stop living and stop enjoying the life you have NOW. Setting goals is a *part* of life. Pursue them in a sensible way. Do not let your future pursuits rob you of the wonder of today.

Many of the strategies we discussed during the last 29 days are designed to put your monetary life on autopilot which, naturally, will allow you to have more time for everything else.

I would like to share with you my personal philosophy and the approach I used while climbing that proverbial ladder of success. I hope it makes the journey less burdensome for you. The manner in which you enjoy the journey *is* more important than where you end up.

Balance

If you were to ask me the most important ingredient for a happy and self-actualized life, my response would be a single word: balance.

Balance is the art of allocating sufficient time, energy, intellect, and passion to each meaningful aspect of your existence. To achieve balance, you must become an expert at focus and efficiency. We each have a precious 24 hours in which to make each day count for something special. Assuming that you currently sleep for eight hours each night, work for nine hours each day, and commute for one (and spend at least another hour eating and grooming), you are left with just five precious hours each day in which to pursue your personal ambitions while also attending to your personal relationships with family and friends.

It is hard to accept, but so many people will spend the bulk of their *free* time in front of the television watching mindless programs or reruns.

Not my readers!

Stop the mindless ogling. Get up and do something constructive with those few precious hours each day! If you find that you are totally unable to control the amount of hours spent in front of the tube, try doing what several of my close friends have done: get rid of your television until you change your habits! It may seem like an unimaginable option to some of you, but for those of you who feel horrified by this suggestion of a TV-less household…I would be willing to bet that you are the ones who need to take this action the most.

Now let's look at the six spokes that represent your *wheel of life* and discuss strategies for ensuring the proper allocation, or balance, to each.

Mental

For way too many people, the thirst for knowledge seems to have been stunted prematurely. I read somewhere that the average male will read only a couple of books after graduating from high school or college (not counting material that is required by his profession or that is related to sports).

Around the age of 20, your educational pursuits and quest for enlightenment should be shifting into second gear, not dropping into neutral. If you want to expand your life experiences, attaining greater wisdom is an invaluable asset. Let's delve into some simple steps that can help you increase your bank of insight and understanding.

Reading can provide you with the vehicle or portal that you need in order to experience a whole new world and an ever-expanding perspective about life. Through reading, everything from agriculture to zoology, atheism to Zen can be explored. There are books on parenting, horsemanship, finances, and science.

The Donald Trumps and Warren Buffetts of the world love to elaborate on how they have risen above the mundane to achieve greatness. They relate these stories to the public through the books they have written. For $25 (or $0 if you get them from these books from the library), you can learn asset acquisition techniques from some of the greatest minds and wealthiest achievers. Tiger Woods will show you exactly how he swings a golf club and how he manages a course. Countless psychologists and relationship counselors provide tips on how to have a more loving and meaningful relationship with your spouse and kids. Everything you could possibly want to know can be found in books (or online). You need to become an avid reader.

Thirty minutes a day spent reading a book can vastly enhance your storehouse of ideas, information, and perspectives. Four or five books per year over the span of a decade will take your mind from average to astute. I am referring to the kind of books that teach you a new skill set or that open your mind to an enlightened way of thinking. A good habit to develop is to keep an interesting book or magazine with you at all times. One predicament we all dislike is becoming bored while waiting somewhere such as in an airport, in a doctor's office, or in any line for *any* reason. With your favorite book on hand, any unavoidable waiting periods will turn into precious, free moments of extra reading time. If you spend several hours per week in your car or commuting by some other means, purchase a collection of books on CD or in digital format. CDs and digital-format "books" can be purchased at lectures, over the Internet, through television advertisements, at bookstores, and may be available for free at your local library. The average American spends at least ten hours per week in his or her car. You could receive the equivalent of an advanced degree while driving! Nurture your brain with idea-generating lectures, biographies, lessons, debates, and other discussions delivered through your audio system. Don't forget the humorous stuff too. Even listening to your favorite comedian holds the possibility of bringing you a certain kind of enlightenment.

Take advantage of the free seminars offered around the country. They offer informative sessions on just about every possible money-making venture ever conceived. Sure, these companies are interested in selling some type of training package or software product, but no one can force you into buying. I have been to dozens of these programs, never purchased a thing, and learned something from every presenter. Most provide a fair amount of useful information as part of their sales pitch.

If you learn more while under the guidance of a teacher or mentor, attend classes on topics that interest you. Junior colleges and state-sponsored universities offer evening classes and online instruction that can be customized to fit around your work schedule and family obligations. If you would like to obtain a real estate license, become a certified financial planner, or acquire your MBA, all of these accomplishments can be achieved through your local institutions of higher learning. Never put limits on your potential by limiting your education—become a student for life.

Physical

Being physically fit pays dividends in every area of your life. People who exercise tend to live longer, have more energy, have a better self-image, and think more lucidly. The No. 1 justification that I hear people use as an excuse for the lack of an exercise program is a lack of time. There are simple things you can do that require no more than 30 minutes a day. Believe me, when your fitness becomes a priority and you see the difference it makes in your life, you will stop making excuses.

One of the easiest things that almost everyone can do is walk. I read that if a person would walk only 45 minutes each day at a brisk pace, they would burn enough calories to lose 18 pounds in a year without changing any other lifestyle factors. What a great investment of time! To add workout minutes to each day, make it a habit to park further from the store entrance or your office building (but always put your safety first, of course). Walk up the stairs instead of riding the elevator. Learn to pace and stretch while you are thinking or chatting on the phone instead of sitting behind a desk or standing still. It is pretty simple math. The more your body moves, the more calories it will burn.

For those who are a bit more ambitious, join a gym. Of course, the trick to getting results from a gym membership is to actually attend on a regular basis! Health clubs operate on the assumption that most of the members who join will stop showing up in less than 60 days. How pathetic! If you are new to the gym scene, hire a personal trainer for a few sessions to show you the ropes. Understand going in that the first 90 days may feel like boot camp. Your body is unaccustomed to the exertion. If you hang in there long enough, your muscles will actually crave the routine, and it will become enjoyable to work out. Most people quit before they reach this point, and they miss out on the reward. Regular exercise is one of the top stress reducers. If you are sitting there telling yourself that you just cannot afford a gym membership or any type of fitness classes at this time, try cutting out the gourmet coffee and junk food for one month. You will have saved enough to pay for a gym membership or exercise classes. Just cutting out cable television will likely net you more than enough each month for a gym membership.

If possible, find a sport that combines exercise with something you genuinely enjoy. My sport of choice is tennis. The aerobic benefits to this activity are fairly obvious. I also enjoy playing golf. Have you ever noticed the large number of overweight golfers? When I play, I like to walk the course, but many others drive in a cart. At the end of play, I feel like I have walked five miles while having a blast and enjoying the beautiful scenery. Bike riding is another enjoyable pastime that incorporates health benefits. One Christmas, I bought my mom a bike for peddling around the neighborhood. Within a few months, she was riding 15 to 20 miles a day in the Arizona sun. And the best part was that she loved doing it! Bike riding gives you a chance to relive some of your childhood happy-go-lucky feelings while strengthening your heart and slimming your waistline.

The message is clear. Get your body in motion. Dance, walk, golf, swim, run around the yard with your kids or grandkids, and you will soon feel your energy increasing every day. It will give you a competitive edge in everything you do.

Spiritual

A person's spiritual life is the most personal and extraordinary part of his or her being. For that reason, I always feel a little reluctant to comment on how anyone else should pursue this facet of life. On the other hand, spirituality is such an important ingredient for living a fulfilled life that I want to share my personal experiences and observations. They have added to my life immeasurably, and I would not want to miss out on the opportunity to possibly help some of you who may find a connection to my perspectives.

Highly spiritual people seem to possess an aura of peace. That is the simplest and best way I can describe how spirituality manifests itself. Spiritually balanced people seem to have an understanding that transcends the ordinary. The source of their peace seems to center on their relationship to the universe and to their Creator. Like everything of value in life, spirituality is something that a person must first make a priority and then must hone continually.

I have always believed it is important to develop a personal *life philosophy*. In order to live the best life possible, you must understand who you are and what you believe—your values, your boundaries (or lack thereof). Also you must recognize and understand your connection to the rest of the universe and everything in it. You need to develop your own philosophy so that you can handle any manner of circumstances. These core beliefs should help provide you with the answers you need to survive and thrive.

Let me share a couple of principles which sustain me through life's most challenging moments.

I believe that we have been endowed by our Creator with everything that we need in order to become whatever we could possibly want to become. We are limited only by our ability to dream, our ability to remain faithful, and by the amount of confidence we muster to embark upon any endeavor. People who refuse to quit cannot be kept down by anyone. Resilient people always find a way to tunnel through, go around, or climb over any obstacles. Their stamina is the by-product of the unwavering belief that the finish line is within reach, regardless of whether it is actually *in sight*. That stamina is attained through FAITH. These tenets have pulled me through some gloomy times and tough situations in which I had to fight to find any viable solutions.

I have also come to understand and accept that life runs in cycles.

As I write this chapter, I realize that I have much for which I am very thankful. My wife is wonderful, and our relationship is incredible. We are grateful for the amazing opportunity we have been given to share each day with one another. My children are doing well and never cease to amaze me. Business is exciting, and I find myself in good health. I am an optimist at heart, but I have been around plenty long enough to know that everything changes—everything. The health status of any family member or friend could change during a routine checkup. My business could take a downward spiral.

How do *you* deal with life's curveballs?

311

I deal with them by recognizing two things: first, my Creator will never give me more than I am capable of enduring; and second, everything changes! Everything runs in cycles. When you understand that all things in this life on earth are temporary, you will refrain from becoming overly invested in either life's troubles *or* triumphs. This message is simple, but its meaning seems to elude most people. It often takes people years of study and exploration before they are able to reach any practical level of understanding. This awareness of my origin and of life's natural laws has been *my* lifesaver on more than a few occasions.

I am certainly not lobbying to become your spiritual advisor, nor do I want you to accept any of my life philosophies without doing your own research and contemplation. If you are looking for guidance in this area, the sources for spiritual enlightenment are virtually endless. In your search, however, do not forget that there are some irrefutable truths. Primarily, you are made of the same substance as the Creator, and the Creator is for *expansion of life*. If you encounter any teachings that contradict these two tenets, you should reject those false teachings that you've come across as they may lead you into a destructive state.

Faith is a powerful ally. God seems to find those who seek him, regardless of their denomination.

Social

In this country alone, there are more than 300 million residents. However, it seems that interacting with fellow citizens, in a meaningful way, is a challenge to many of us.

It is practically impossible to achieve any great level of accomplishment without the aid and contribution of others. It is imperative that each of us learns how to win people over and convince them to join our team. Remember, who you know may be as important as what you know.

To gain people's confidence and trust, you must be able to place their interests ahead of your own. If you allow the other party to dominate the conversation, his or her true nature will be revealed in a relatively short period of time. Your strategy should be to facilitate the conversation by asking leading questions such as: *What kind of business are you in? Do you have children? What do you do for fun? Where were you born and raised?*

The challenge for most of us is that we talk too much and forget that the best thing we can do is to take time to listen to others. With practice, you can improve your communication abilities by learning to listen carefully.

So, which qualities should you look for when choosing your friends and associates? Compassion, generosity, intelligence, a good sense of humor, an outgoing demeanor, and ambition are a few excellent traits. The presence of any one of these may mean enough to you that it will encourage you to invite this person into your life. As for *my* preferences, the single best quality a person can possess is sincerity. I look for this same attribute whenever I need to choose business associates or close personal friends. Without sincerity, all that remains is an empty shell.

To a large extent, a person will associate with others who behave and believe just as he or she does. Just as a parent is mindful of a son or daughter's playmates, you should be very careful regarding who you invite into your life. Your choices will facilitate (or hinder) the attainment of your dreams and personal missions. Choose wisely!

Financial

If you can fill a need in the marketplace, you will be financially rewarded. There are few things more satisfying than owning a business or engaging in a profession that is guided by your sense of purpose. When you can link your values to your income sources and strive to find balance, you will find the path to greatness.

A person will become conflicted if he or she attempts to fill a role or roles that are not in harmony with his or her principles. Whenever you conduct yourself in a style that is contrary to your beliefs, problems will evolve over time. You may keep the chaos capped for a while, but in the end, the truth is always revealed.

These chaotic and conflicted life situations are usually the ones that end up on the evening news.

Since work and business commitments play such a dominant role in most of our lives, the method you use to earn money will have just as much impact on your life as the amount of money you make. Find an enterprise that provides opportunities for you to use the gifts your Creator has bestowed upon you so that, as you make your living, you can make a beneficial difference in the lives of others, too. In order to live life to its fullest, you must feel passionate about your chosen livelihood.

Make no mistake that money is an essential ingredient for a happy, productive, and full life, but it is not life itself. Your net worth does not match your value as a human being. Your financial statement is not your soul. Your finances should be a priority but not your dominant one. Is the attainment of money more important than your family relationships, your health, and your spiritual life? Most would say that it is not, but their actions would belie that claim.

Today's lesson is to maintain perspective. Finances are truly important, but they are no more important than the other five spokes in *your wheel of life*.

Family

I am amazed at the number of people who declare again and again that *family* is their No. 1 priority, but then the way they live life contradicts those assertions. Business investments, golf games, time spent at the gym, social events, and sometimes raiding the liquor cabinet, all take higher priority over family involvement.

Through the years, I finally learned that family life requires a massive investment on the part of each member. I am not referring to financial investment. More than anything else, your children and your spouse (and even your extended family) need your time and energy. There is no substitute for your presence.

Be sure that your family is making it to the top of your priority list. Spending time with them should not be some kind of afterthought that occurs to you once you have completed everything else. Family is the easiest thing in the world to take for granted. Do not take family time for granted. Be passionate and be generous with your time and attention.

Verbalizing your love for your family is wonderful, but you cannot use sentiments as a replacement for action. Children pay more attention to what you do than to what you say. Lead by example. Children will pick up on any discrepancies between what a parent does and what a parent says. Never forget that your kids will (most likely) grow up to be much like you. Be the kind of person you want your kids to be.

You Made It!

I hope you have enjoyed our journey together.

The purpose of this last day together is to remind you to maintain balance among all of the essential ingredients needed to experience real success and happiness in life.

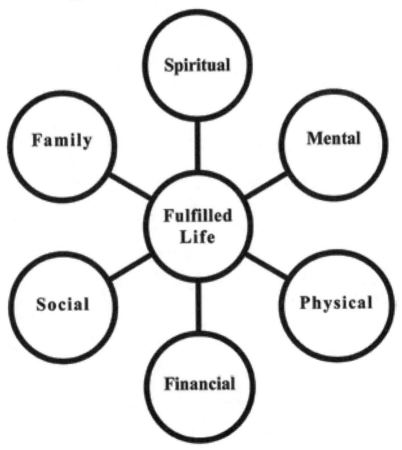

If *your* personal wheel of life is missing a spoke, it is likely that you will feel a sense of emptiness or imbalance. However, when you allocate the necessary resources to each of these six dimensions, a sense of peace and balance will prevail.

This sense of balance has become increasingly rare in our world.

My wish for you is that you will acquire all that you want and want all that you acquire. Let's make our one and only journey count, for our own well-being and for all those we touch along the way.

About the Author

Steven Sitkowski has spent his entire professional life in the financial services industry. He knows the financial landscape from the vantage point of an insider. He has been a Certified Financial Planner, Registered Investment Advisor, has run a $2 billion stock brokerage operation, has been a general and limited partner in real estate holdings, was president of two financial planning organizations, and is currently President of the Growing Wealth Network. Steven has held licenses in real estate, securities, insurance, and as a mortgage broker. Mr. Sitkowski has been the host of a nationally syndicated radio talk show and has lectured to over 1,000,000 people in the United States, Canada, and England. Audiences love his "tell it like it is" communication style.

Steven uses his breadth of knowledge to show consumers how to protect themselves against slick-talking financial salespeople and others who attempt to separate his clients from their hard earned money.

Steven's message is easy to understand, and more importantly, will help you to make more money and save more money!

If you are interested in additional information or personal coaching, you can send Mr. Sitkowski an email @ 30DayMoneyMakeover@ gmail.com.